Blessing It All

Rituals for Transition and Transformation

Allison Palm and Heather Concannon
Editors

Skinner House
Boston

Copyright © 2024 by the Unitarian Universalist Association. All rights reserved. Published by Skinner House Books, 24 Farnsworth St., Boston, MA 02210–1409.

skinnerhouse.org

Printed in the United States

Cover design by Jeenee Lee
Text design by Tim Holtz
Author photos by Shannon Stockwell

print ISBN: 978-1-55896-920-9
eBook ISBN: 978-1-55896-921-6

5 4 3 2 1
28 27 26 25 24

Library of Congress Cataloging-in-Publication Data
Names: Palm, Allison, editor. | Concannon, Heather, editor.
Title: Blessing it all : rituals for transition and transformation / edited
  by Allison Palm and Heather Concannon.
Description: Boston, MA : Skinner House Books, [2024] | Summary: "An
  expansive collection, the rituals in Blessing It All foster community,
  joy, and healing in moments like the joining of a blended family,
  changing names and pronouns, honoring Pride Month, having an abortion,
  getting a prosthesis, surviving sexual assault, ending a marriage, and
  so many others. The rituals-written by a diverse array of contributors
  with lived experiences that add depth and authenticity to each
  offering-are designed to be led by anyone inspired to do so, with clear
  instructions and additional insights and guidance. They are suitable for
  communities, congregations, family, and individual use. And they can
  happen anywhere our lives happen, wherever people or families or
  communities gather, because that is where we encounter the holy"--
  Provided by publisher.
Identifiers: LCCN 2023052882 (print) | LCCN 2023052883 (ebook) | ISBN
  9781558969209 (paperback) | ISBN 9781558969216 (ebook)
Subjects: LCSH: Rituals (Liturgical books) | Rites and ceremonies. |
  Unitarian Universalist Association.
Classification: LCC BL600 .B57 2024 (print) | LCC BL600 (ebook) | DDC
  264--dc23/eng/20240222
LC record available at https://lccn.loc.gov/2023052882
LC ebook record available at https://lccn.loc.gov/2023052883

Scripture on page 194 taken from the New American Standard Bible ®, Copyright © 1960, 1962, 1963, 1968, 1971, 1972, 1973, 1975, 1977, 1995 by The Lockman Foundation.

"the mother" by Gwendolyn Brooks reprinted by consent of Brooks Permissions.

"The seven of pentacles," 1982 by Marge Piercy; from *Circles on the Water* by Marge Piercy. Used by permission of Alfred A. Knopf, an imprint of the Knopf Doubleday Publishing Group, a division of Penguin Random House LLC. All rights reserved.

David Whyte, "Much Has Been Said," from *The Bell and the Blackbird*. © 2018 David Whyte. Reprinted with permission from Many Rivers Press, Langley, WA www.davidwhyte.com.

Dedicated to Katie Tyson, with gratitude and love.

Contents

Rituals for Congregations and Communities

Introduction

Our lives and the lives of our communities are marked by moments of transition and transformation. As individuals, we grow up, we move, we start new schools and new jobs, we begin and end relationships, we have children and—if we are lucky—we get to watch them grow, we discover more about who we are, we lose people and pets. As communities, we honor people entering new life stages, we acknowledge harm and seek repair, we reckon with natural disasters and national traumas, and year after year we mark the cycles of the seasons. As humans, we grow and we change, we grieve and we celebrate.

Often we mark only the big moments: birth and death, birthdays and holidays, becoming an adult, and committing to a partner. And yet these are not the only moments that touch our lives and shape who we are. In this book you will find rituals for other moments, for moments that occur once or come around again and again—in the cycle of the year, in the cycle of life, in the cycle of the universe. With this book, we invite you to bless it all: the big and the small, the happy and the sad, and everything in between.

The rituals in this book are for moments that are ordinary and profound, tender and heartbreaking, joyful and celebratory, and often a little bit of each. They are for moments of transition and loss, transformation and growth. They are for communities, congregations, friends, small groups, families, and individuals. They are meant to be done in church sanctuaries and basements, in living rooms, in the woods, in the streets, in hospital rooms, in backyards, and online, because we might need to ground ourselves, to connect with something larger than ourselves, and to mark a loss or a joy in any of these places—or in others. These rituals happen where our lives happen, wherever people or families or communities gather, because that is where we encounter the holy.

In these pages you'll find texts ranging from stand-alone blessings to fully scripted ceremonies. They were written by a wide variety of people: ministers, other religious professionals, and laypeople. The vast majority of our contributors have lived in and through the circumstances for which they wrote. Their lived experience gives the rituals depth and authenticity, and they hope that their work may speak to others in similar circumstances.

This book is for you: for religious professionals, members of faith communities, and nonreligious people; for families, groups of friends, and individuals; for children and people caring for them; for all who have rejoiced in new life, who have mourned a loss, who have struggled to name the transformation taking place in their hearts. May you find in these pages connection and commitment, inspiration and invitation, a blessing and a balm.

Why Do We Need Rituals?

We, the editors of this book, Allison Palm and Heather Concannon, are Unitarian Universalist ministers. This book is grounded in the Unitarian Universalist tradition, yet we know that many reading this book may be part of other traditions or may not belong to any religious or spiritual community. And we know that you still may long for spiritual resources and rituals to honor transitions or transformations in your own life.

Unitarian Universalism is a noncreedal tradition with a strong emphasis on love, community, and honoring the many paths that people take to find the meaning and truth. Historically, Unitarian Universalism has held that individual quest for truth and meaning as a central value—though we are coming to understand some of the limitations of that emphasis on individualism. We know that we need shared spaces for meaning making and a sense of shared grounding in times of transition. And the freedom offered by an individual search for truth and meaning can also make it harder to find something to hold onto when everything is changing.

We both know intimately the longing for and power of ritual. This book is inspired by our own experience of facing moments when we needed the sacred space offered by ritual, yet found little in our Unitarian Universalist tradition that was designed to create that space.

In many ways, the story of this book begins on a hot summer day in Boston in early July 2009, when Allison got a call from a church friend with terrible news.

Eighteen hours earlier, Heather had woken up disoriented in an emergency room in Colorado. She had to have it explained to her that she was in the hospital, that there had been an accident. She and our mutual friend Katie had been driving cross-country on their way home from the 2009 General Assembly of the Unitarian Universalist

Association when they were in a head-on collision on a rural two-lane highway. Katie was killed instantly. Heather survived.

We met Katie when all three of us were in college, through our church's young adult group. Katie was effusive, loving, hilarious, nerdy, charming, and always ready for a debate. We became close friends. Now, as the news of her death spread, we and all our community were in shock. Allison remembers not knowing quite what to do with herself until she got a text: "We're gathering. Come join us." She made her way to Katie's partner's apartment, where most of the young adult group had gathered.

Those of us in Boston gathered because it was what you do when someone has died. But then we didn't know what to do next. We stared at the floor and passed around a baby. We went for a walk and took turns breaking down in tears. It was the first of many gatherings over the next weeks, months, and years, gatherings where we bumbled through the messy work of grief together without a road map.

A week after the accident, Heather flew home from Colorado with her family. Again, the whole young adult group gathered, meeting her at the Boston airport, awkwardly, tenderly hugging, trying not to break her broken body any more. We sang "Love Will Guide Us," a song familiar to most Unitarian Universalists, in the airport terminal as other passengers skirted around our group, trying not to stare. We sang because it was what we knew how to do, because singing was the closest thing we had to a ritual for that moment. Because we knew that song by heart, because it connected us to our faith when we needed to feel like something larger than ourselves was holding us.

In the months that followed Katie's death, our community continued to gather as we sought to make sense of this terrible tragedy. There were two big memorial services—one in Katie's hometown and one in Boston a few months later. Beyond that, we were on our own. Each time a new "first" came up, we'd wonder together how to mark it. The first church retreat without Katie. Her first birthday after she died. The first anniversary of her death. We were searching for a way to process our grief as a community that went deeper than the standard memorial service, but the only option Unitarian Universalism offered us was to create it ourselves. At times, it felt like yet another burden to take on in the midst of our grieving.

We both love the freedom and openness of the Unitarian Universalist tradition in which we were raised. Yet when we faced a grief and trauma bigger than we could manage alone, we felt like we were lost at sea. We longed for something to anchor us; we wanted our faith tradition to offer us wisdom and comfort. But it seemed to be asking us to forge our own anchor while we were already adrift in a vast ocean of grief.

Katie's death was not the first time we had wished for more ritual in the tradition that raised us, but it was the first time that we didn't feel good about having to create it ourselves. In the midst of grief, we didn't want freedom and openness, we wanted to be held and cared for. We wanted someone else to give us a structure through which to process all we had lost. We needed a guide, a container to hold us.

We thought carefully about how we wanted to mark the first anniversary of Katie's death. Since we were offered no structure for such a ritual, we made one up—we and other young people who loved and missed Katie dearly got together and created something we hoped would give us what we so desperately needed. We invited all of Katie's community, and about fifty people came to the ritual we held. It was deeply meaningful, but we still wish we hadn't had to create it for ourselves.

Now, as ordained ministers serving Unitarian Universalist congregations, we have heard others express the same longing we felt then. We have spent late nights trying to figure out how to hold our communities in the face of all that the world throws at us. We have seen colleagues searching for ways to build rituals around particular moments, and to help congregants mark particular life events. We know that our longing for guides, for containers, for rituals is not unique, or even unusual.

With this book, we offer a response to this longing. We offer rituals that bless it all—the sacred, beautiful, tragic, ordinary, *human* moments in our lives.

What Is a Ritual?

The urge to create rituals to mark life passages is a deeply human one, almost instinctual, and can be seen across time and across cultures. From Stone Age burials to "Taps" on the trumpet, from confirmations to quinceañeras, from jumping the broom to breaking the glass, humans find ways to mark the important moments in their lives and in their communities.

The word *ritual* can mean many different things, both secular and religious. Sometimes people use it to mean just repeated actions; other times it implies an element of intention or tradition or spirituality. In this book, we define a ritual as an embodied and participatory way to mark a transition or facilitate a transformation. In so doing, rituals connect us to something larger than ourselves—to community, to the holy, to the seasons, to the cycles of life and death.

Rituals Facilitate a Transformation or Mark a Transition

Rituals can serve two distinct yet related functions. On the one hand, a ritual can connect us to our aspirations, facilitating a transformation; for example, it can help us discern something or let something go. On the other hand, it can mark a transition that has already occurred, affirming a change that has already taken place, such as using a new name or pronouns, or making a commitment to a life partner. In either case, at their core rituals create a container for change, whether that change is simple and mundane or profound and even life-changing.

Rituals do not have to happen at one specific point in a transition. They can be useful at various stages, serving different emotional purposes at each. A ritual done prior to a transition can help ease the way into it, help us say goodbye to what we must let go of in order to grow in a new way. A ritual may help us to name who we want to become or to commit ourselves to living differently in the world. A ritual held in the midst of a transition can facilitate change, healing, and growth. And a ritual done after a transition can help us to process what has just happened, to more fully accept a change we did not want, or to name a new stage that we have entered. Often, rituals serve more than one of these purposes.

The congregation that Heather served for many years as the minister of faith formation had a yearlong Coming of Age program for young people that includes two important rituals at different times: one at a fall retreat, and the other as part of a Sunday service in the spring. She explains,

> The second night of the fall Coming of Age retreat is when the magic begins to happen. I have led our yearlong eighth-grade Coming of Age program enough times to know that I cannot assess the maturity or investment of the group in the Coming of Age program until after that Saturday night in November.
>
> On Saturday night, after sharing a meal together, the youth, adult mentors, and program facilitators move into a circle, where I hand out slips of paper. After sharing a bit about how special it is to have a group of young people and a group of trusted adults who are not their parents together learning and growing and sharing our wisdom with one another, I invite youth to write down questions they have for the adults, and vice versa. I then first invite the adults to answer questions from the youth.

The questions always blow me away. The youth wonder, "What is it like to have kids, and watch them grow up? What is it like to have a parent die? How did you choose where to go to college? Do grades really matter that much? What if I choose a job or career path and then I don't like it? How do you know when you are falling in love?"

And the adults always offer such tenderhearted, affirming answers to these young people.

And then we switch. And I ask the youth the questions the adults submitted earlier.

"What is it like growing up in a world that's so much online? What do you think are the most important values to your generation? What makes an adult worthy of your trust? Who do you most admire? What do you worry about when you think about the future?"

Invariably, every year, in this moment I watch the youth get more vulnerable with each other and with the mentors in the room.

This is where I begin to see the transformation happen: the deepening from a collection of individuals into a connected and cohesive group. This ritual facilitates it. And almost without fail, after that first retreat, our conversations are suddenly deeper, more vulnerable, more invested, more authentic. The youth trust each other and the adults in the room enough to really go deep, push themselves to think carefully about the topics at hand. The adults see the youth with so much more respect—no longer just as "kids of the church" but as thoughtful, growing, interesting, particular young people who have wisdom to share with them.

At the end of our yearlong program, our eighth graders, like many Unitarian Universalist young people, offer credos, descriptions of their faith and their values, to the congregation in our Sunday morning Coming of Age worship service. This worship is unfailingly beautiful, symbolic, and powerful—yet I always tell our eighth graders prior to the service that it is not their credo that defines their Coming of Age experience, it is all the experiences and thinking and community building and openheartedness and reflection that got them to a place where they *could* write a credo. Too often, people think that the Sunday Morning credo service is *the* Coming of Age moment. But, unlike that Saturday evening in November, this culminating service does not *facilitate* a transformation; rather, it is the moment that the rest of the congregation *marks* the transformation—from child to youth—that has been in process throughout the course of the year.

Rituals Are Participatory

By their very nature, rituals are participatory. Although many rituals are led by one or a few people, everyone present has some role in making the ritual experience happen. Rituals are designed to include everyone in the gathering, whether large or small, and it is through their presence and participation that a ritual becomes powerful.

There is something uniquely powerful about the whole gathered body creating something together. Allison describes this happening in her congregation in the spring of 2020:

> The Covid-19 pandemic brought new and unexpected challenges to all of us who were tasked with leading communities in worship. Not only were we leading our people through an unprecedented time of isolation and fear, with sickness and death seeming to be around every corner, we were also doing it all in an entirely new medium as we shifted from meeting in person to meeting online. We were truly making it up as we went and hoping we might create something that would hold us through all that we were going through.
>
> At the congregation I serve, we moved our worship quickly onto Zoom, almost not missing a beat. Sometime in the first few weeks, we started inviting members of the congregation to respond in the chat box. Sometimes service leaders read their responses aloud, and sometimes we just let them be there for people to read on their own. It was a way of making space for people to connect with one another in a small way, to break through the isolation that was so intense in those early days of quarantine.
>
> About a month in, I decided to try something a little different. The service was about taking things one day at a time, and instead of preparing a benediction or ad-libbing one on my own, I invited everyone to share one word in the chat box describing what got them through the day. For the benediction, I read their answers aloud as they came in. It was one of those moments as a worship leader when I had no idea what exactly was going to happen or if it was going to work, but I just crossed my fingers and took the leap.

The result was better than I ever could have expected. Even over Zoom, as I read that list of words aloud, you could just feel the connection, the spirit moving among those little boxes on our screens. As I look back at the words now, they are not particularly poetic or profound. We named naps and gratitude and family, books and music and love. Some of the words were mundane, some were humorous, some were even a little confusing. The magic of that benediction was not the content, it was the fact that we created it together. In a moment when we all felt very far apart, when we needed one another so deeply, the co-creation of that experience added meaning and depth that no polished, poetic words I might have come up with on my own could have offered.

In the months following, we did many similar rituals of sharing and co-creation—sometimes for benedictions, sometimes for prayers. Each time I wondered if it was going to work, each time I worried that it wouldn't come together the way I was hoping, and yet, each time, the magic happened again—community, connection, co-creation.

This co-creation is a powerful expression of Unitarian Universalist theology. Unitarian Universalists believe that there is no special ritual authority reserved for clergy. It is the intention and attention of the people who have gathered, whether one or many, that consecrate a place and a moment. We believe that all people—young and old, clergy and lay, religious and nonreligious—have the capacity to offer wisdom, love, and connection, and to find and create meaning in the ordinary stuff of life.

Rituals Are Embodied

Christian hegemony and white cis-heteropatriarchy have left us with a legacy of disconnection from our bodies. These systems of power and control have taught us to privilege minds over bodies, intellect over emotion, theories over experience. Any body that is considered less than the ideal—including black and brown bodies, women's bodies, trans bodies, fat bodies, disabled bodies—is devalued at best and excluded, threatened, or killed at worst.

Rituals reclaim our connection with our bodies. They call us back into our bodies, into the present moment, into the room with one another. They remind us that the only way that we can experience the world, the holy, our relationships is through the bodies we inhabit. In that way, they are an act of resistance to disconnection from and disdain for our bodies.

Several of the rituals in this book have to do with the direct experience of having a body. They mark such things as weaning a child, surviving sexual assault, and undergoing surgery. And even those rituals that do not directly connect to the body invite people to use their senses in order to get in touch with their emotions. Taste, touch, smell—all of these help us to connect with an experience in a way that is deeply meaningful and memorable. Many of these rituals invite participants to physically *do* something: to lay down a burden, to burn away regrets and anger, to bless another's body with lotion or water.

The embodiment of ritual also helps connect us more deeply to our values, to our beliefs about the world, and to our hearts. There is a reason we turn to ritual in the face of tragedy and transition. Our emotions live in our bodies, and so embodied ritual helps us to take what we intellectually know to be true and process it more fully.

Allison tells this story about using a Glitter Blessing at the first Pride service her congregation held:

> As I was planning for my congregation's first ever Pride service, I came across the Glitter Blessing written by Rev. Caitlin Cotter Coillberg, which is included as an element in the "For Pride" ritual in this book. We had wanted to do something with glitter, and some kind of ritual, and this felt just perfect. I loved the theological message about the sacred beauty inherent in every person, as well as the embodied practice of placing glitter on people to symbolize that theology.
>
> As with many new rituals I introduce to the congregation, I wasn't sure exactly how people would respond. I spoke Caitlin's beautiful words of introduction and then invited people to come up or raise their hand from their seat for a blessing. We gave people the option of putting the glitter on their hand or their face. As we spread the glitter on each person's hand or face, we spoke the words "May the beauty that you are shine as bright as the stars."
>
> The sacred feeling of this ritual was so much more powerful than I expected. I was especially surprised at how many of my humanist-leaning, ex-Catholic people wanted the glitter right in the center of their forehead, reminiscent of the crosses on Ash Wednesday. Some even requested I place

the glitter "where the ashes go." Even these folks who I knew had left those ashes behind had a muscle memory of that ritual and wanted this symbol of original blessing, of the beauty that they are, to go right in that same place.

As I spread the glitter gel on hands and foreheads, and spoke the words of the blessing, I looked right into people's eyes and could see the way it touched their hearts. The physicality and embodied intimacy of the blessing went deeper than the simple words ever could have on their own.

Afterward, I heard stories from people who had gone about their day with that glittery reminder of their inherent worth, and had even shown it off to others. Not only did the embodiment matter in the moment of the blessing, the physical reminder that they left with kept it present in their hearts throughout the day, and allowed them to share that blessing with the world.

Rituals connect us to our bodies and to our hearts. Using our senses, they remind us that we are bodies as well as brains. Rituals invite us into a different way of knowing—a way of experiencing our values or theology as more than words on a page.

Rituals Connect Us to Something Larger Than Ourselves

There is a reason that many religious and cultural traditions have rituals that are repeated generation after generation. Rituals connect us both to our deepest selves and to something larger than ourselves—to our community, to our faith, to the generations that have come before us and will come after us, to the grand story of the universe, and to the love that holds us and will not let us go.

Rituals connect us to our community by reminding us that we are not alone in this hard and beautiful work of being human. Rituals connect us as individuals to a people, whether it is our family, our congregation, or those with whom we share an identity or cultural heritage. In "For Mending Broken Covenant," for instance, the community is invited to name the ways that the bonds holding it together were broken and share in a ritual to repair those bonds. The ritual helps everyone remember that the work of being in community is messy and hard, beautiful and powerful, all at the same time, and that spirit and grace and love show up to guide us in that work.

Rituals also connect us to a larger human story that spans generations. Regardless of whether a particular ritual is newly created or a long-standing tradition, the knowledge that other people in other times have had the same longings, questions, worries, and sorrows can be powerful. In "For the Beginning and End of a Congregational Year," stones are brought by each member of the community at the beginning of the year, and taken by each member at the end of the year. The bowl that holds the stones, along with any leftover stones, is used each year, over and over again. There are always some stones left over, reminding the community that people have died, moved away, or left, and that others have joined, but that through it all, the community persists, generation after generation.

Finally, rituals connect us to our faith, to our sense of what some people call the holy—you might use that word or a different one. They remind us of the love that holds and sustains us, of the sacredness of our earth, and of the most deeply held values that guide our living. In "For Blessing Backpacks," participants are invited to fill their bags with courage and love, so that they carry their faith with them as they go about their everyday lives. Both in our everyday lives and in times of transition and change, we need these reminders of our faith, of all that holds and sustains us.

Heather tells this story about the creation of the ritual "For a Blended Family":

Jeff and Karin were two members of my congregation who had met through the church and fallen in love. When we met to plan their wedding, they said, "We want a way to acknowledge our kids in the ceremony, and to leave space for any of the feelings they might be having about it."

Between Jeff and Karin, they had six young adult children. Jeff's first wife, Nancy, had died of cancer when his two girls were in high school, and Karin's marriage had ended five years earlier. They had both raised their children in the congregation, and now, years later, they were starting a new chapter of their lives together.

They reflected, "This is a happy day for us, but it has been a hard road of loss, especially for our kids, to get to this moment." They were looking for a container to hold it all—the history and the potential, the merging of their two families, the grief and the love.

As we thought about the symbolism they wanted, we remembered the water communion that the congregation holds each year. Each fall, this congregation, like many other Unitarian Universalist congregations, uses water to symbolize the merging of our separate journeys. Water represents so much: it is cleansing, nourishing, healing, and powerful, the sustaining essence of life. In this congregation, people are asked to bring water and share what it represents to them. Then they bless the water and the coming together of their shared journeys. We decided to adapt this ritual to use it as a container to hold this moment—to symbolize Jeff's and Karin's families merging together, their separate family histories and their shared future, and the sacredness of it all.

Jeff's and Karin's families each brought water from their homes, and during the ceremony, with grandchildren peeking their heads up over the table, each of the six young adult children came up to the altar table and one by one poured water from their childhood homes into a shared vessel. We blessed it all—the tears of grief and the tears of joy that brought these families to this place, the love that grew out of loss, the hope and the promise, the past and the future.

This is the task of ritual: to give structure and meaning to the human experience in a way that connects us to our family and community, to the grand arc of the human story, and to the mystery in which spirit and love reside.

Conclusion

We need rituals that meet us in our lives and in our shared practices of meaning-making. We need rituals that connect us with our traditions—faith traditions, family and cultural traditions, and others, with our theology and values, and with our sense of being part of something bigger than ourselves. And we need rituals that we don't have to create for ourselves in the moments we need them.

We hope that this book will offer you rituals to hold you in your tender moments, to give you courage when you most need it, and to capture your joy. Just as there is a love that holds us and will never let us go, so too are there rituals, grounded in our faith, values, traditions, and communities, that can hold us through it all.

For Unitarian Universalists in particular, we also hope that this book will bring more ritual in general to the shared practice of our faith. Engaging regularly in ritual, both individually and collectively, moves us out of our heads and into our hearts, making space for more embodiment, more co-creation, more connection, and more transformation.

Handle with Care
Context and Covenant for Rituals
By Rev. Aisha Ansano

A few years after I became a Unitarian Universalist, I was visiting my mom, and we decided to attend the local UU church for a Sunday morning service. As we walked into the sanctuary, I glanced down at the order of service I had been handed and almost turned around and walked back out—because the service that day was going to be a Kwanzaa service.

Why did that make me want to leave? Because, as a multiracial Black woman, I was extremely wary of what a Kwanzaa service might be like in a UU congregation. Even in my limited experience of UU churches, I had all too often witnessed UUs taking customs and rituals that were not theirs and using them as if they were, with no acknowledgment—or even, it seemed, understanding—of the harm this could cause. Using rituals in this way can both dilute their meaning and disrespect the people and culture from which they come.

I'd been in worship services where the congregation was invited to sing African American spirituals that were presented without introduction or context, as though they were just fun songs that fit a theme, rather than being deeply rooted in a particular history. I'd watched UUs light the candles of a menorah incorrectly in worship and mispronounce the words of Spanish texts and songs. Often I had wondered if the people attempting these rituals had any relationship with people of the culture or tradition being showcased. And if not, were the rituals being used appropriately, or was something important missing from the observance, since those whose tradition it was weren't involved?

That day, home on vacation and with my mom, I didn't know if I had the energy to endure more rituals taken out of context. I especially did not want to experience white UUs celebrating Kwanzaa without any relationship to folks who celebrate it as a personal or community practice, or to see a couple of Black folks, whether UUs or members of the wider community, asked to present the holiday like a show and tell, whether or not they actually celebrated it themselves, simply because they were Black.

I'm glad I stayed at the church that day. The service was indeed led by Black staff members, congregants, and wider community members—but they were people with personal and familial experience of celebrating Kwanzaa. The white minister shared some reflections about commonalities between the principles of Kwanzaa and the UU principles. It was a truly wonderful and powerful service—but my previous experiences almost made me miss it. Even though I hadn't been UU for long, I was already weary of Unitarian Universalist appropriation of rituals without cultural context or relationship with their communities of origin.

Like many noncreedal spiritual communities, Unitarian Universalism is not devoid of ritual. From weekly practices like lighting the chalice or sharing joys and sorrows to annual rituals like the flower communion and water ceremony, our tradition has a number of rituals grounded in our theology and history, and individual congregations often also have rituals of their own that are rooted in their particular history and community. And it is also true that, as a tradition with historical roots in Christianity but with many members who don't identify as Christian, we can struggle to discern which rituals from our history still feel like ours.

When we yearn for rituals that we aren't finding in our own tradition, it's easy to turn to other cultures and religious traditions, to take customs and rituals that speak to us and try to make them our own. It may be a relief to find that a ritual already exists to give us what we are yearning for, to feel that we do not need to create our own from scratch. The long history of a ritual might help it feel even more powerful. When we are longing to remember and honor the people in our lives who have died, it is tempting to reach for established customs such as Dia de los Muertos even if we do not have Mexican heritage, or the yahrzeit even if we do not hold a Jewish identity. These observances already exist, and we know that they are deeply meaningful for many—and so we may convince ourselves that they can be meaningful for us, as well. But the power of these particular rituals is rooted in specific cultural and religious histories and experiences, and if we do not share those, then the rituals are not ours to use. When we choose to use them anyway, whatever our intention, we risk diminishing their meanings and harming the potential relationships between us and those for whom they hold familial, cultural, or religious significance.

We can participate in rituals from other cultures and traditions as invited guests, but they are not ours to lead or to adapt to fit our needs. Instead, we must turn to our own rituals—that is part of the goal of this book, to offer rituals grounded in Unitarian Universalism that UUs can use to mark important occasions and moments in their personal and communal lives. And since Unitarian Universalism excludes no one on the basis of belief, readers who are not UU are invited to connect with these rituals as well, and to infuse them with their own traditions—as long as the adaptations they make are consistent with the values and intentions inherent in the original rituals.

Using Rituals Responsibly

The rituals in this book are being offered as a gift. They exist because people have needed them. And the existence of these rituals—the existence of this book—is proof that we are capable of creating and holding our own rituals. The rituals offered here are grounded in Unitarian Universalism and often use UU symbols and language, but they demonstrate a larger point: whoever we are—Unitarian Universalists, members of another noncreedal faith community, followers of a creedal faith, spiritual but not religious, or entirely secular—we can create rituals that meet our needs and those of our communities.

In accepting and using these gifts of ritual, however, it's important to recognize that some of them were written by and for people with particular experiences and identities. Even if you too are a Unitarian Universalist, that does not mean that you can always freely use work created by and for UUs with marginalized identities simply because you share religious identity.

When a transgender UU writes a poem about their experience as a transgender person, it is not an invitation for cisgender UUs to adapt that poem to fit their own identity and experience and then share it in worship. When a Black UU creates a ritual grounded in the Black experience, non-Black UUs should consider how the ritual needs to be contextualized if they use it, and whether they are best suited to lead it. When a UU with a disability writes a reflection on their experiences with welcome— or its lack—in UU spaces, temporarily able-bodied UUs should not use it to talk about other forms of welcome in UU spaces.

Whenever you use a ritual in this book, I invite you to think about why its author might have written it, and what it might mean to the community for whom it was written. I hope that, as you dig into the resources offered here, you do so with deep intentionality, respect, and humility. And I hope this book inspires you to create the rituals that *you* need, that meet your needs and the needs of your communities, grounded in your own religious, spiritual, and/or ethical values.

Some of the rituals in this book are meant for small groups, and some are for larger gatherings or congregational worship services. Some focus on a specific individual, while others invite equal participation by everyone present. In smaller gatherings, it is easier for those present to stay in deep relationship with one another, to think and talk through the process and the ritual itself with intentionality, and to hold each other accountable in love. In larger gatherings, such as congregational worship, it can be easier to drift away from the deep relationship and accountability we'd like to have with each other. That's when it can be particularly easy to use a ritual in a way that might be painful or harmful, however unintentionally. When some participants have not been involved in planning the ritual and discussing its meaning, they may not understand why it is being led in the way that it is, or why certain words or songs are being used and should not be changed. When a ritual is offered to a large gathering, therefore, extra context or framing can be helpful. For instance, the leader could talk about the community from which the ritual emerges or give some background on the songs and readings.

Covenant

Since we may unintentionally and unconsciously perpetuate harm and replicate systems of oppression, rituals from this book should be planned and led through the lens of the following covenant. This covenant is intended to ground your engagement with these rituals in humility, intention, accountability, and gratitude.

As I use the rituals in this book, I covenant to engage with them through the following values:

- Humility, acknowledging and sitting with any discomfort that arises.
- Intention, giving the rituals my attention and focus, and engaging with them with reverence and respect.
- Accountability, learning about and alongside the centered community through relationship and context.
- Gratitude, participating in the ritual with appreciation for those who offer it.

In preparing to lead a ritual from this book, read through the covenant and share it with everyone involved in the planning and leading of the ritual. If you or someone else has questions about the covenant, create space for a conversation to bring you all to a deeper understanding of it and the values that underlie it. Everyone who is planning or leading the ritual should agree to this covenant and understand what it means. With rituals that are written by and for people with a particular identity or experience, it may make sense to give all participants, not just the planners and leaders, some explanation of the covenant's values and invite them to engage with the ritual through its lens as well.

Humility

Approaching these rituals with humility means recognizing that aspects of some of them may make us uncomfortable. Unless the ritual was written by or for those with a marginalized identity that we also hold, the invitation here is to acknowledge and recognize that discomfort and to process it together, without making substantive changes to the ritual.

If you are planning to lead the ritual "For Lamenting and Setting Intentions to Heal White Supremacy Culture," you may want to tell participants that it was adapted from one written for a 2017 campaign by the Unitarian Universalist Association called "The Promise and the Practice of Our Faith" and share with them some of the campaign's context and history. (Information is included in the ritual's description.) At the same time, while the words "white supremacy culture" might make you or others uncomfortable, do not remove them from the ritual. Instead, invite yourself and other participants to reflect on why those specific words might have been chosen, and what about them is making you uncomfortable. A moment of conversation about this discomfort might be a welcome way to ground yourselves in humility.

Intention

When you lead a ritual, how might you invite those who are participating to approach it with intention? As you use the rituals in this book, especially ones that might come from or honor a community or identity that is not your own, think about what context and grounding you may wish to offer. Is there something in the ritual's description or setup that might be helpful to explicitly tell people? Should you share the context of any individual elements of the ritual, explaining the biography of a reading's author or the history of a song? Is there language that should be defined or explained so that no one is confused during the ritual? What context would be helpful to provide in order to invite participants into the space?

The more information you can share, the more everyone can enter the ritual with deep intentionality.

The first time I led worship for Martin Luther King Jr. Day, I remarked to the staff team planning with me that I really wanted to sing "Lift Ev'ry Voice and Sing," which is sometimes called the Black national anthem—but that I was also hesitant to use it. I had been in UU congregations where people seemed to sing this song as though it were any other, only half paying attention and not really noticing the words. I felt that it had often been sung in UU spaces without its history and power being recognized. And so the staff suggested that I share this reflection with the congregation as an introduction to the song, that I give them some historical and personal context, and then invite them to sing with intentionality and even discomfort.

So I did. I introduced it by saying,

> This song deserves to be sung with attention. It is a song that starkly names the horrors and violence of racism in this country, and it is a song that should make us uncomfortable: uncomfortable with the history that it calls upon, uncomfortable with the fact that the struggle for racial justice continues, and has not come quite so far as it should have by now. How can anyone sing the words "treading our path through the blood of the slaughtered" without a deep, deep discomfort?

By sharing this with the congregation, I enabled them to be more deeply connected with the song, its history, and my experiences. I believe that this allowed us to all have a more deeply spiritual and intentional moment in singing it.

Accountability

Accountability invites us to lead and participate in rituals through the context of relationship with those who created them or those for whom they were created. Do you, or does your congregation, have a relationship with someone whose identity the ritual is focused on? If so, consider inviting them into the planning process and offering to let them lead the ritual—but without assuming or expecting that they will want to take on that labor. If they express concerns about the ritual being led in your setting, take that as an opportunity for you to learn more, rather than just leading it anyway. If the ritual was written by or for people with a marginalized identity that you do not hold, do not adapt pieces of it to be about your identity instead. Consider whether you can offer participants information about the ritual, such as its historical context, to help them understand it better.

In the setup for "For Release from Prison, Jail, or Detention," Jason Lydon explains that "all quotes and readings in this ritual (aside from the biblical quote) come from currently or formerly incarcerated writers." You may want to explicitly say that when introducing the ritual, so that those present can understand the context in which the readings were chosen. Follow Lydon's request and "do not include additional writings from people who have not experienced incarceration," even if you think they might be a perfect fit.

In "For Coming Out Day," Rose Maldonado Schwab says that she wrote the ritual to be led by a leader who is part of the LGBTQ+ community and that some language might need to be adapted if the leader is an ally, so that they don't claim identities they don't hold. Since she has directly invited it, this adaptation is okay; but this is not an invitation to change the identities listed in the "Invitation to the LGBTQ+ Community" section just because they might be unfamiliar to the person leading the ritual.

Gratitude

Engaging with these rituals from a place of gratitude means appreciating the people who wrote them and the communities and experiences from which they come. This can be as simple as making sure that you name the author of the ritual (and anyone else who may have written elements of it) for participants. If the ritual is one you've been wishing for, or one that perfectly fits a moment in your life or the life of your community, you might express your gratitude directly to its creators. Finally, sharing the rituals with others who might be in need of them is a powerful way to show your gratitude for the work of their creators.

Conclusion

Approaching and engaging with these rituals from a place of humility, intention, accountability, and gratitude can be difficult work. At times it might feel overwhelming or even impossible. The reality is, you will not do this work perfectly. You are going to make mistakes, or wish you had done things differently, and it will be frustrating at times. However, the goal is not perfection; instead, the goal is to continue to learn and grow, to connect in relationship to others, and to repair covenant and rebuild relationships when something isn't right.

The rituals in this book have been lovingly created and offered as a gift, and the best way that we can honor that gift is by receiving it with a spirit of humility, intention, accountability, and gratitude. May these rituals anchor your roots and feed your spirit.

Rev. Aisha Ansano believes that deep relationship building is crucial in the struggle for justice in our world and is called to serve as a prophetic and pastoral presence to those seeking spiritual community and connection. She is a cofounding minister of Nourish, which helps Unitarian Universalists feel fed in body and spirit through embodied worship experiences. Aisha also serves as the denominational counselor to UU students at Harvard Divinity School. She lives in Malden, Massachusetts.

Practical Tips for Rituals

In this book you will find a variety of rituals for different settings and circumstances. These rituals are for you to use, adapt, and turn to as resources. To help you use them, we offer these practical tips: to make the space serve the ritual, to ground leaders of rituals in their role as facilitators, and to make the experience of the ritual as inclusive as possible. This is not an exhaustive guide, but rather an invitation to think through some practical and relational elements as you prepare to use the rituals in this book (and, perhaps, to create your own).

Space and Setup

Rituals happen in all kinds of different spaces. Sometimes a ritual happens spontaneously, with no time to prepare the space. That is okay. Your own energy as leader may be all you need to create the kind of environment in which powerful transformation can occur.

When you are able to take the time to set up a space, remember that the environment of a ritual sets the tone before any words are spoken. As you are creating the space for the ritual, think about the kind of atmosphere you want people to enter into. What is the emotional goal of the ritual? Is it celebratory, somber, reflective, empowering? How can the space reflect that through its lighting, imagery, altar decorations, and sound as people enter the space?

Consider also the flow of the space. In addition to being beautiful, is it practical? Is there room for people to move around if they need to? Or are there places that risk traffic jams and collisions? For example, if people need to move to the front of the space and then back to their seats, is there enough space to do that? Is there enough space for people using assistive devices like wheelchairs or scooters? What instructions will you need to offer?

Gather all of your materials in advance, and think about where and how they will need to be used during the ritual. Do you have a place to lay your script down if you will need both hands? If you are passing around stones, do you have a container to hold them? Do you have a way to play recorded music or a way to project any slides or videos?

Many of the rituals included in this book involve lighting candles or a chalice. The flaming chalice is a symbol of Unitarian Universalism and lighting and extinguishing a chalice is often used to mark the beginning and end of sacred time. If a ritual includes flame, there are several specific considerations you may wish to think about ahead of time. If the ritual is taking place outside where it may be windy, or if some participants may not be able to inhale smoke or safely handle flame, you may want to use battery-operated artificial candles instead. Similarly, if you will need to extinguish candles, consider providing a snuffer or another way to extinguish the flame in case anyone would have trouble blowing one out.

Look through the script of the ritual and consider what words and music participants might need in front of them to participate fully. Print copies or create slides for any words or music that cannot be easily repeated after a leader or taught in the moment, and plan how and when you will distribute any handouts without disrupting the ritual.

Taking the time to think through the space and setup can ensure that the space works in service of the ritual rather than against it and that logistical challenges will not impede its beauty and transformative power.

Accessibility

The embodied, participatory nature of rituals makes it particularly important to be mindful of accessibility. In making rituals accessible, we are embodying our values and theology: Unitarian Universalists, along with many others, believe that all people are whole and holy, that all bodies are good bodies, and that we are called to place justice and love at the center of our faith.

It is important to consider how participants with a wide variety of mobility, sensory, allergy, and processing needs will experience all parts of the ritual: how they will enter into its space, how they will eat any food or drink involved, how they will perceive what is happening, how they will join in any shared words or movements. A ritual offered to the public will probably need to allow for a wider set of needs than one planned for a few people, but don't assume you know all the needs even of close friends. It is always better to err on the side of greater accessibility.

We have woven adaptations into the rituals in this book to make them more accessible to and inclusive of a wide variety of participants. If you know certain participants have disabilities or chronic illnesses, are neurodivergent, or have allergies, remember that they are the experts on their needs. When possible, ask them what would make the ritual most accessible to them. And of course, you are the expert on your own needs! Adapt the instructions in these rituals as you need to; for instance, you might place items on a higher or lower surface than is suggested, invite participants to come to you instead of moving toward them, or recruit a helper to lift or handle things for you.

Many excellent resources for making worship spaces accessible are available from the Unitarian Universalist Association and the UU organization EqUUal Access. We know that our understanding of how to be inclusive keeps growing and changing, and we trust that this list will be incomplete. Here we offer some general thoughts about making rituals accessible.

- If there will be more than ten people present, if people will be moving around, if they will be more than about ten feet apart, or if they will be outside, use a sound system and microphone at all times. Assisted listening devices are also a good idea. Sign language interpretation may be desirable.
- Make sure any texts that participants will need are either printed or projected in an easily readable font and size. Have some large-print paper versions or a link to a downloadable document available for low vision participants. Microsoft Word documents are usually compatible with screen readers; PDFs are not. Consider describing aloud what is happening in the ritual, as well as the appearance of significant people and items.
- Avoid using scented candles or other materials, especially when you are designing a ritual for a large group. Remember that even natural scents that many people enjoy, such as pine, eucalyptus, sage, and rose, can trigger allergies, so it is important to keep natural decorations away from people, and not to burn them or otherwise release their scent into the environment. If scents are a specific and necessary part of the ritual, check in with participants ahead of time to make sure there are no allergies or sensitivities.
- If you are using food in the ritual, be sure there are options for people with food sensitivities or allergies, or who are in recovery. For instance, if serving bread and wine, include gluten-free bread and both sulfite-free and nonalcoholic wine. Avoid using foods that might produce airborne allergens.
- In guided meditations and breathing exercises, remember that some people struggle to breathe easily. Instead of or in addition to suggesting deep breaths,

try inviting people to breathe intentionally, or to pay attention to the rhythm of their breath without trying to change it.

- Whenever you invite participants to stand, explicitly offer the option to sit as well. Also consider inviting people to stand or move around the space during the ritual as they feel necessary. If the ritual takes place inside a bounded space, clearly lay out the area included and explain how people should exit and reenter it if necessary.

- When movement is part of the ritual, make sure that people who cannot do that movement have an equally meaningful option. For instance, people could be invited either to stand or to raise their hands; to come forward to light a candle or to have one brought to them; to bring items to a gathering spot or to have someone else bring them. You could also alter the movements according to the needs of your group, such as by having a focus person go to participants instead of asking all participants to come forward to them.

- Be mindful of the height of tables, signs and posters, and other surfaces that people need to engage with. Avoid making the floor or ground the main ritual surface. Placing materials at multiple heights (floor, low table, higher table) makes them accessible to a wider variety of participants.

- If you are in relationship with minority language communities, including the Deaf community, or expect minority language users to be present, arrange in advance for interpretation. Make sure that invitations and other publicity include the fact that the ritual will be interpreted, and if it is a public event, publicize it in the relevant language communities.

- Remember that people process information in different ways and at different speeds, and offer multiple options for doing so: time to think before offering responses, the option to speak later (or not at all) rather than at an assigned moment, paper to jot down notes before sharing, etc.

It is important that you be mindful of the particular group for whom you are leading a ritual. If done well, accessibility adaptations can make a ritual deeper and more meaningful for all participants.

Music

Music is an important way to enhance the tone, flow, and mood of the ritual. Many rituals in this book suggest songs, as well as places where musical underscoring might add to the experience. The majority of the songs suggested in the rituals can be found online or in the Unitarian Universalist hymnals *Singing the Living Tradition* and *Singing the Journey*. The authors have been thoughtful about choosing music that fits well with the theme and tone of each ritual, but you are welcome to choose your own music instead. Here are some tips for choosing and arranging for music:

- Consider the overall mood and tone of the ritual. At this point in the ritual, are people going to be feeling upbeat, reflective, or somber? Choose music that will match that emotional space.
- Will this be a song that everyone sings together or music that is performed by one or a few people (or recorded)? If it is a song that will be sung by everyone gathered, consider how familiar the group might be with the song. If it is a song that is new to many people, make sure it is easily taught and that you have a song leader arranged in advance to teach the song. Consider if people will need printed or projected lyrics for a song.
- Many rituals have times where participants are silently participating in movement or reflection. This is an excellent opportunity to use musical underscoring (quiet background music, often instrumental) to enhance the moment. It smooths over any awkwardness and can help participants sink more deeply into the emotional experience of the moment.
- Arrange the music in advance, either recorded or live. Make sure you have the equipment necessary for everyone to hear the music.
- If the musician/song leader is a different person than the ritual leader, make sure you communicate in advance about cues and how to know when the music should begin and end.

We strongly encourage the use of music in rituals. Music allows us to access emotion and touch our souls in ways that words sometimes can't. When done well, music can help participants integrate the overall experience of a ritual in ways that are powerful and transformative.

Adaptations for Online Rituals

All the rituals in this book are designed to take place in person. However, as the Covid-19 pandemic taught us, it is important to be able to adapt rituals for virtual use.

The authors of all of the rituals in this book have given permissions for their rituals to be used both in person and online.

Adapting a ritual for use online is always easier if you are doing the ritual live and on a platform on which people can interact with one another. This allows for participation and for organic co-creation of the ritual experience.

If you are adapting a ritual to be used in a multiplatform context, where some people are online and some are in person, make sure to give the people online a meaningful alternative to each in-person element of the ritual. This may mean that the two groups are doing slightly different rituals. As long as the meaning-making remains the same, that is okay. Ideally there will be a way for the two groups to connect, such as by reading aloud contributions that online participants have shared in the chat or by making online and in-person participants visible to one another.

When some or all participants will be online, go through each element of your ritual and consider how it might work in an online format. There are a number of ways you can adapt participatory elements of rituals for use online. They include:

- Using a chat function in place of spoken sharing.
- Inviting people to engage in the same physical movements in their own spaces, such as reaching out hands to connect across screens.
- Substituting items that people commonly have in their homes for traditional ritual items, so that each person can participate in the ritual action at home. You may need to tell online participants what to provide themselves with in advance.
- Providing relevant materials in advance to people who will be participating online for them to use during the ritual.
- Collecting photos from participants in advance to share during the ritual.

In general, make sure that online participants have things to do just as in-person participants do; they should not be simply watching others act. Remember that online platforms also offer tools and options that are impossible in person, such as close-ups of what is happening and word clouds created on the spot by participants. While the experience of attending a ritual in person cannot be exactly replicated online, we have discovered that online rituals provide unique opportunities for creativity, connection, and transformation.

Ritual Roles

Rituals are, by their nature, participatory, and so it is the entire gathered body—whether one person or a hundred—that co-creates the ritual together. However, people may take on a variety of roles in that co-creation. In this book, we distinguish between four different roles: participant, helper, leader, and focus person.

> A **participant** is anyone who is attending and taking part in the ritual. This is the broadest category. Rituals are meant to include everyone in the room, and so, while people may take part in the ritual in different ways, there is no role for people who are simply observers.

> A **helper** is someone who assists in the ritual in some way. In several of our rituals helpers pass out supplies, direct the flow of traffic, or manage other details.

> A **leader** is a person who creates and holds the container in which the ritual experience can occur and guides the participants through it. In the Unitarian Universalist tradition anyone, minister or layperson, can lead a ritual, but most rituals do require a designated leader or leaders.

> A **focus person**, if there is one, is a person for whom the ritual is being performed. Such a ritual marks a personal life passage or moment, enabling a group or community to witness and mark it.

In this book, we have rituals that are designed to be done by individuals for themselves; rituals designed for families or small groups, where one of the participants may also serve as a leader; and rituals designed for groups of any size in which the leader is distinct from the participants.

Notes about Ritual Leadership

A good ritual leader is someone who can remain mindful both of the plan and flow of the ritual and of the needs of the group that may arise during it. So much of the experience of a ritual is influenced by the tone and presence that its leader brings. A good ritual leader projects a sense of calmness and confidence, even when things don't go according to plan (which will happen!). They read the mood of the room, model appropriate sharing, allow time for participants to reflect and share as well, and are comfortable with silence.

If you are planning to lead a ritual, it is important to think through every step in advance. It can be helpful to do this in the space in which you will be leading the ritual. Think about who will be where, where materials will be set up, when participants will move and where they will go, how you will phrase explanations and directions, and any other concerns specific to your space and the participants.

Sometimes a ritual leader is also a participant, or even a focus person. This is most often the case in rituals that are done in the home or by a family, when it may not make sense for an outside leader to be present. On the other hand, if you are a participant or focus person, you may want to have another person hold the space for you so that you may simply concentrate on the experience of the ritual, without needing to also attend to the needs of the group.

Children in Rituals

Rituals are one of the best tools for multigenerational worship and community building that we have. Rituals are often accessible to kids in ways that word-centered practices may not be, because they are embodied and participatory. In order to participate fully in a ritual, however, children may need some additional preparation or explanation from caregivers or other adults. Adults may need to repeat or interpret directions, explain actions, or demonstrate or model how to participate.

As you are preparing for a ritual in which children will be participating, make sure that the materials are child-friendly, or that child-friendly alternatives are available (for example, offering battery-operated candles or washable markers).

Keep an open mind about what children are capable of doing and understanding. You may be surprised by how much of the meaning and metaphor they take in. Children love rituals and the predictability and participation they offer. If you are looking for a way to create meaningful and memorable multigenerational worship services or other events, ritual is a great place to start.

Consent and Comfort in Rituals

People come to ritual spaces, especially religious ones, with a wide variety of experiences in spiritual communities. For some, those experiences have been profoundly healing and beautiful, while for others they have been painful and exclusionary. Some people are simply unfamiliar with being in a ritual space and may be uncomfortable or nervous that they won't know the right way to move, speak, act, or otherwise participate.

Whatever associations and past experiences people bring, there are many ways to make a ritual space more comfortable for all in attendance, and to attend to both spiritual and bodily consent throughout the ritual.

It can be extremely helpful to give participants a sense of what will happen in the ritual ahead of time, to allay any nervousness. A leader might say, "Today we are going to share in a ritual of [*theme*], and in a few moments, I will invite you to [*action*]." Always make clear that participants can choose not to engage in any part of the ritual, without needing to justify or explain themselves. They can simply not do the suggested action, say "Pass" or shake their head when invited to speak, or otherwise indicate that they plan not to engage in that part of the ritual.

If an element of the ritual involves touching other people (such as a laying on of hands or an anointing) give people the explicit option to participate in a meaningful way that does not involve touching or being touched. For some people touch is healing and connecting, but others may find it takes them out of the ritual headspace or feels threatening. Always give clear directions for how people should indicate if they do not wish to be touched (crossing their arms, for instance) and remind participants to respect one other's bodily autonomy.

One way to help people feel safe and comfortable is to use the right language for them. Especially when working with focus people, it is important to make sure that both the pronouns and the ways you describe their identities are the words they would use for themselves. The ritual scripts here default to the gender neutral pronoun *they* for a focus person, but be sure you know which pronouns you should use for the specific person or people you are working with—or if you shouldn't use a pronoun for them at all.

Permissions and Guidelines for Adaptations

Most of the rituals in this book were written with a specific location, set of materials, physical space, group size, or set of participants in mind, and these specificities are described in their introductions. Of course, your own circumstances may or may not match them. Purchase of this book brings with it permission to use the rituals it contains in both online and in-person formats and to adapt them to suit your and your group's or community's needs. Feel free to use the materials presented here as a launching point for crafting rituals that fit your particular situation—while always preserving the values and intentions inherent in the original authors' work, and crediting them in whatever way makes sense in your context. Whenever you change a ritual, you will want to read through its setup and script to make sure that the flow, directions, metaphors, and language still work with the changes you have made.

The vast majority of these rituals have been created by people who hold an identity or experience relevant to the ritual. If the ritual is for an identity or experience that you do not hold, please be cautious about how you adapt it. Consult with the focus person to make sure the ritual is speaking to their own experience. There are some things that should not be adapted, or should only be adapted in relationship with people with the identity or experience the ritual is about. You can read more about best practices for ritual adaptation and implementation in the chapter "Handle With Care: Context and Covenant for Rituals in Pluralistic Communities" on page [xxi].

Rituals for Individuals and Families

Grounding and Centering

For Daily Reflection

Rev. Tandi Rogers and Rev. Sue Phillips

This ritual is a gentle, daily experience of shared reflection. It uses the same format and reflection materials for a whole week, so that the shape and substance of the experience have time to sink in for participants. Repetition is important because new meaning is revealed over time. The ritual invites each participant to enrich and explore their own spiritual life, evoking that which is beyond ourselves but to which we are connected by essence and aspiration. The authors originally designed this for their immediate family and have hosted what they call "family chapel" for both friends and complete strangers. Others have picked up the concept and made it their own as individuals, small groups in a retreat setting, online as a virtual pop-up community, and in religious communities.

Materials

- ☐ Chalice
- ☐ Timer
- ☐ Short piece of music (preferably no more than four minutes)
- ☐ Short reading (preferably less than 125 words)
- ☐ Optional: Bell or chime

Setup

The sweeter and more intentional the environment the better, just for loveliness's sake, but no formal setup is required! The authors enjoy using meditation cushions and floor chairs—something about sitting on the floor together is especially calming for them, but of course folks should just be as comfortable as possible. The authors have used the same space for this ritual for years, and the space has become part of the reflection experience, as they notice the light, sounds, and temperature changing with the seasons.

Choose a reading and a piece of music that are meaningful to you. Consider using music with rich metaphors, evocative tunes, or contemplative words. Try to match the tone and content of the music with the reading so there's some thematic integration.

Do this ritual every day for a week, using the same music and reading each day. With fewer than five participants, it will last about half an hour; allow more time for more people.

Script

Opening Words

Welcome to this time out of time to empty our hearts and minds. To let our spirits rest a bit together in the communal silence. In the music. In the reading. Let whatever rises rise. We will light our chalice, take a time of shared silence, hear some music, and listen to a reading twice. After the second reading, you are invited to share as you are inspired. Let's take some thoughtful breaths and arrive.

(Take a breath and wait a few seconds before continuing.)

Chalice Lighting

(Light the chalice or candle.)

Shared Silence

(Move right into three minutes of silence, ideally ringing a bell or using a timer with a lovely sound to mark the beginning and end of the time.)

Music

(Play the music the first time.)

Reading, First Voice

(The first reader names the author and title of the piece, then reads the reading slowly and intentionally. Allow 30-45 seconds of silence after they have finished.)

Reading, Second Voice

(The second reader reads the piece aloud, not repeating the author and title but with similar calm and intention.)

Reflection

(Ask simply, "What is rising for you in the meditation, reading, or music?" Be patient with silence. Leave time for each participant to speak, but also be content with someone choosing not to.)

Blessing

(Offer a brief blessing, prayer, or meditation, rooted in what you heard in the participants' reflections. Try to use generous, expansive language so that as many people as possible see themselves reflected in what you say.)

Music

(Play the music for a second time.)

Chalice Extinguishing

(Extinguish the chalice. Linger for just a moment as the smoke clears.)

Closing Words

(Thank everyone for coming and wish them well.)

For a New Year

Rev. Tandi Rogers

This is a reflection ritual to help participants focus their intentions for the coming year. This ritual can be done solo or in a small group. The candle collage was inspired by an exercise the author created for a youth leadership school. After an especially busy year, she wanted a way for her family to talk about all the changes they were going through, and this ritual emerged. It's become an annual event for them.

Materials

- ☐ Chalice
- ☐ Small table for chalice and completed candles
- ☐ Tables for crafting
- ☐ Pillar candles in plain glass holders, one for each participant
- ☐ Art supplies: glass or acrylic paint, tracing paper, tissue paper, permanent markers, pictures and words cut out of magazines, etc.
- ☐ Scissors and glue
- ☐ Guiding questions, either posted where everyone can see them or on handouts
- ☐ Optional: Music

Setup

If you are doing this ritual for a group, you will need two spaces very near each other: an intimate space where people can sit in a circle around a small table and chalice, and a separate crafting space. Make the crafting space inviting, ensuring that people have room to lay out materials and plan their candle art. Place a variety of art supplies on each table, with scissors and glue within reach, and a candle at each seat. Make sure table surfaces are protected appropriately. Encourage people to wear clothing that can get glue or paint on it. Perhaps have ambient music set up to create mood.

To honor that some people are internal processors and appreciate ample time to think through the prompts, send the guiding questions out with the invitation.

If the group is very music-oriented, when inviting them you may ask that they each send you two or three songs to invite in a fresh new year. From their suggestions you could make a playlist to offer up while people are working on their candles.

When setting this up for a group, invite people who may need some help maneuvering craft tools to sit by you. That way you can offer aid as requested.

Script

(Gather people in the intimate space first for an opening reflection.)

Opening Words

Welcome to a ritual of making New Year's candles to guide our intentions on this fresh year. The New Year can bring a mixture of emotions and memories. Some people have experienced the best year ever, and some have crawled across the finish line. The freshness of a clean slate brings hope for things to get better.

Chalice Lighting

"On the Brink of a New Year" (Lois Van Leer)

> We light this chalice on the brink of a new year
> Letting go of what has been
> Open and hopeful for what may come
> Renewed, restored, ready
> To live life fully anew
> May we move forward with intention.

(Light the chalice.)

Crafting

We're going to hear some guiding questions, and then we will move over to the sacred tables of craft supplies, where you will have a full hour to paint, glue, glitter, collage—however your intention for the New Year is calling to be expressed. And then we will meet back here for some closing sharing. We will go around the circle, each person who wishes to taking a turn reading one of the guiding questions, with ample time after each question for inspiration to arise. If you prefer not to read aloud, just say "Pass." Feel free to jot down ideas as they come, but please don't answer aloud at this time.

(Invite someone to start by reading the first question aloud. After they finish, pause for a few moments and then invite the next person to read. After a few questions, you will probably not need to prompt further readers.)

- What are you looking forward to this year?
- What is something new you want to try this year?
- This time next year, what do you want to have accomplished? What impact do you want to have made?
- What do you need to learn?
- What do you need to let go of?
- Who do you need to partner with?
- Who is your posse, the people you can count on?
- What ancestor or ancestors, familial or spiritual or cultural, will you call upon?
- What is your spiritual replenishment plan? What will you do when your spiritual well is dry? How will you keep yourself spiritually nourished?
- What do you want to ask of the Universe or the God of your understanding?

We will meet back here with our candles at [one hour from now].

(Decide as a group whether you will work in silence or welcome light conversation. You may or may not want to put soft, instrumental music on in the background. Leave the chalice lit, as the creation of the candles is part of the ritual. After an hour is up, invite people to place their candle in a circle around the chalice.)

Sharing

What came up for you? Who would like to share your candle with us first? As you pick up your candle, please light it from the light of the chalice. You can share what came up from a few guiding questions, or talk about your intention for the New Year. You can share as much as you like—and you may also pass, and just light your candle without saying anything.

(People share as they are moved. As the leader, make it clear through your modeling that silence is holy and welcome before and after sharings, and instead of speech.)

Chalice Extinguishing

(After everyone who wishes to has shared, extinguish the chalice with these words.)

This chalice flame has become many. May the community, inspiration, and intention of this time be embodied by our individual candles. May we take these candles and incorporate them into our individual spiritual practices that guide our living—living with courage, clarity, love, grace . . . and with what other qualities, friends? [Incorporate words offered up.]

May it be so. Amen.

For Everyday Adventures
Barbara Seidl

The purpose of this ritual is to acknowledge when someone is facing a challenge and to provide a physical reminder that they are not alone. It is appropriate both one to one and in a small or large group, and for most challenges: a math test, surgery, a trip. It can also serve as a general reminder to a congregation that their community is with them in their struggles; it can have one focus person or many. It is not appropriate for children under age 8, because of the sharpness of the safety pin. The author first received this ritual from her college debate coach, the late Tracey Anderson Wayson.

Materials
☐ Safety pins, one for each focus person
☐ Optional: Basket to hold pins

Setup
If you are doing this ritual with one other person, no setup is necessary. You'll just need a safety pin and a somewhat private moment.

If one person is offering the ritual to a group (such as a minister to a congregation), safety pins can be distributed during a worship service, or people can be given pins as they arrive. Assume that some people will not get them or will misplace them, though, and be prepared to distribute more as needed, or set baskets of them where people can easily reach them during the service.

If a group is offering the ritual to one person (such as a family to a child), everyone should be present in the room at the same time and, ideally, for the duration of the ritual. The person leading the ritual stands next to the person receiving the safety pin. It's helpful to designate someone to ensure the pin comes back to the leader after it has been passed from hand to hand.

See variations for groups of more than seven or eight people.

In all cases, the safety pin can be offered for the recipient to pin on themselves.

Script

ONE TO ONE

I have something I'd like to give you.

(Show the focus person a safety pin, or instruct them to select one from a basket.)

You are about to [take a big math test, go see your doctor, etc.].

I want you to have this safety pin for two reasons. Reason 1: it's always good to have a safety pin on important or challenging adventures. They come in handy. Reason 2: I want you to have this safety pin as a physical reminder—something you can touch and hold if things get hard on your adventure—a reminder that you're not holding it together all on your own. I am here thinking of you and helping you hold it all together. There are forces as strong as metal supporting you, and even the smallest and most ordinary things—a breath, a smile, a moment, a safety pin—can be very powerful. Where would you like this pinned to help you remember these things?

(The focus person chooses where it should be pinned, though you may offer suggestions. Many people choose to have it pinned over their hearts. Pin it on the spot they have chosen.)

As you [take this test, see your doctor, etc.], may you remember that you carry me with you on your adventure, and you don't have to hold it all together alone.

ONE PERSON TO GROUP

I believe you all picked up a safety pin when you came in today. If not, please raise your hand and the helpers will bring one to you.

Whatever challenges or adventures you may be facing in your lives—[name potential adventures]—I'm giving you this safety pin today for two reasons. Reason 1: it's always good to have a safety pin on important or challenging adventures. They come in handy.

Before I explain reason 2, I invite you to turn to your neighbor, hand them the safety pin, and say "This is for you. I thought you might need it on your next adventure." Let's try that now—turn to your neighbor and say, "This is for you. I thought you might need it on your next adventure."

(Participants exchange safety pins. When they have finished, continue.)

Reason 2: I want you to have this safety pin as a physical reminder—something you can touch and hold if things get hard on your adventure—a reminder that you're not holding it together all on your own. We are here thinking of you and helping you hold it all together. There are forces as strong as metal supporting you, and even the smallest and most ordinary things—a breath, a smile, a moment, a safety pin—can be very powerful. Where would you like this pinned to help you remember these things?

I invite you now to pin this safety pin on your shirt, the zipper to your jacket, or wherever you have chosen, and to help each other as you're willing and able.

(Continue speaking as people attach the pins.)

As you [repeat the adventures named previously], may you remember that you carry us with you on your adventure, and you don't have to hold it all together alone.

SMALL GROUP TO ONE PERSON

We have something we'd like to give you.

(Show the focus person a safety pin, or instruct them to select one from a basket.)

[Name] is about to [take a big math test, go to the doctor, etc.]. We're going to pass this safety pin around to each person in the room. When it reaches you, please hold it and silently offer your good wishes to [Name] on [this test, this appointment, etc.].

(Continue speaking while the safety pin is passed among participants.)

[Name], you are about to [take a big math test, go see your doctor, etc.]. We want you to have this safety pin for two reasons. Reason 1: it's always good to have a safety pin on important or challenging adventures. They come in handy. Reason 2: We want you to have this safety pin as a physical reminder—something you can touch and hold if things get hard on your adventure—a reminder that you're not holding it together all on your own. We are here thinking of you and helping you hold it all together. There are forces as strong as metal supporting you, and even the smallest and most ordinary things—a breath, a smile, a moment, a safety pin—can be very powerful.

(Retrieve the pin from the last person to hold it.)

Where would you like this pinned to help you remember these things?

(The focus person chooses where it should be pinned, though you may offer suggestions. Many people chose to have it pinned over their hearts. Pin the safety pin in the designated spot on the focus person.)

As you [take a big math test, go see your doctor, etc.], may you remember that you carry us with you on your adventure, and you don't have to hold it all together alone.

LARGE GROUP TO ONE PERSON

(If the safety pin is unlikely to make it around the room in the allotted time, such as because the group is larger than seven or eight people, consider options below.)

Option 1: Attach a note to the safety pin

(Attach a note to the pin saying, "We'll be using this safety pin for a blessing later today. [Name] is [having surgery on Monday, taking a big test, etc.]. When this safety pin reaches you, please hold it, silently offer any good wishes you have for [Name], and pass it along to the next person." Attach a long ribbon to the pin and note to make them easy to hold, pass, and track. Begin passing them early in the event, well before the ritual, and designate someone to track them, keep them moving, and bring them to you when needed. You may want to provide yourself with an identical backup pin in case the one being passed gets lost.)

(Insert this line in the script.) This safety pin has been passed hand to hand among us and now holds all our hopes and good wishes for you. Where would you like this pinned, to keep us with you on your adventure?

Option 2: Don't pass the safety pin

(Insert this line in the script.) Friends, please take a moment to summon your good wishes for [Name] silently into your hearts and minds. And now send them into this small but powerful reminder of our love.

(Hold the safety pin up in the palm of your hand, angling your hand down slightly so the pin is visible to others. Wait 5-10 seconds.)

Where would you like this pinned to keep us with you on your adventure?

For Discernment

Rev. Liz Weber

This ritual is for when you need to choose between options. It is for individual use, though two or more people could do it individually and then come together for further discussion. It could also be done with another person present as a supportive witness—not commenting or participating, but just being present and listening. The ritual was inspired by the process the author used to approach a big decision she had to make early in seminary.

Materials

- ☐ Chalice
- ☐ Sheet of paper for each option (bigger than 8½" × 11" is nice but not necessary)
- ☐ Pen or pencil
- ☐ Optional: Markers, pastels, or colored pencils
- ☐ Optional: Voice recorder

Setup

On each sheet of paper, write the name of one option. Set the pages so that you can spend time with them one at a time, such as in a circle around you or in a row along a table in front of you. It can be nice to do this ritual in the center of a labyrinth or sacred space, or just seated on the floor if that's comfortable. Set your chalice in a central or anchoring place.

Before you do this ritual, you may want to consciously set aside the thoughts you've been wrestling with to make space for a more heart-centered way of knowing. You could journal or picture placing your thoughts in a basket. Remind yourself that you can come back to them later.

This ritual can be done without the paper. You could use a voice recorder or just try to remember the most important moments and sensations.

Script

Chalice Lighting

I kindle this flame
with an open spirit
and with hope for clarity.

(Light the chalice.)

Centering Prayer

Spirit of Life,

I have an important choice to make.

I have wrestled with this decision
sought advice
weighed my options.
I have given it good time, heart, and thought.

I am not sure what to do.

I come here today
with the intention of spiritual discernment.
May I listen for new feelings and insights.

Help me to be open
to my inner wisdom
to new ways of knowing
to surprises
to what I have known but not yet accepted.

I give thanks
for those who have supported me
on my path.
I invite their wisdom

to join with my own
and be my guide.

I know that my choice will impact others' lives as well as my own.
May the path ahead be as gentle and kind to all of us as possible
and may I remember that this is my decision.

May my truest choice be uncovered.

May this time of discernment bring clearness
and a way forward.

Amen
and blessed be.

Silence

(Be still for two to five minutes. You can use the chalice flame as a focal point if that's helpful. You do not have to do or be anything right now. These few minutes are for continuing to settle in and clear space in your heart and mind. When you notice yourself thinking, come back to your intention of settling in, becoming centered and grounded for this ritual.)

Sitting with the Options

(Look at the first paper and consider the option in front of you. Imagine holding the option in your hands. Spend a few minutes with it, or longer as you feel led.)

(You may sit with the option quietly, imagine conversing with it, or both.)

(Notice what arises. Especially notice any images that come to mind, how your body feels, any words or phrases that emerge. Is there tightness or spaciousness in your throat, chest, or belly? A sharp silence, an expansive stillness? Movement, warmth, or coolness? Colors? Lines of music? Memories?)

(Make any notes, doodles, or sketches on the page as you are moved to. Especially note any "aha" moments or sensations. These could be new realizations and understandings. Or they could be a feeling in your heart or your body that is telling you something important that you want to remember.)

(When you feel ready, picture setting the option back down. Thank it.)

(Move to the next paper. Take up that option, and consider it in the same way. When you are ready, put it down and thank it. Repeat until you have considered all the options at hand.)

(Sit back and take in the collection of pages. What has become clear? What wisdom have you gathered? Which option(s) are you pulled toward or away from?)

(Close the space by stacking the papers.)

Chalice Extinguishing

May I move forward with clarity.
May I remain open to my inner wisdom
and centered in what I have discovered here.
May I move courageously and confidently
toward the choice I am making.

I extinguish this chalice
and continue on the path of my life.

(Extinguish the chalice.)

For Entering and Exiting Silence
Rev. Karen G. Johnston

This ritual offers a way to intentionally enter and exit a time of sacred silence that might be part of a centering prayer or a meditation retreat. It has a symmetrical form, with participants doing nearly the same actions in exiting as in entering, though in reverse order, enhancing its elegance. It can be done by an individual or, when coordinated, by a group. The author devised this ritual as part of a twelve-day solo meditation retreat informed by somatic healing and Buddhist practices.

Materials
- ☐ Candle
- ☐ Song (preferably one you know by heart)
- ☐ Slip of paper with "I choose to enter into silence" written on it in pencil
- ☐ Pencil with an eraser
- ☐ Chime

Setup
Set up an altar with the ritual materials. You may want to add others that are important to you.

Choose whatever posture (sitting, lying down, standing, swaying, walking around, or something else) helps you to bring your full attention to this ritual, allowing it to wash over you, helping you to move in the liminal spaces between silence and regular life.

If you use sign rather than (or in addition to) voice, you can express the song verses with increasing and decreasing emphasis. If you find humming a positive sensation, you can hum. You could also lightly tap a finger on your collarbone, or an open palm gently on your upper chest.

Script

Entering

Companion

(For some, entering into silence allows in unwelcome emotions, memories, or projections. It can be helpful to have a friendly or protective companion with us to help us access whatever resilience we need to experience silence as beneficial. A burning candle can be such a companion.)

(Light your candle. It may represent someone living or dead or a safe place or space, from either your past or your imagination. You are invited to name it aloud, to welcome your companion and/or express gratitude for their company, bowing to their presence.)

Voice

(Sing your song. If it has fewer than three verses, repeat one so that you sing at least three. Sing each successive verse more softly (so you might want to start louder than you normally would). Do not sing the final verse aloud. Hum it if humming is comfortable for you; humming can positively activate the vagus nerve, engaging our parasympathetic nervous system to help calm us. If humming does not work this way in your body, trust your body's wisdom and do not hum. You can express the final verse in some other physical way, such as swaying or tapping.)

Vision

(Read, silently or aloud, the slip of paper with the words "I choose to enter into silence" on it. At whatever pace you choose, erase the words as an affirmation of this choice. Keep the now-blank slip of paper.)

Sound

(Ring the chime, at first almost as loudly and quickly as you can tolerate, and gradually softening and slowing down. This may take twenty seconds or five minutes; it is up to you. As the chime sounds, observe the feeling in your hands as you strike it and allow the vibrations, rather than your intellectual thoughts, to be your primary sensation of this experience. See if you can experience the slowing and quieting of the sound of the chime as an invitation to settle your body into the silence.)

(It is now time to begin your extended practice of silence.)

Exiting

(If you want to include your companion candle in the exit ritual, be sure it is lit.)

Sound

(Begin to ring the chime slowly and softly, gradually speeding up and getting louder until it is almost more than you can tolerate. This may take twenty seconds or five minutes; it is up to you. As the chime sounds, observe the feeling in your hands as you strike it and allow the vibrations, rather than your intellectual thoughts, to be your primary sensation of this experience. See if you can experience the swelling sound as an invitation to exit from the silence, perhaps by moving or shaking your body.)

Vision

(On the same slip of paper, write the words "I choose to exit from silence" at whatever pace you choose.)

Voice

(Begin humming your song [unless humming does not feel good to you], then sing it. Repeat verses as necessary so that you sing at least three, with each verse louder than the previous one, perhaps moving or shaking your body at the same time, as a proclamation that you have exited the silence.)

Companion

(If your friendly candle is still lit, express gratitude for its company, its protection, its witness. Call its name before you blow it out. As you blow it out, use your hands to waft the smoke and heat that are leaving the extinguished wick toward yourself to affirm the connection between you and your companion even as you have exited the silence.)

Milestone Moments

For Preparing to Give Birth
Rev. Elizabeth Carrier-Ladd

Childbirth can be one of the most profound moments in one's life. As we prepare for it, there can be power in gathering with a community of beloveds to gather strength and love for the process. The purpose of this ritual is to help ground the pregnant person and surround them with love and strength in preparation for the experience of labor and birth. Whether this ritual is a part of a larger gathering or not, be intentional and mindful about who the pregnant person and their close family want to be present.

Materials

- ☐ Chalice
- ☐ Optional: Item to be blessed for the pregnant person to have with them at the birth

Setup

This ritual can be done with or without touch, and can be just as powerful either way. What matters is what would be most meaningful to the focus person. Ask them ahead of time whether they would like hands on them or near them, and which body part or parts others should touch or gesture toward: belly, heart, hand, shoulders, or something else.

If you wish, invite the focus person to choose an item to be blessed.

This ritual asks participants to move to the focus person to provide a blessing. It could be modified by having the focus person move to each participant, or by inviting participants to say if they would like the pregnant person to come to them. Keep the circle clear of unnecessary objects so that everyone can easily move around.

Script

Chalice Lighting

From a tiny cluster of cells, a life

A whole being has grown

Has been becoming

Has prepared to emerge from within our beloved [Name].

In honor of this life

Their spark of the divine that we can already sense

And the love we already feel toward them

We light this chalice.

It is so good to gather in celebration of new life.

(Light the chalice.)

[Name], will you please place one hand on your heart and one hand on your belly.

This child has grown slowly within you. You have made room for them. You have changed the way you walk. Your organs have moved. Your center of gravity has shifted. You have been rearranged in a way that cannot be undone. You will not go back to where you were before. This journey has already changed you. And birth will change you further.

You are capable and strong. You will welcome your [or "this"] child with love and grace. There may be fear and anxiety in this transition. And you are grounded in love. You are held in love. You are love. Inside you is a great well of peace that can carry you through whatever comes.

Song

"Meditation on Breathing" (Sarah Dan Jones)

(Lead participants in singing.)

Embodied Meditation

Let us all take a moment to get centered in our own bodies. Let us first find a comfortable position. Maybe you wish to be seated on a chair or on the floor, or maybe you'd prefer to lie down or stand tall. Find the position that is calling to you.

(Pause to let participants settle themselves into position.)

And first just check in with your whole body. Take a few rounds of breath.

Now, let us move our awareness to wherever we touch the earth. Noticing the sensations where we connect to the earth and finding our own grounding. Finding a sense of safety in our connection to the ground. A sense of knowing that all will be well, no matter what comes. A sense of deep calm amidst the storms of life. Breathe.

I invite us all to put one hand on our hearts. To connect to the love that overflows from within us. To feel the capacity of our own love. The power of it. The force it holds for transformation.

Breathe.

Here may we feel that we are safe.
Here may we feel that we are loved.
May we know that we are powerful forces of love in the world.
May we know that all we must do is breathe.

Breathe.

May it be so.

Blessings

We invite each of you to offer your blessing to [Name] and the baby. Birth is something that the baby and the pregnant person do together.

[If the focus person is holding an item to be blessed] [Name] is holding an item of meaning to them that will accompany them to the birth space, as a reminder of this moment and this community that blesses them and journeys with them into this moment of transition. [Describe the item if the focus person wishes you to.] As you bless this person and the [or "their," "her," "his"] baby, this item will be imbued with your love and blessings.

As you feel so moved, please come to [Name] and rub your hands together like this. [Rub your palms together quickly.] Then put your warm, energy-filled hands on [or "a few inches from"] [Name]'s [chosen body part]. You are invited to share a few words of blessing. You may choose your own words, or you can say something like "You are a gift. This baby is a gift. May you be held in love as you bring this baby into the world." You may come forward, one at a time, now.

(One by one, participants come forward to offer their blessings.)

Chalice Extinguishing

As we extinguish this flame, may you remember:

You are enough.

You are strong.

You are powerful beyond measure.

You are grounded in love.

You are held by this community.

[If the pregnant person is planning to raise the child] You are exactly the [mother, father, parent] that your child needs.

(Extinguish the chalice.)

For Adoption

Rev. Christina Leone-Tracy

This ritual marks the finalization of an adoption. It is meant to be used by the family (and close community, if desired) of the adopted child, including most centrally the child themselves. The script assumes one child and multiple parents and family members, but it can be easily adapted to suit single parents, several children being adopted at the same time, and other variations.

It has two versions: one for when the biological or first family is willing and able to participate (whether in person, online, or by sending written messages), and one for when it is not possible or desirable for the biological or first family to participate.

(Note that the family of the child's biological origin is called the "first family" here. Families may use or prefer different terms: "first," "biological," "bio," "birth," or something else. The word *real* should never be used for either the first family or the adoptive family. Both are real.)

This ritual can be held in the family's home, outdoors, or in a sanctuary or other sacred space, though it is unlikely to be part of a worship service.

The author of this ritual is a mother to two children through the gift of adoption. She reached out to, and is grateful for the input and editing of, UUs and others who themselves were adopted or are first parents, including the first mothers of her children. While some requested to remain anonymous, the following contributors wished to be acknowledged for their input in the creation of this ritual: Kent Doss, Katie Gilroy, Robin Tanner, Corey Torres, and Marlene Walker.

Materials

- ☐ Chalice
- ☐ Tea lights
- ☐ Four votive candles
- ☐ Additional candle for the adopted child, if they are old enough and willing to participate

☐ Small table or other place for chalice and candles

☐ Taper candle

☐ Optional: Photos of child and family (including the first family, if possible and appropriate)

Setup

This ritual is intended to be led by a minister, religious leader, or other representative of the adoptive family's faith community. As leader, you should carefully review the script in advance with the family to determine which version you will use and what changes, if any, need to be made to accommodate the number of participants and the presence or absence of the first family or others.

If family members want to add any additional words of promise to the child beyond the "I do" and "I will" statements in the script, there is time for them to do so either during the ritual or in the form of a letter which will be presented to the child and read in private by the family when they are ready. Each participating family member, whether they are adoptive, first, or extended family, needs to decide whether and how they wish to make those promises, and come prepared with their words or letter.

The ritual assumes that the child being adopted is too young to actively participate. However, it does include an optional line at the end for an older child who would like to participate. Work with the child and family to find words that feel most fitting to their feelings and circumstances.

If the first family is participating, find out ahead of time how they and the adoptive family want them to be identified and described.

This ritual relies on candle lighting. If a participant will have difficulty holding or lighting a candle, someone else can help them or do it for them.

Set up the table, chalice, candles, and photos or other objects as desired.

Script

IF THE FIRST FAMILY IS PARTICIPATING

Opening Words

Today we gather, a beautiful and beloved community, brought together by love: brought together by our love for this child, whose very life brings blessing and widens the circle of family. We gather to honor the love we each have for [Child's name] and to commit ourselves to their continual growth and connection.

Chalice Lighting

The first love we honor, the spark, comes from [Name(s) of first family], [Child's name]'s [identify the relationships of the family members present: birth mother, uncle, etc.]. We light our chalice flame with words to honor that spark and that love.

First family: We light this chalice flame as a symbol of the life and love we gave to [Child's name]. May this light burn brightly, fueled by our love and the love of everyone who holds this child in their heart.

(The first family lights the chalice.)

Leader: We acknowledge the flame of our chalice as the flame ignited and sustained by love. We recognize that, like the flame of a candle, love that is shared is only expanded and never diminished. May our love in this circle do the same for [Child's name], so that they may always feel confident in the love and commitment of family in their life.

Naming

Who gave this child their name?

Naming parents: We did.

Leader: And what name did you give this child?

(The naming parents give the child's full name. They may also want to say something about it or why they chose it.)

Pledges of Love and Support

Our commitment to [Child's name] is lifelong. As we help them to grow, we honor the complexity of feelings, questions, hopes, and longings that will arise in them. I ask you, then, each to make a pledge to [Child's name] on this day, as we expand the circle of love and light around them.

Do you, [Adoptive parents' full names], promise to care for, support, and love this child unconditionally, throughout their life, and wrap them fully into the circle of your family?

ADOPTIVE PARENTS: We do.

(The adoptive parents may speak additional words of promise, or present the child with a letter to be read when the family is ready, in private.)

LEADER: Do you promise to support [Child's name]'s unfolding identity, and honor their search for their own path? Do you commit to maintaining an open relationship with their first family, in whatever ways are possible, throughout [Child's name]'s life?

ADOPTIVE PARENTS: We do.

LEADER: Then please light a candle, symbolic of the love you have for [Child's name], which only grows and never diminishes in its sharing.

(The adoptive parents light a votive off the chalice flame.)

Do you, [First family's full names], promise to love this child unconditionally throughout their life, and offer your support as needed to their adoptive family?

FIRST FAMILY: We do.

LEADER: Do you promise to support [Child's name]'s unfolding identity, and honor their search for their own path? Do you commit to maintaining an open relationship and free exchange of information with [Child's name], in whatever ways are possible, as they grow?

FIRST FAMILY: We do.

(The first family may speak additional words of promise, or present the child with a letter to be read when the family is ready, in private.)

LEADER: Then please light a candle, symbolic of the love you have for [Child's name], which only grows and never diminishes in its sharing.

(The first family lights a votive off the chalice flame.)

I turn now to the extended community: siblings, grandparents, friends. Do you, also, promise to love this child, unconditionally, throughout their life, and offer your support as needed to them and their family?

EXTENDED COMMUNITY: We do.

LEADER: Do you promise to support [Child's name]'s unfolding identity, and honor their search for their own path? Do you commit to providing a safe place for their questions, hopes, and concerns?

EXTENDED COMMUNITY: We do.

(A representative of the extended community may speak additional words of promise, or present the child with a letter to be read when the family is ready, in private.)

LEADER: Then I ask [name of the extended community's representative and their relation to the child] to please light a candle, symbolic of the love you all have for [Child's name], which only grows and never diminishes in its sharing.

(The representative of the extended community lights a votive off the chalice flame.)

LEADER: On behalf of this whole community, I promise to love and support [Child's name], their family, and their unfolding identity and to honor their inherent worth and dignity and free and responsible search for truth and meaning throughout their life. I will light a candle in honor of our faith community and the love we have for this child, which only grows and never diminishes in its sharing.

(Light a votive off the chalice flame.)

Optional Affirmation by Adopted Child

[Child's name], as you see here, you are so deeply loved, by everyone in the circle of your family. They have promised to love you, support you, and honor your questions as you get older. As a symbol of the circle of love, of which you are a part, and the love shared by all members of this family, will you light the final candle in this circle?

CHILD: I will.

(The child lights a final votive candle off the chalice flame.)

Closing Words

The love surrounding [Child's name] is evident. May it always light the path for them to find their way forward. Our prayer for each member of this family is that they may always know and feel their connection and belonging, interconnected through the complexity of adoption. We honor those promises that were made today, to and with [Child's name], and we pray for the lifelong growth and deepening of those commitments, through all the joys and challenges that are to come.

(Warm your hands over each of the votive and chalice flames, and place your warmed hands on the child's head and heart.)

Chalice Extinguishing

We extinguish these flames, but not the love they represent. May the lights kindled through this adoption continue to burn brightly, and the warmth of the love they represent always be felt by [Child's name], all the days of their life. Amen.

(Extinguish the candle flames, beginning with the chalice.)

IF THE FIRST FAMILY IS NOT PARTICIPATING

(Adoption sometimes comes after a long, painful struggle that may include abuse or trauma in a first family. If this is the case, mention of the first family must be carefully handled. The role of the first family's representative in this script may be played by one or more of the adoptive parents, or by someone else. If the child is old enough, follow their lead in choosing a representative and developing words that might be useful and healing.)

Opening Words

Today we gather, a beautiful and beloved community, brought together by love: brought together by the love for this child, whose very life brings blessing and widens the circle of family. We gather to honor the love we each have for [Child's name] and to commit ourselves to their continual growth and connection.

Chalice Lighting

If the story of the first family is not painful

The first love we honor, the spark, comes from [Child's name]'s first family. While they are not physically present in this circle, we light our chalice flame with words to honor that spark of life and the loving choice they made through adoption.

If the story of the first family is painful

[Child's name], across generations extraordinary gifts were implanted in your very bones, as dust from the stars. We acknowledge this ancestral and ancient spark, even as we bear witness to the long journey to this day.

REPRESENTATIVE OF THE FIRST FAMILY: I light this chalice flame as a symbol of [Child's name]'s life, whose spark was born in the body of [their birthing parent] [Use whatever term is preferred by the family; if the birthing parent's name is known and the family wishes, name them.] May this light burn brightly, as [Child's name]'s life continues to grow.

(The representative lights the chalice.)

LEADER: We acknowledge the flame of our chalice as the flame ignited and sustained by love. We recognize that, like the flame of a candle, love that is shared is only expanded and never diminished. May our love in this circle do the same for [Child's name], so that they may always feel confident in the love and commitment of family in their life.

Naming

Who gave this child their name?

(The adoptive parents answer "We did," or "Their first mother did," or whatever is the case.)

LEADER: And what name was given to this child?

(The adoptive parents give the child's full name. They may also want to say something about it.)

Pledges of Love and Support

LEADER: Our commitment to [Child's name] is lifelong. As we help them to grow, we honor the complexity of feelings, questions, hopes, and longings that will arise in them. I ask you, then, each to make a pledge to [Child's name] on this day, as we expand the circle of love and light around them.

Do you, [Adoptive parents' full names], promise to care for, support, and love this child, unconditionally, throughout their life, and bring them fully into the circle of your family?

ADOPTIVE PARENTS: We do.

(The parents may speak additional words of promise, or present the child with a letter to be read when the family is ready, in private.)

LEADER: Do you promise to support [Child's name]'s unfolding identity, and honor their search for their own path? Do you commit to remaining open about their adoption story, in whatever ways are possible, throughout [Child's name]'s life?

ADOPTIVE PARENTS: We do.

LEADER: Then please light a candle, symbolic of the love you have for [Child's name], which only grows and never diminishes in its sharing.

(The adoptive parents light a votive off the chalice flame.)

We acknowledge that [Child's name]'s first family is not in this circle. But we honor the role they had in creating their life. Do you promise to honor your child's identity and culture of origin, in whatever ways are possible, throughout their life?

ADOPTIVE PARENTS: We do.

Omit or adapt the following section if mention of the first family is painful or traumatic

LEADER: Will you support [Child's name] in whatever path they wish to follow as they grow, neither forcing reconnection with their first family nor denying them the chance to seek it if they so choose?

ADOPTIVE PARENTS: We will.

LEADER: Then please light a candle, symbolic of [Child's name]'s ties to their first family, which are not visible in this circle. We acknowledge the love which only grows and never diminishes in its sharing.

(The adoptive parents light a votive off the chalice flame.)

I turn now to the extended community: siblings, grandparents, friends. Do you, also, promise to love this child, unconditionally, throughout their life, and offer your support as needed to them and their family?

EXTENDED COMMUNITY: We do.

LEADER: Do you promise to support [Child's name]'s unfolding identity, and honor their search for their own path? Do you commit to providing a safe place for their questions, hopes, and concerns?

EXTENDED COMMUNITY: We do.

(A representative of the extended community may speak additional words of promise, or present the child with a letter to be read when the family is ready, in private.)

LEADER: Then I ask [name of the extended community's representative, and their relationship to the child] to please light a candle, symbolic of the love you all have for [Child's name], which only grows and never diminishes in its sharing.

(A representative of the extended community lights a votive off the chalice flame.)

LEADER: On behalf of this whole community, I promise to love and support [Child's name], their family, and their unfolding identity and to honor their inherent worth and dignity and free and responsible search for truth and meaning throughout their life. I will light a candle in honor of our faith community and the love we have for this child, which only grows and never diminishes in its sharing.

(Light a votive candle off the chalice flame.)

Optional Affirmation by Adopted Child

[Child's name], as you see here, you are so deeply loved. These people, your family, have promised to love you, support you, and honor your questions as you get older. As a symbol of the circle of love, of which you are a part, and the love shared by all members of this family, will you light the final candle in this circle?

CHILD: I will.

(The child lights the final votive candle off the chalice flame.)

Closing Words

The love surrounding [Child's name] is evident. May it always light the path for them to find their way forward. Our prayer for each member of this family is that they may always know and feel their connection and belonging, interconnected through the complexity of adoption. We honor those promises that were made today, to and with [Child's name], and we pray for the lifelong growth and deepening of those commitments, through all the joys and challenges that are to come.

(Warm your hands over each of the votive and chalice flames, and place your warmed hands on the child's head and heart.)

Chalice Extinguishing

We extinguish these flames, but not the love they represent. May the lights kindled through this adoption continue to burn brightly, and the warmth of the love they represent always be felt by [Child's name], all the days of their life. Amen.

(Extinguish the candle flames, beginning with the chalice.)

For Weaning

Rev. Elizabeth Carrier-Ladd

This ritual is to honor and mark the transition of a child weaning from nursing. It can be done either as part of an intentional weaning process or after a child has weaned on their own, and it can be done by the nursing parent and the child alone, or with family members, or others whose presence the nursing parent feels would be meaningful, as witnesses to the transition. Whether or not the child can understand that this change is significant, it can be powerful for both parent and child to mark it. There are two versions of this ritual: one to be used with a child who cannot understand or participate in it, and one to be used with a child who can.

Materials
- ☐ Embroidery floss
- ☐ Child-friendly scissors
- ☐ Safety pin

Setup

Choose a location for the ritual that feels comfortable. Put the scissors and safety pin somewhere you can get them but the child cannot, such as in a pocket. Place the embroidery floss nearby.

You may want to practice ahead of time to determine how large the bracelet or bracelets you will make should be. They should be tied around your wrist and, as appropriate, your child's tightly enough that they will not fall off accidentally, but not so tightly that they can't be taken off if you wish to.

Script

FOR A CHILD WHO CANNOT UNDERSTAND

(Hold the child on your lap or in your arms.)

I want us to mark a shift that has happened. Our relationship is evolving. You will always be my special little one. And our relationship changing is exciting and sad at the same time. You are no longer drinking milk from my body.

(Name any feelings you have. It is normal and okay to have a lot of complex and even contradictory feelings around this transition.)

I love being able to watch you become yourself each day. So I would like to do a little ritual with you in order to mark this change in our relationship.

(Pick up the embroidery floss.)

This string represents our relationship. It is so beautiful. So special. And you and I are wrapped closely together no matter what. I will always be your [use whatever name your child calls you]. I will always love you so, so much.

(Wrap the floss around both of your bodies three times.)

And our relationship is changing right now. As you grow up and you no longer need to eat from my body, we are able to take more space from each other sometimes. You need me in different ways. You may even need me less. And that is okay. It's wonderful. Even as it may be hard sometimes for either or both of us.

We can cut this cord to show how you are growing up. And how our physical relationship is changing.

(Cut the floss, severing the binding around you. You may want to hold the child's hand as you do so. If you like, take a moment to share with them some of your feelings about the moment of cutting; you might feel like cheering, or sighing, or talking through the complexity of your feelings.)

And our relationship continues. It just changes. So I will make myself a bracelet out of this floss, so that I can hold close our special relationship even as it is changing right now, and you can touch it or hold it when we are snuggling, which we will still do a lot. We know that our relationship will keep changing as you keep growing. And as I keep growing. So this is just one step in our ever-evolving relationship. And no matter what, we will always be special to each other. And you will always be my little one. And I will always love you so completely.

(Cut the floss into three equal pieces and tie them in a knot together at one end. Put the safety pin through the knot and attach it to something to anchor it so that you can braid the strands of floss. Choose any braiding pattern you like.)

(When the braid is long enough, tie it off, cut away any trailing ends, and tie it on your wrist as a bracelet. You may say these words to yourself or hold your child again for this part.)

This is to remind us of how special our relationship is, was, and always will be. I can wear this to remember as long as I want. And we know that we will not forget, even long after I stop wearing this particular keepsake. Because we do not need reminders to know how important we are to each other.

(Offer your child a hug, a kiss, or whatever form of affection they like best.)

FOR A CHILD WHO CAN UNDERSTAND

Sit with me a minute. I want us to mark a shift that has happened. Our relationship is evolving as you grow up. You will always be my special little one. And our relationship changing is exciting and sad at the same time. You are no longer drinking milk from my body. Right?

(Allow time for a response.)

How do you feel about this change?

(Allow time for a response and honor every feeling expressed.)

(Name any feelings you have. It is normal and okay to have a lot of complex and even contradictory feelings around this transition.)

I love being able to watch you become yourself each day. So I would like to do a little ritual with you in order to mark this change in our relationship. Okay?

(Allow time for a response. Then offer your child some different colors of embroidery floss.)

Which color should we use?

(Put the unchosen colors aside.)

Good choice! What a pretty color. So, this string represents our relationship. It is so beautiful. So special. And you and I are wrapped closely together no matter what, right? I will always be your [use whatever name your child calls you]. I will always love you so, so much.

(Wrap the floss around both of your bodies three times.)

And our relationship is changing right now. As you grow up and you no longer need to eat from my body, we are able to take more space from each other sometimes. You need me in different ways. You may even need me less. And that is okay. It's wonderful. Even as it may be hard sometimes for either or both of us.

(Hand the child the scissors.)

You can cut this cord to show how you are growing up. And how our physical relationship is changing.

(If necessary, help your child cut the floss to sever the binding around you. Take a moment for each of you to share feelings about the moment of cutting, if that feels appropriate: you or they might feel like cheering, or sighing, or talking through the complexity of your feelings.)

And our relationship continues. It just changes. So I will make us both bracelets out of this floss, so that we can hold close our special relationship even as it is changing right now. We know that it will keep changing as you keep growing. And as I keep growing. So this is just one step in our ever-evolving relationship. And no matter what, we will always be special to each other. And you will always be my little one. And I will always love you so completely.

(Cut the floss into six equal pieces. Bring the ends of three pieces together and tie a knot, put the safety pin through the knot, and attach it to something to anchor it so that you can braid the strands of floss. Choose any braiding pattern you like. When the braid is long enough, tie it off and cut away any long trailing ends. Do the same with the other three strands. Your child may be interested, or even want to participate, but it's fine if they just want to play while you do this. When both braids are finished, tie one on your wrist and the other on your child's as bracelets.)

This is to remind us of how special our relationship is, was, and always will be. We can wear these to remember as long as we want. And we know that we will not forget, even long after we stop wearing these particular keepsakes. Because we do not need reminders to know how important we are to each other.

(Offer your child a hug, a kiss, or whatever form of affection they like best.)

For Starting at a New School

Rev. Allison Palm and Sadie Kahn-Greene

This is a family ritual to mark a child's transition to a new school, but it could also be done at the beginning of a new year at a familiar school. It is designed for preschool and elementary school kids. It could be done the night before or the weekend before school begins, and by a single parent or caregiver and child or with multiple family members present.

Materials

- ☐ Chalice
- ☐ Bag that will go to school (such as a lunch box or backpack)
- ☐ Different-colored ribbons (or another special object to be attached to the bag) and scissors
- ☐ Optional: Book about starting school or transitioning to a new school

Setup

Have the bag and ribbons ready. Set up your chalice where you will be doing the ritual.

Script

Chalice Lighting

We are going to take a little time together to think and share about starting at your new school. Let's start by lighting our chalice, which is a good way to show that this is a special time.

(Light the chalice while you, another parent or caregiver, or the child says these words:)

We light this chalice together for new beginnings,
to celebrate the new beginning of going to a new school.
We light this chalice for all of the hopes and wonderings you [or "I"] bring to this new beginning.

Story

(If you'd like, you can read a book together about starting school or starting at a new school. Here are some suggestions:

- The Kissing Hand, *by Audrey Penn, illustrated by Ruth E. Harper and Nancy M. Leak, is good for a child first starting school, ages 2–5*
- The Invisible String Backpack, *by Patrice Karst, illustrated by Joanne Lew-Vriethoff, is good for a child first starting school, ages 3–7*
- The Day You Begin, *by Jacqueline Woodson, illustrated by Rafael Lopez, is good for a child who has a unique identity in their school, ages 5–8*

(After the book, you can spark some conversation using these questions:)

- *I wonder what you noticed in that story?*
- *I wonder where you see yourself in the story?*
- *I wonder how the story makes you feel?*

Sharing Wonderings

When anyone starts something new, they often have questions or wonderings about what will happen. [Tomorrow, on Monday, etc.], you are starting at a new school. What are you curious about? Do you have any wonderings? We can write them down if you'd like, and we can see what's on your mind.

(The child can share as much as they'd like, writing it down if that feels good. A parent or caregiver can encourage sharing.)

Sharing Hopes

When anyone starts something new, they often have hopes about what it will be like.

What are you hoping you will see or do when you are at your new school?

(The child can share as much as they'd like, writing it down if that feels good. A parent or caregiver can encourage sharing.)

You have a lot of wonderings and hopes about your new school. That makes sense!

(You may want to summarize what they shared.)

Ribbons of Courage and Love

I wonder what might help you feel ready for this new beginning. Do you need something to help you feel brave? Or to remember that I love you even when you are at school?

(Invite responses.)

Sometimes different colors and objects can represent ideas and remind us of things. We have all these ribbons today that you can use to help remember some of the things that we just talked about—the things that you want to bring with you as you go to your new school. Let's pick some out for your [backpack, lunchbox, etc.].

(Pick out ribbons and tie them on to the bag, talking about what they represent.)

Chalice Extinguishing

I'm glad we could spend some time talking together. Let's extinguish our chalice by naming all the things that are going to help you be ready for this new school:

We extinguish our chalice flame, but carry with us [name what each ribbon represents].

As you carry this bag, may you know that you have everything you need for this new adventure and that you are loved.

(Extinguish the chalice and offer a hug, a kiss, or whatever form of affection your child likes best.)

For Life Transitions for a Person with Intellectual Disability and/ or Autism Spectrum Disorder

Li Kynvi and Rev. Elea Kemler

In honor of Lars and Caleb, and in memory of Steven

This ritual marks a significant life transition or occasion, such as moving, leaving school, or beginning work, for a person with intellectual disability and/or autism spectrum disorder (ASD). Since the range of intellectual disability and ASD is so wide, the ritual offers options and guiding questions for leaders to consider as they construct what's meaningful and possible for their situation. It is designed for participants who are special to the focus person, but offers suggestions for adapting it to a congregational setting. Elea Kemler has a young adult child with ASD and Li Kynvi has one with profound intellectual and physical disabilities.

Materials

- ☐ Chalice
- ☐ Recorded music
- ☐ Meaningful gift symbolizing the place or people the focus person is leaving
- ☐ Meaningful gift symbolizing the place or people the focus person is going to
- ☐ Short fun song for closing
- ☐ Cake, snacks, or other party food

Setup

This ritual needs ample space for the dancing and the transition path. Chairs and spots for wheelchairs can be set in a large circle to begin, with these elements happening in the middle of the circle and participants then returning to the outer circle for the ending, but many other setups are possible.

Design the space in a way that suits your context and the focus person's circumstances and preferences. In particular, consider placing yourself directly in front of the focus person, speaking right to them. Since directionality of address is an important sensory factor, this arrangement might be best for them. If this means that you have your back turned to some other participants, that's all right, though you may want to use a microphone to be sure everyone can hear you well. Be careful not to speak in the singsong manner typically used with young children. Use adult vocal inflection, even if you need to simplify your language.

For focus persons with significant intellectual disabilities, repetition is key. In the weeks leading up to the ritual, talk with them not only about the upcoming transition itself, but also about the celebration that will take place. Perhaps share with them the opening words that will be used, play the song that will be played, talk about the important people who will be there to help them move forward with their life. Consider incorporating words from the closing prayer into their daily rituals, as appropriate. Preparing the focus person by using language from elements of the ritual will help ground them in it, making it familiar, personal, and safe. Make sure the ritual incorporates music or items that they find comforting and enjoyable.

There is always a chance that the focus person will opt out of all or some of the plans. This may be more likely if they have ASD. Have a backup plan that simply creates a celebratory atmosphere where people can have fun together in a way that is tolerable for the focus person, and in which they feel honored. Adapt in the moment to what the focus person needs; flexibility is key.

A focus person with ASD may not be comfortable making consistent eye contact. This does not mean they are not paying attention. You can look directly at them whether or not they are meeting your eyes.

If the focus person has visual impairments, you may need to clearly describe everything that is happening. They may want to feel or handle items that are being used in the ritual.

In general, emphasize senses and sensory experiences in the ritual that are significant to the focus person. Some people will benefit from sensory supports that help them feel settled and well organized, especially in highly charged situations when they are the center of attention. This could be a weighted blanket, a fidget, or having someone they know and trust near them and offering comfort. They might like to have a printed copy of song lyrics or the ritual's text.

For the music, choose an upbeat song that the focus person likes to move or dance to. Think about where you will place the player; the music should be audible but not overwhelming. Consider talking beforehand with attendees who might not be naturally inclined to dance or sing, explaining how meaningful their participation would be to the focus person. When participants understand that this is an opportunity for them to deepen their connection with the focus person, the ritual is more meaningful for them as well.

Think about how those lining the path should interact with the focus person as they move along it. The script offers some suggestions.

The focus person's family and loved ones will have their own work of transition to do. Keep in mind that this ritual centers the needs of the focus person. Especially if you end up using your backup plan, their loved ones may need their own, separate ritual of transition.

The script offered here assumes a family setting, but if the focus person attends religious services regularly and feels comfortable and at ease there, and if they will be able to continue to attend after their transition, then it would be appropriate to incorporate this ritual into a congregational worship service. The people most significant to them should stand at the beginning and end of the path, and congregation members can line up between them. During the ritual, mention that [church, synagogue, etc.] will stay the same. Congregants can join in the singing, encouragement, chanting, and warm wishes.

Script

(This sample script assumes that the focus person is moving from their mother's home to a group home. Adapt it as needed, using your creativity and specific circumstances.)

Chalice Lighting

(If the focus person needs additional support to orient themselves to what's happening, perhaps introduce the chalice lighting by saying, "Just like we do when we're in church, we are going to start by lighting a chalice together and saying the words that go with it." If they regularly attend church services in which specific opening or chalice lighting words or music are used consistently, consider using them here, as well.)

We gather on this important day
So we can be together to celebrate [Name].
We light this chalice full of hope and love.
It is good to be together.

(Light the chalice. If a sibling or other family member wants to participate but isn't comfortable speaking, they could light it. The focus person could also light it themselves.)

Opening Words

Welcome, welcome, welcome!
We are so happy to be together for this big day.
We all have lots of regular days in life, and a few special days.
This is a special day because today we celebrate [Name] as they move from living with their mother, [Mother's name], to living in a residential community on Strom Street.

Sometimes special days can feel like a little too much. If you start to feel like it's too much, find a way to let us know and we will slow it down, or quiet down, or take a break.

It's normal to have lots of different feelings on big days. We might feel happy, sad, nervous, shy, maybe even mad sometimes. Or we might feel more than one thing at the same time. It's all okay; all the feelings are okay to have.

Today we feel super proud of [Name] and happy for you, and we want to celebrate this big move together!

Now let's listen and dance to one of [Name]'s favorite songs. [Name the song.] Feel free to sing along!

(If the focus person startles easily, say explicitly, "I'm going to start the music now" or have them start it themselves.)

Music and Movement

(Play the music and encourage everyone to mingle, dancing and singing in whatever way works for them and interacting with the focus person in ways that person treasures.)

(If the focus person is a wheelchair user who does not propel their chair independently, remember that that chair can dance too! If they enjoy it, take the brakes off and dance and spin them.)

Path of Transition

This is a special time in your life, [Name]! We will make a path for you to move through now, to show how you're moving from home with Mama to home on Strom Street.

You've been home with Mama for [number] years now, since you were a baby! At home with Mama, you like to [swing on the porch, play with the dog, sing with the ukulele, etc.]. And you spend time with [name the people the focus person lives with, and any other people they frequently see—other family members, neighbors, teachers, etc.—who are participating in the ceremony]. All these people are going to stand over here.

(Have these people stand together on one side of the space, holding or displaying the gift that symbolizes what the focus person is leaving.)

(If there's a logical comparison available that can help the focus person understand, consider using it. For instance, "Just like your sister moved and now she lives at her school, you are growing up too, and it's your turn now.")

(A parent, guardian, or caregiver can express their love and reassure the focus person about things that will remain the same. They might say something like, "I have loved you every minute I have known you, and I will keep on loving you. We have always had a ukulele at home, and here is a new one you can take with you to your new home on Strom Street. Your friends there can play ukulele with you, and I will play with you when I visit! Lots of other things will stay the same too. You will still get to eat mac'n'cheese and goldfish crackers and wear your favorite soft sweatshirt." They should give the focus person the gift that symbolizes what the person is leaving.)

The time for living at home with Mama is finished now. The time for living on Strom Street is starting.

(Describe clearly what is to come, with specific sensory details. For instance, "On Strom Street your room is at the end of the hall, and Pedro will be with you! You go by the bubbling fish tank and Tyler's room on your way there. All your favorite music and clothes will be there for you, and your posters will be on the walls." Name the people who will be entering the focus person's life, and have the ones who are present stand on the other side of the space, across from the first group, holding or displaying the gift that symbolizes what the focus person is going to. Say something like "Courtney and Angel, who you met when you visited Strom Street, are here with us now. They have a new quilt for your bed in your new room!")

(Have both groups, along with others who may be participating, form two lines facing each other, creating a path from the old location to the new one. If possible, place people from where the focus person is leaving at the beginning of the path, those whose role or presence will remain largely unchanged—extended family, church and school friends, etc.—in the middle, and those from where the focus person is going on the far end, holding the arrival gift.)

So now you get to move through the path we made for you, just like you are moving from home with Mama to home on Strom Street. Here you go!

(As the focus person moves along the path, have the people lining it interact with them in the way that suits the focus person best. For instance, if they like the sound of cheering and yelling, each person could begin chanting their name as they pass by, so that by the end everyone is chanting together and then breaking into cheers. If that much noise would be overwhelming, each participant could murmur a word of encouragement as the focus person goes by. If they like to be touched, each participant could hold their hand or pat them on the back. Consider other ways to enhance the focus person's experience of walking the path as well. If they enjoy the feeling of wind in their face, put a fan at the end of the path, blowing toward them; if they like pretty rocks or flowers, line the path with them or pile them at the end.)

(If the pressure and attention are too much, the focus person may want to move down the line as quickly as possible, or not participate at all. Be prepared to shift smoothly to your backup plan, and make sure that everyone knows that doing so is just fine.)

Focus Person's Expression

(This is a time for the focus person to express anything they might want to. They might do so in words, whether spoken in the moment, prerecorded, or read for them by someone else. If the focus person is nonverbal, they might use a voice output device. If they don't engage at all with symbolic language, they could dance or blow bubbles! You could play a recording of them vocalizing, show a video of them doing something fun, or show photos of them through the years, with music and a little narration.)

Regathering

[Name], we are so proud of you and we love you so much!

(Summarize the ritual that just happened in reassuring language: "We came together and lit a chalice, we talked about feelings we might have, and we danced and sang to [name of song]. Then we talked about your big move from home with Mama to home on Strom Street. We gave you a new ukulele, and you moved through the path while we said your name over and over! Then you got your new quilt, and you told us you're excited and a little scared. We get that! We know the people who will be living with you at Strom Street are very kind and you will feel safe and loved there, too.")

Prayer

Let's pray together.

(If there is a prayer—embodied or in words—that has long been a part of the focus person's life, use that here. Otherwise, address the Divine with whatever name or term is most familiar to the focus person: Spirit of Life, Loving God, etc.)

What a joy it is to be together on this special day!
We are so thankful for each other and for [Name].
This is a big change.
[Name for the Divine], help us through it.
Be with [Name] in the mornings, in the afternoons, and at night.
Bring [Name] a feeling of love and belonging, no matter what.
Thank you!
Amen.

(If the focus person likes to be touched, it will be very important during the prayer for those close to them to touch or hold them in whatever way is customary and calming for them.)

Chalice Extinguishing

Now let's blow out the chalice and sing our last song before we have cake!

(Extinguish the chalice.)

(Sing a short, fun song the focus person enjoys.)

Thank you, everyone, for coming to celebrate this special day with [Name]!

For Coming Out

Rev. Kimberly Wildszewski

This ritual is designed to recognize, affirm, and celebrate any person who is coming out from a previously assumed sexual orientation or gender identity. It is meant to be used by an individual who is in relationship with a small group, community, or congregation, in the context of a congregational worship service or small group gathering. This ritual was inspired by one the author had written for others who had claimed new or true names, genders, or pronouns, and needed these claims recognized and affirmed. The author is a queer cisgender woman who was raised within Unitarian Universalism. She hopes to give congregations language and ritual to help create and maintain allyship and affirmation.

Materials

None

Setup

Review the script with the focus person prior to the ritual to make sure it resonates with their story and their experience. Personalize it as appropriate. Be sure the focus person is comfortable being touched in the laying on of hands, and have participants just hold out open hands if they are not.

Script

Henri Nowen said that "to give someone a blessing is the most significant affirmation we can offer." Today, we are here to give [Name] our blessing and our affirmation, as they [say what identity the focus person is naming or claiming in the ritual].

[Name], you have come with stardust in your hair, with the rush of planets in your blood, your heart beating out the seasons of eternity, with a shining in your eyes like the sunlight. As you present yourself here before this congregation, may it be known that we count you among our blessings.

You were born into a world filled with boxes, boundaries, closets, and enclosures. Some were bold and loud; others were built up around you without your knowing. And in your own true growing you have had to discover and dismantle each.

Piece by piece you tore down assumptions.
Piece by piece you pulled away expectations.

Piece by piece your spirit mended.
Piece by piece you laid a new foundation on which
Your true self danced, sang, flourished,
wholly, holy, free.

Let it be known that this journey of resistance,
of discovery, of alignment
has been a sacred one.

Whatever boundaries you were given that stifled your spirit,
Whoever you were waiting on to offer their affirmation,
Whatever made you question your place in the world,

May you be released from these.

However you choose to identify
No matter how many times you must say the words
And even if they change over time

May you be reminded that this journey,
Your journey,
Is a sacred one.
And you are not alone.

Beloved village, will you please come forward and, as you're able, circle round [Name].

Those closest to them, please place a hand somewhere on them or hold out your open palms toward them. Others further out, please place a hand on someone who is connected to them, or hold our your open palms in turn, until everyone in this space is connected.

(Pause while people arrange themselves.)

[Name], what surrounds you now is neither boundary nor border. What envelops you now is love—is affirmation for who you are.

Knowing this, feeling the weight of this truth, receive our blessing:

[Name], you were loved before you had words. Before you could tell us who you are. You are loved now, worthy of love now, will be loved as your life, relationships, and identity continue to unfurl.

May you know our affirmation and celebration of all the ways in which you experience sacred, intimate, connection—with others, and for yourself. We not only respect you, we honor your [sexuality, gender identity] as a beautiful part of who you are.

To give someone a blessing is the most significant affirmation we can offer. I cannot do that alone. All who gather today, will you join me in saying the words of blessing:

[Name], we dedicate you in the name of goodness, beauty, and truth. We bless you. We are blessed by your authenticity and your trust.

May you remember this moment as a time when you were seen, known, and loved.

Amen.

For Affirming Names and Pronouns

Rev. Shige Sakurai

In memory of Jude Maloney

This is a ritual for affirming someone's name and/or pronouns, particularly those of a trans and/or nonbinary person. It is written to recognize one person, but may be easily adapted. It could affirm multiple focus people at once, for example as part of an annual service. It could also be adapted for name changes unrelated to gender, such as because of a shift in relationship or family, or to reclaim a heritage or personal agency.

The author is nonbinary and goes by they/them pronouns.

Materials

- ☐ Chalice
- ☐ Plant selected by the focus person (preferably one that has roots and requires water)
- ☐ Water in a container for pouring
- ☐ Optional: Poem or short reading
- ☐ Optional: Closing music

Setup

It is important to work closely with the focus person to customize this ritual. They may or may not want you to explain their name and pronouns, and how they should be referred to, in detail; they may even wish to do so themselves. If they have been using their name for a while, the ritual might be designed more to reaffirm it than to declare it or mark their claiming of it.

The focus person may wish to choose a plant that represents something about their personality, their interests, or even their gender or heritage.

Some focus people may wish to provide poetry or music that speaks to their experiences, or incorporate into the ritual phrases or actions derived from their own traditions or that allow them to reclaim power from traditions that have taken it away from them in the past. If you want to include a reading, find out if they would like to choose one, perhaps relating to their heritage, culture, or background.

When leading the ritual, be sure to use the focus person's correct pronouns when referring to them. After the ritual is over, the plant could be donated to a congregation or kept by the focus person as a memento. If it is kept at a place of worship, it may make sense to display alongside it the name and pronouns of the focus person, as a reminder to the community.

Script

Chalice Lighting

As we light this chalice, we join in this special time together in warmth and support.

(Light the chalice.)

Let us witness, reflect upon, and affirm our communities in their wholeness, and in recognizing both common humanity and the uniqueness of each individual.

Opening Words

Today, we recognize a particular beloved member of our community, who has brought a plant. Let us remember that this plant is a sacred symbol in this moment, and that whatever may happen to it in the future will not in any way diminish the inspiration and affirmation of this moment and the ever-flowing powers of love and care that this ceremony carries.

Plants are our siblings. Plants grow and change over time, they make transitions, and they become rooted. Some plants flower or produce fruit—sometimes regularly, sometimes only after many years. Some produce pollen, and some do not. Some change drastically over time. Some grow better in one climate than another. But the vast majority of plants have roots, they live in the earth, they need and create air, they take in water as nourishment, and they require the fire of the sunlight. Like humans, plants are diverse, they are complex, and they change and develop over time. Like us, plants are both deeply individual and interdependent with their environments.

The roots of this plant represent the autonomy and rootedness of the individual to name themselves. Today, let us witness the proclamation of our beloved community member, and the invitation to pour in our love and support, symbolized by our ritual of watering this plant.

Rite of Self-Naming

In this rite of self-naming, I invite our participant to first release a previous name [and pronouns], and then to declare a name [and pronouns] before our community.

Focus person: I release to the universe the name [and pronouns] by which I have previously been known.

Leader: We hold you in love and liberation.

Participants: We hold you in love and liberation.

Focus person: I now declare before you that my name is [Name] and my pronouns are [_____].

Leader: [Name], we hold you in love and liberation.

Participants: [Name], we hold you in love and liberation.

(The focus person may choose to offer brief personal comments or thanks, or describe the plant they brought and what it represents for them.)

Optional Reading

(Read, or invite a community member to read, a short poem or other text.)

Community Commitment

As a community gathered here today, we now offer our support for [Name] and [their] freedom, protection, and well-being. We commit ourselves to centering those who have been pushed to the side. We commit to our own learning, and to the correcting of mistakes that can cause harm. [Name], we delight in your right to declare your own name [and pronouns], and we commit to respecting this most personal aspect of your selfhood.

May it be so.

PARTICIPANTS: May it be so.

LEADER: We now pour in this water to nourish your plant, a symbol of the connection between the community and your individuality, a symbol of our love for your rootedness and our collective opportunity for growth. We hold each other in love and liberation.

PARTICIPANTS: We hold each other in love and liberation.

(Pour the water into the plant pot. Alternatively, the focus person could choose one or a few significant people to pour it.)

Chalice Extinguishing

May we always uphold the humanity of ourselves and others, and may we cherish the proclamations witnessed today. Even as we extinguish this chalice, may we each hold ourselves and each other accountable, and may we carry this flame, a light of liberation, in our hearts.

(Extinguish the chalice. If you wish, close with a song or other music.)

For Release from Prison, Jail, or Detention

Rev. Jason Lydon

This ritual is designed for welcoming one or more people out of prison, jail, or detention. It is intended to be a celebration, with family and community in attendance. The ritual can be adapted for as many focus people as needed.

Materials

- ☐ Altar table for chalice and candles
- ☐ Chalice
- ☐ Tea lights, at least three for each focus person
- ☐ Taper candle
- ☐ Bowls of water, one for each focus person
- ☐ Towels, one for each focus person
- ☐ Paper, at least one sheet for each participant
- ☐ Markers, crayons, or pens
- ☐ Music

Setup

Set up the altar table with the chalice, the tea lights, and the taper candle for lighting the tea lights. Participants can be arranged either in a circle or in rows, theater-style. Set a bowl of water and a towel by each focus person's place, and set paper and markers, crayons, or pens where they will be accessible to everyone.

If any focus person was released from incarceration less than three months ago, be sure that they do not have to have their back to a door that is used for entering or exiting.

Recruit a formerly incarcerated participant to do the chalice lighting.

All quotes and readings in this ritual (aside from the biblical quote) come from currently or formerly incarcerated writers. Do *not* include additional writings from people who have not experienced incarceration.

Consult with the focus people ahead of time to find out how they would like you to speak of their time incarcerated and the people they knew there. Some may have good memories of people who helped them; some may associate certain figures with pain or trauma; some may have had many friends inside, or only a few, or none. Do not assume that an individual had—or did not have—any particular experience of incarceration.

Script

Gathering Music

(Choose one or two of the following to be playing as people come in.)

- *Prison Break (Taina Asili)*
- *Freedom (Nicki Minaj)*
- *I'm Like a Bird (Nelly Furtado)*
- *Ella's Song (Sweet Honey in the Rock)*
- *Love (Mos Def)*
- *God Bless the Child (Billie Holiday)*
- *Changes (2Pac)*

Chalice Lighting

(These words should be offered, and the chalice lit, by a formerly incarcerated participant.)

As we gather in this ritual of healing, this ritual of release and freedom, we light our chalice together.

(Light the chalice.)

It is a blessing to be together. Our time together on this day is dedicated to honoring [Name(s)]. The journey from the outside of prison to the inside and then out again can be a lonely one. Though all of our lives are interconnected and the loss of even one to a prison cell can ripple outward to others, time for those inside can become frozen. During this ritual we will wash away some of the pain, burn away disconnection, and write a path forward. We gather with humility, reverence for life, and an openness to transformation. May we journey together with love.

The Washing

From the beginning of life, we have been held in water. Our bodies, our planet, and this bowl here are all filled with the sacred power of water. Ritual washing crosses religious traditions. When washing feet, hands, or body, one prepares for that which comes next. We are gathered here, in this moment, with [Name(s)], to witness this transition and their preparation for what comes next.

[Name(s)], before you is a bowl of water. As you begin to wash your hands in this bowl of water, imagine washing away the isolation of prison cells. As the water moves between your fingers, imagine washing away the guards, the COs, the administration, all those who refused to see your humanity. As your hands bump against the glass and you feel the firmness of the bowl, imagine washing away the concrete and steel cages that kept your body locked away.

(The focus person or people wash and dry their hands as the leader speaks.)

As you dry your hands, I invite all gathered to join me in this affirmation, three times:
"I am not forgotten. I am unafraid. I am free."

ALL: I am not forgotten. I am unafraid. I am free. [Repeat three times.]

LEADER: Please join in singing "Circle 'Round for Freedom."

Song

"Circle 'Round for Freedom" (Linda Hirschhorn)

(Lead participants in singing.)

The Flame of Remembrance

The ancient prophet Isaiah spoke with righteousness about the need to set all the captives free. In chapter 61, verse 1, we hear Isaiah proclaim:

The spirit of God is upon me,
because God has anointed me;
God has sent me to bring good news to the oppressed,
to bind up the broken-hearted,
to proclaim liberty to the captives,
and release to the prisoners.

(Adapt this section to what you know about the focus person's or people's experiences and whether there are people or experiences they want to remember. Do not assume that you can safely mention "my cellie," "my friends," etc. without confirming in advance that doing so will not retraumatize anyone.)

When returning to this side of the prison walls, one can experience pains of guilt. What about those still left behind? What about my cellie? What about my beloved? What about my friends? The questions can swirl around in our minds. At times the swirling can turn into a spiral downward, with moments of fear, loss, and confusion. Know this: you are not alone.

Around us there are candles that await your spark. Light as many or as few as you would like. Each candle represents a person you want to offer love and care. During your time inside, did someone offer you a toothbrush with no strings attached? Did someone look out for you in the yard? Did someone make sure you had canteen even when your commissary ran out? Who must you not forget? Light a candle for them. You are welcome to share out loud who you are lighting candles for, or do this in silence.

(Allow time for the focus person or people to light candles. Silence here is welcome, though you could also play quiet instrumental music.)

(Once the focus person or people have finished lighting candles, invite the unison affirmation below.)

Leader: Please join in our affirmation.

All: A spark to remember, a flame to illuminate the truth, a fire to warm the spirit.

Writing and Drawing a Way Forward

We have, before each of us, some paper and markers, crayons, or pens. One step toward healing from the trauma of incarceration can be imagining a world free from prisons. In the essay he wrote from his prison cell, Tiyo Attallah Salah-El offers these words: "Creating a new way of 'Thinking About Prisons' requires the best efforts, ideas, and experiences, and honest, careful, sharp, and critical reflection from all those who are willing to take on this daring and daunting task. We could and must construct the groundwork for future generations to build a world that is safe and just. Let us begin working at the edges of what is possible. Let us strive toward a new possibility."

Let us, in this sacred space, begin creating a new way. Use your paper to write, draw, or create what justice, healing, transformation, and accountability might look like without the violence of incarceration. What do we need? What do you need? Breathe into your imagination. Allow your body to guide you. Maybe you want to use your paper like an architect, creating new structures for liberation. Maybe you want to use your paper like a poet, finding just the right words to express your dreams. Maybe you want to use your paper like an artist, blending colors and shapes, or tearing it to create a picture of freedom. We will take fifteen minutes, even as we know that there are many lifetimes of work to express.

(Allow fifteen minutes of time to create. Let everyone know when there is five minutes left, when there is one minute left, and when it is time to return attention to the group.)

(When time is up, encourage everyone to briefly share what they created. When everyone who wishes to has shared, invite the group to sing.)

Song

"How Could Anyone" (Libby Roderick)

Chalice Extinguishing

Our time together is coming to a close, though our commitment to one another is only growing stronger. [If this is a Unitarian Universalist gathering, add "Unitarian Universalism is a religious tradition created by heretics and criminals. Our faith has persevered throughout history because our religious ancestors refused to be silenced."] We know there is nothing salvific about punishment; we will not be saved by police or prisons. We keep each other safe. We do the work of healing and care. As we close, hear these words adapted from Mumia Abu Jamal.

We are in need of a religion of Life that sees the world in more than merely utilitarian terms. A religion that reveres all life as valuable in itself; that sees Earth as an extension of self, and if wounded, as an injury to self.

We need a religion that recognizes the interdependence of [humanity] and this world; which sees that the atmosphere surrounding our globe is the same air we breathe, and part and parcel of our lungs—that Earth's water is no different from the saliva in our mouths.

We need a religion that rediscovers the idealism that existed before institutionalism; to rediscover the primordial awe felt by ancient [humans] when [they] first beheld creation spiraling outside of [humanity's] insignificant self.

May we practice this religion together.

Amen. Let it be so. Blessed be.

(Extinguish the chalice.)

For Retirement
Rev. Anne Bancroft

These rituals are an opportunity to acknowledge a significant and often overlooked transition in our adult lives. Retirement comes to each of us differently. For some it is the end of a particular career and identity. For others, it is a gentler transition into a less structured or time-bound lifestyle. Some people have planned to retire, looked forward to it, and enter retirement joyfully. Others may have become unable to work and may be angry, worried, or afraid. In the myriad ways we experience retirement, it is important to recognize the impact of this change on our identities, our time, and our interests or capacities for engagement.

Three options are offered here:

A community ritual, designed to be included in a congregational worship service or a brief ritual celebrated in the company of a larger community.

A small group ritual, to be observed or celebrated alone or with a small gathering of family or friends, at home or at a special place chosen by the retiree.

A personal ritual, an extension of the first two rituals, to encourage and support the retiree's ongoing awareness of how they are settling into this new phase of life and how their life and relationships may be changing.

Materials

For the community ritual:
- ☐ Altar table
- ☐ Two identical candles
- ☐ Optional: Music

For the small group ritual:
- ☐ Altar table
- ☐ Two identical candles
- ☐ Collection of small stones
- ☐ Basket to hold the stones

For the personal ritual:
- ☐ Journal
- ☐ One or several pens
- ☐ Candle
- ☐ Timer

Setup

The environment for the community or small group ritual can be as elaborate or as simple as desired. Set up the altar table with the two candles, and with enough room for the retiree to stand behind the table. If several retirees are being honored in a community ritual, provide two candles for each. A special table covering or flowers might be appreciated, or meaningful photographs of colleagues or professional events or awards. However the environment is embellished, the candles are the significant element.

For the community ritual, light one candle (or one of each pair of candles, if there is more than one focus person) before the ritual begins. For the small group ritual, leave both candles unlit and make sure there is space around them for stones to be placed. Place the stones in a basket on the altar.

For the small group ritual, give the focus person time beforehand to think about what effects, good and bad, their work has had on the rest of their life, and which of these they will want to mark by placing a stone. They may not want to name all of these effects aloud. For instance, they might feel proud of their professional achievements, or sorry that work kept them from spending time with their family, or pleased that their work was useful in other contexts (such as a cook who cooked for friends, a designer who created a beautiful home, someone who used their work network to find jobs for others). They should similarly consider in advance what they want to say about their hopes and fears for life in retirement: excitement of a new challenge, worry about their financial circumstances, disorientation at losing a familiar identity, etc.

Setup for the personal ritual is simple—choose a place that is quiet and comfortable and make sure you have the materials listed above.

Script

COMMUNITY RITUAL

Song

"Oh, We Give Thanks" (Wendy Luella Perkins)

(Lead participants in singing. As they sing, the retiree comes forward to stand behind the altar table.)

Candles of Transition

Today it is our honor and joy to give thanks for the presence of [Name] among us, and to acknowledge the transition of retirement in their life.

(Describe what the focus person is retiring from; name their roles or titles and summarize the trajectory of their career, as appropriate.)

This candle [gesture to the lit candle] represents that time and those efforts, all the joys and challenges of a career that [Name] found [describe how the focus person experienced their work: "both invigorating and exhausting," "always surprising," etc.].

This candle [gesture to the unlit candle] represents a new and different source of light, a new and different source of energy that will shine uniquely, though no less brightly. I want to invite [Name], when they are ready, to light this new source of energy. For a brief time, these candles shine together as [Name] imagines the transition in their heart, accepting the end of one light as a new light kindles.

(The focus person lights the second candle.)

Whether we come to retirement enthusiastically, or cautiously optimistic, or equally sad and hopeful, change brings loss. As [Name] extinguishes their first candle, may we celebrate with them the beauty of what their work has been and delight in the possibilities beyond its extinguishing.

(The focus person extinguishes the first candle.)

Prayer

> Dear and Holy Spirit of Life and Love and Living that guides our days of labor and service,
>
> Be with us as we acknowledge and celebrate our beloved's retirement, their transition from a familiar path and sense of self to a new way of being and engaging with their community and world. Bestow the blessings of patience, curiosity, and resilience as they travel this new road, and the grace—dear Spirit—to weather and celebrate the change.
>
> So may it be.

Song

> "Go Lifted Up" (Mortimer Barron)

SMALL GROUP RITUAL

Song

> "Oh, We Give Thanks" (Wendy Luella Perkins)
>
> (Lead participants in singing.)

Welcome

> Thank you for being with us today as we acknowledge and honor this time of transition for [Name]. Retirement brings with it all kinds of expectations, not just for [Name] but also for those who know and love them. This is a time to share the potential enormity of this change and to celebrate what the future may bring.

Candle for the Past

> As they light this first candle, [Name] will share with us some of what they are transitioning from—how it has formed or affected their life up to this point, and what it has meant to them. We have stones to represent the varying attributes of these years—both the positive ones and the less positive.

(The focus person lights the first candle and places a stone near it for each attribute or effect of their work that they want to mark, naming the effect aloud if they wish to.)

If something about [Name]'s work has benefited you in your life, you are invited to share that with us now. Please take a stone, place it near the first candle, and say how [Name] used their skills, or network, or experience to help or support you.

(Participants share as they are moved to.)

Let us now take some time in quiet together to acknowledge and honor all that the stones before us represent—all the beauty and nuances of this time in [Name]'s life.

(You might choose to play music, or simply pause for a time of silence.)

Candle for the Future
(The focus person lights the second candle.)

We light this second candle with joy and curiosity, wondering what expectations accompany this new adventure. I invite [Name] to share their hopes and their fears about what lies ahead, and to place a stone for each feeling next to the second candle.

(The focus person places a stone for each of their feelings, naming each aloud if they wish to.)

[Name] has shared their hopes and fears about what may be ahead. Let us lovingly affirm those thoughts—the hopeful ones and the worried ones—knowing that the journey forward is unknown, and unfolding even as we speak. I invite each of you to share your hopes for [Name] and, if you feel moved, to offer a way in which you commit to support [Name] on their journey. For each thought, please place a stone near the second candle.

(Participants share as they are moved to.)

Let us take another short time to breathe together, to allow our hearts to absorb the love and affirmation that we have shared for [Name] as they move along their life's path.

(Pause in silence for a time.)

Song

"Oh, We Give Thanks" (Wendy Luella Perkins)

Closing Words

As [Name] extinguishes the first candle, symbolizing the end of one path in hopeful celebration of the next, we offer a prayer for the journey.

(The focus person extinguishes the first candle while you say the following words.)

The angel of hope appeared.
God is change, she said.
You will not be alone.
Where there is a new path,
there is love and possibility abundant.
Embrace it, as you are able.
Travel gently in this new land
until it feels, again—or for the first time—
like home.

PERSONAL RITUAL

This ritual is an invitation to notice and name both the joys and challenges of a retirement transition. It acknowledges that a shift is in process. Such a shift is not always straightforward or easy; conversely, it is not always convoluted or difficult. However you experience it, it is wise to attend to it as regularly as possible. You could plan to hold this ritual daily or less frequently, but ideally not less than once each week.

Make sure you have thirty minutes of unhindered time: clear your calendar, turn off your phone. Set your timer for twenty-five minutes, and begin.

Light your candle and read aloud these opening words.

All that I have done, all that I have been, has brought me to this point in time. May I be grateful. May I be curious. May I be willing to be changed.

Take a minute to breathe with intention, settling into the willingness to collect your thoughts and feelings and write them down. Then let your responses take form on the pages of your journal. Any form is fine, and none is better than any other; you may want to doodle, fold origami, write, draw, or something else. If you find yourself becoming distracted, simply take another breath and restart.

Consider these prompts:

- *How am I feeling right now, in this moment? How does my retirement, my shift to something new, inform these feelings?*
- *How do I feel connected, and to whom? Or disconnected, and from whom?*
- *What one thing will I do today to move forward? Who will I share it with?*

When your timer rings, stop working and take five minutes to sit with what you have created. Honor this transition time. Then extinguish your candle before continuing with your day.

Partnership

For the Union of More
Than Two Partners
Rev. Lyn Cox

This ritual includes an exchange of vows and other elements solemnizing a lifetime commitment between any number of partners. It is similar to a two-partner wedding, but is especially designed for partnerships of three or more people practicing ethical nonmonogamy. The version here is written for three people, but it can be adapted for more. The author is a UU minister who has been a resource to colleagues on ethical nonmonogamy in Unitarian Universalism since 2003.

Materials

- ☐ Altar table
- ☐ Clear jar with lid for sand ceremony
- ☐ Decorative sand in four different colors (one for the base, one for each partner)
- ☐ Clear vases or other pourable vessels to hold each color of sand
- ☐ Two rings for each partner
- ☐ Table or music stand from which the partners can read their vows

Setup

People who practice ethical nonmonogamy connect with their partners and meta-mours (the other partners of their partners) in many different ways; they organize their relationships in many different configurations. But in all cases, the core values of ethical nonmonogamy include honesty, consent, listening, communication, consideration, and respect. This ceremony is designed for people who consider one another primary partners and are making a lifetime commitment to one another. This is not to say that such an arrangement is the best or the default, simply that this is one possible constellation of people who may be seeking such a ceremony. Adapt the text offered here to suit the people you are working with.

Go through the script with the partners beforehand and personalize it as needed, including asking them to help phrase the statement of intentions, to choose a reading and a person to read it, to decide whether they will exchange rings or some other symbol or token, and to decide how they will refer to one another in their vows. The ceremony is written with the partners' names in the same order throughout, but you and they may wish to vary the order. Rehearse the ceremony with the participants in advance, in the space where it will take place. (If you rehearse pouring the sand for the sand ceremony, use only one color of sand—or no sand at all, with partners just rehearsing the motions of pouring.)

Set up the altar table with the clear jar in advance, and pour a layer of the base sand color into it. Set each partner's colored sand near the main jar, in a container that will be easy to pour from. Have the rings in a secure but easily accessible location, and ensure that you and all participants have your scripts if you need them.

Script

Opening Words and Statement of Intentions

Dear ones, we are gathered together for the joyful and spiritual purpose of joining together these three people in a covenant of commitment. These beloveds, [Name 1], [Name 2], and [Name 3], will make vows and participate in rituals today as a testament to the abundance of their love and the centrality their partnership has in their lives.

The joys of life are multiplied, the sorrows of life more sustainably held, and the mysteries of life more deeply explored with the companionship of those who have promised to share those things with one another. By joining their lives in this ceremony, [Name 1], [Name 2], and [Name 3] are recognizing the mutual responsibilities, deep respect, and room for growth that come with life partnership.

[Name 1], [Name 2], and [Name 3], may you enter into this next phase of your life partnership with abundance in all of the things that help you sustain commitment: trust, patience, creativity, and love. You have not come with an expectation of uninterrupted and eternal bliss, nor with a demand that anyone make themselves smaller; you recognize and bring reverence to the work and play of daily life, the need for resourcefulness, and the mysteries of growing as individuals and as partners alongside one another.

Have I properly expressed the intention you bring to this partnership, the spirit of your union, and the purposes you have in bringing us together today?

PARTNERS: You have.

Acknowledgment of Families

The values [Name 1], [Name 2], and [Name 3] bring to their partnership, and the encouragement that will lead them to strengthen it over time, are nourished by the wisdom and love that you, dearly beloved, have provided and continue to provide by being here today.

In particular, [Name 1], [Name 2], and [Name 3] mentioned their families [specify "chosen families" and/or "families of origin" as appropriate] as sources of support and understanding as they have learned how to build their lives together. Your past influence and ongoing love will help sustain them in the years ahead.

If the partners are raising children

As we lift up the love that [Name 1], [Name 2], and [Name 3] have for one another, we also honor that the bond they affirm today makes a family of [number] people. [Children's names] are also held in this union and celebrated in this ceremony. May this family provide the strength and support that each member needs to grow into the fullness of their being.

Reading

To help express their feelings on this occasion, [Name 1], [Name 2], and [Name 3] have selected a reading about love. I invite [identify the reader: "their friend Kai," "[Name]'s mother Charl," etc.] forward to offer the reading.

(The partners should choose a reading that feels appropriate to their relationship. Some possibilities include:)

- *"A New Constellation" (Marge Piercy) from* The Moon Is Always Female
- *"Hug O'War" (Shel Silverstein) from* Where the Sidewalk Ends
- *"How to Fall in Love with the World" (Jess Reynolds) from* Love Like Thunder
- *"Love Is Becoming a Safe Word" (adrienne maree brown) from her website*

Sand Ceremony

A lifetime commitment includes both togetherness and individuality. Partners encourage one another to be their best individual selves, even as they come together as a family. By joining together, [Name 1], [Name 2], and [Name 3] pledge to continue growing as people, to recognize one another's unique needs and gifts, and to honor the ways their hearts are forever mingled.

[Name 1], [Name 2], and [Name 3] will symbolize this pledge with sand art. At the bottom of the glass jar, there is already some sand, a foundation of friendship and shared values that this family will build on. [Name 1], [Name 2], and [Name 3] will add layers of sand, each in a different color, symbolizing their individuality. Yet, once the sand art is complete, the combination of colors forms a pattern more complex and beautiful than any of the colors could make alone. Nor can one color be removed without affecting the others and altering the pattern, just as each partner matters to your union.

I invite you now to pour your sands into the glass jar, one at a time.

(Each partner takes a turn adding a layer of their sand to the jar. They may wish to pour several times each, creating multiple layers. When they have finished, put the lid on the jar.)

Sustaining a family is everyday work, as common as sand. Yet when we step back, we see the sparkle and variation that makes this mission into a miracle. May this art be for you a symbol of the balance of unity and individuality, a place to begin on the shores of a vast ocean of love.

Prayer

I invite you to join me now in opening our hearts to the sacred, our bodies to stillness, and our minds to centering in this very moment.

Spirit of Life and Love, known by many names and yet fully known by none, our hearts lift in a chorus of blessing for [Name 1], [Name 2], and [Name 3] and the commitment they solemnize today. May they resonate with the love and support with which we surround them. May they know harmony in the blending of their individual voices, and may they know serenity in their times of rest. When there is joy, may it rise to the rafters and bring joy to others. When there is struggle, may we join together with them in songs of persistence. Eternal one of blessing, accompany [Name 1], [Name 2], and [Name 3] through their shared life, in echoes of the past bringing wisdom and in voices from the future calling them onward. May it be so.

Exchange of Vows

[Name 1], [Name 2], and [Name 3], before I ask you each to make your vow, I ask you each to affirm your intentions, one at a time.

[Name 1], do you accept [Name 2] and [Name 3] completely as life partners, committed to love, to care for and be cared for by, to sustain in sickness and in health, to grieve with in sorrow and to celebrate with in joy, from this day forth?

PARTNER 1: I do.

(Repeat for the other partners.)

LEADER: The vows through which you affirm your life partnership are only one sign of your dedication to each other as individuals and to your family as a whole. The consideration, listening, patience, service, and commitment that you practice every day are what will bring meaning to these vows.

I ask you to join hands in a circle and face each other as you exchange your vows.

(The partners may, if the ceremony space and their mobility needs allow, choose to rotate the circle as each one speaks, such that the partner who is speaking faces the congregation as well as their partners. They may prefer to read their vows from a table or music stand in the center of the circle or to repeat after you.)

Partner 1: I, [Name 1],
join with you, [Name 2], and you, [Name 3],
as my [partners, spouses, life mates, etc.].
I pledge to be truthful, openhearted, and supportive in word and deed.
I vow to honor each of you and our family as a whole by keeping our agreements.
I promise to cherish each of you and to encourage your individual well-being, as well as the health of our partnership.
I will sustain this covenant through all of the changes in our lives from this day forward.

(Repeat for the other partners.)

Ring Ceremony

As a sign of your partnership, you have chosen the gift of rings, two for each partner to wear, an embrace of the hand from each of your other partners.

A ring is a circle. A circle can symbolize an embrace, a gateway, the cycle of life, a renewal of the spirit. All of these things can be found in a living and loving partnership. In a multipartner family, rings may remind you of ebb and flow, the support that flows in many directions, not merely back and forth but swirling and surging among you all, in a network of care. May the endlessness of the circle lead you to move with courage in the world and with peace in your family. May these rings be blessed by the Spirit of Love and be true symbols of love for all the years of your lives.

[Name 1], please bestow a ring on each of your partners and repeat after me.

(Read the following text line by line, pausing after each to let the partner repeat what you have said.)

[Name 2] and [Name 3], I give you these rings as signs of my devotion.
The center of the circle is as open as my heart.
The completeness of the circle is as endless as my love.

(Repeat for the other partners.)

Pronouncement of Union

(Turn toward the gathered community.)

Now that [Name 1], [Name 2], and [Name 3] have committed to one another their love and devotion, and have made a public pledge of their covenant, I declare that they are now [life partners, spouses, life mates, bound in holy union, etc.]. May their partnership be long sustained in love and happiness.

(Turn toward the partners.)

You may now kiss one another [or show affection in some other way].

Closing Words

And now, with confidence in the spirit and practice of abundant love, we send you forth to build a life together of beauty, warmth, and understanding. May the truth and trust that you show to one another bring you strength. May your love and your partnership endure as a grace upon this world. Go in peace. Return to one another in love. So be it.

For Acknowledging Community in a Wedding

Rev. Allison Palm

This ritual is intended to be a part of a larger wedding or union ceremony. It is designed to acknowledge that the partnership exists in the context of community and to honor the role that others play in supporting the couple.

Materials

- ☐ Small altar table to hold the tree, water, and other materials
- ☐ Small tree that can be easily planted in a pot or in the ground
- ☐ Pot with soil or a hole in the ground ready to plant the tree in
- ☐ Water in a container that is easy to pour from, with enough for all who will be offering blessings
- ☐ Optional: Cloth for the partners to clean their hands after planting the tree
- ☐ Optional: Music

Setup

Set up an altar table with all the materials needed. If you will be planting the tree in the ground, dig the hole beforehand and set up the table with materials next to it.

Consider the needs of all the participants in the ritual as you set it up. Make sure the altar table is a comfortable height for everyone who will be participating and that the water container is not too heavy. Planting in a pot makes this ritual more accessible, as it removes the need to bend over to reach the ground.

Consult with the couple to decide who will offer a blessing, and ask those people to compose one. In some cases, it may help to offer a template.

Partners who use this ritual should consider how they will feel if the tree does not survive and should be assured that the length of the tree's life is not indicative of the length of their relationship's life.

This ritual is written for two partners but could be adapted for more.

Script

All trees start from small seeds, whether dropped or borne willy-nilly by animals, water, or the wind; but once grounded, they can become one of the longest-lived things in the world, silent guardians of forests, parks, and even street corners in a crowded city. A partnership, too, starts from a small moment, from the meeting of another person. We meet thousands of people in our lives, but only sometimes does the relationship take root, growing, stretching like a seed grounding itself in the earth, and then growing strong and tall, reaching toward the sky.

[Name 1] and [Name 2], your relationship began as a seed. Over the years it has taken root, as you have learned each other's stories, cared for each other, and created a life together. Your relationship will continue to grow in the years to come, just as a tree adds circles to its trunk, holding steady through the seasons of life, reaching to the sky as you reach toward your future together.

In honor of your partnership and love, the roots of your ever-growing relationship, I invite you to plant this tree now together. [Add details about the kind of tree it is or where it is being planted, as appropriate.]

(The partners plant the tree. They may wish to have members of their families or of the wedding party help them or even plant it for them, especially if they would have difficulty doing so themselves.)

Despite their dignified solitude, trees are never truly alone. They depend on water from the skies, the soil of the earth, and the activity of countless animals, birds, and insects.

[Name 1] and [Name 2], your relationship is grounded in the fertile soil of the families and communities that nurtured you from childhood to adolescence and finally to adulthood. As you look out at those who have gathered here to witness your union today, may you feel the strength of those relationships and know that they will keep you grounded in your journey together.

And we know that your relationship will continue to be fed by the communities that surround you. Just as trees cannot exist without the help of water, earth, sun, and wind, so too does any partnership need the support of family and friends to thrive.

In that spirit, we, their community gathered here, are going to offer our blessings to this union by watering the newly planted tree of this partnership. [Name 1] and [Name 2] have invited a few people to offer blessings. [Identify and call forward the people who will do this.]

(The designated people come forward one at a time, water the tree, and offer the blessings that they have prepared.)

We now invite everyone forward to add their water and silent blessings for [Name 1] and [Name 2].

(Give any necessary instructions, including asking people to add just a few drops of water if the tree is in a small pot. You may want to play some music as people are watering the tree.)

[Name 1] and [Name 2], may the blessings of this water and the love of your communities sustain you as your partnership and love continue to grow.

For a Blended Family

Rev. Heather Concannon

This ritual marks the blending of two families into one. It is intended to be used as a component of a full wedding or commitment ceremony.

Materials

- ☐ Altar table
- ☐ Two vessels of water, one provided by each family (preferably water from a place that is special to that family)
- ☐ Larger vessel to hold the blended water

Setup

Create an altar table with the three vessels, two filled with water and one empty when the ceremony begins.

This ritual should be personalized to reflect each family's specific circumstances. In particular, discuss with the participants ahead of time how they plan to use the blended water—to water a plant at home, to use in another ritual, etc.—so that you can mention this in the ritual.

Script

Opening Words

> [Name 1] and [Name 2],
> You come here today
> Not as sole individuals,
> But as members of families and communities.
> You come as parents, you come [widowed, separated, divorced],

You come as friends, as children, as members of a larger community, an interdependent web.

Today is a day we celebrate the love and commitment which has brought you together
And the journeys that have brought you to this day.
Whatever places your journeys have taken you,
Whatever feelings have been your companions on the journey to this day,
We invite all of you—[Name 1] and [Name 2], and especially [Children's names]—
To bring your whole selves to this new manifestation of family that we celebrate and honor today.
To bring your whole selves means bringing all of who you are:
All of the stories,
All of the emotions,
All of the loss and the change and the joy,
And all of the people
Who have made this day and these families coming together possible.

Water Ceremony

And so,
To honor the paths you have taken to arrive at this moment
And to honor the blending of these two families into something new,
We'd like to invite you now to participate in a water ceremony
To mark the merging of separate journeys and lives
Into a shared journey, shared life, shared family.

We use water because it is the very essence of life.
It is common,
Yet it is also so miraculous.
Water is refreshing, cleansing, nourishing, soothing, healing, powerful, sometimes overwhelming.
Water represents our humanness: Our tears of joy and frustration, tears of sorrow and of laughter.
Water sustains life,
And, like streams feeding into a larger river,

It represents our separate journeys merging into one.

And today, this water becomes holy by our shared intention
And by our blessing it together.
It becomes holy by our bringing each of our separate journeys
And choosing to share them with one another,
With intention and love.

And so, today we use water taken from [describe the source and meaning of each family's water]
And we pour it into one shared vessel
Which they will [describe how the blended family will use the blended water].
And we invite you now
To come forward
And share your separate waters, merging them into one shared future.

(All participants, both children and parents, come forward and pour a small amount of the water from their original family's vessel into the shared, larger vessel. If some family members are unable to do so, they could all could put a hand on the vessel while one of them pours.)

I invite [Name 1] and [Name 2] to hold this water, and [Children's names] to gather around it and place a hand on the water for a moment of blessing.

(If the partners are not able to hold the vessel, they could place their hands on it and have the children place their hands on them.)

Blessing

Let us bless this water together,
As we bless the merging and mingling
Of your lives together:

[name all the participants, being careful not to group members of an original family together].

Bless the fullness of the journeys that have led you to this joyous day.

Bless the tears, both of sadness and of joy.

May this water represent both the winding rivers of the past

That have brought you to this moment

And the present moment, as you enter a shared future.

May it bless you with a future of hope, connection, and love

As you continue to create family together.

For Separation or Divorce
(for Both Partners)

Arran Morton

This ritual is for people who are ending their marriage or romantic partnership, but who want to continue their relationship in a new form. It is written for two partners but could be adapted for more, and offers ways to include and affirm their children, if desired. It is ideal for a smaller, intimate gathering.

Materials

- ☐ Altar table
- ☐ Chalice
- ☐ Two taper candles
- ☐ Tea light
- ☐ Wedding rings (or other tokens that were exchanged at the wedding)
- ☐ Item symbolizing the relationship (such as a copy of the marriage certificate, wedding picture, handfasting rope, etc.)
- ☐ Fireproof bowl or cauldron containing a small amount of wood shavings or shredded paper (enough to ensure the symbolic object will burn completely, but small enough to keep the fire contained)
- ☐ Fire extinguisher or fire blanket

Setup

This ritual is ideally held in an outdoor, well-ventilated space, or a private residence where a small, contained fire can be lit without setting off fire alarms or sprinklers.

Set up the altar table with the chalice, the bowl or cauldron, and any other non-flammable decorative items you would like. Place the two taper candles and the tea light on the table as well, but try to make them less visible. Light the tea light before the ritual starts.

Keep a fire extinguisher or fire blanket nearby, just in case!

Script

Chalice Lighting

I invite [Name 1], [Name 2], and [Children's names] forward to light our chalice.

In the spirit of love, we light our chalice
To guide us through the difficult times
To celebrate the good times
And to honor our transitions.
To acknowledge our community
Who are by our side through it all.

(Focus people light the chalice.)

Opening Words

Thank you for being here to support [Name 1] and [Name 2] today.

As you know, we are here to witness and hold space for [Name 1] and [Name 2] as they end their marriage. They welcome each and every one of you. You have all supported them throughout their life together—many of you were at their wedding [number] years ago—and they hope you will continue to support them in this new stage of their lives.

This is not a day of sorrow, though of course there is sadness and grief in every ending. This is a day in which [Name 1] and [Name 2] hold space for all that has been in their relationship, honor the gifts they have given to one another, let go of what was, and prepare to move forward in their lives. Though we will undoubtedly touch sorrow, and that is important, we will also share in the excitement of a new beginning, and most likely many other feelings!

Releasing Vows

[Number] years ago, [Name 1] and [Name 2] stood before you and asked you to recognize their relationship. To recognize them as a family and to support their journey together. They have appreciated your support when times have been difficult and they have delighted with you in joys both large and small.

Their relationship began and has continued to be rooted in love and respect for one another. Over the last [number] years, their paths have been bound closely together. Their relationship, their family, and this community have shaped their lives. And for many years that has fed their growth and happiness.

Now, after considerable reflection and exploration, they have come to realize their journey as a couple has come to an end. They have not taken this decision to separate lightly. Ultimately the love and respect for each other that brought them together are the same forces that now ask them to end their marriage and to forge new paths in the future.

And, as they had their community here to witness and support them in joining their lives in marriage, they invite you to witness and support them in ending it. They have prepared some words to say to one another.

(Invite the focus couple to come forward.)

Partner 1: [Name 2], I am grateful for the time we have had together,
for the love and care you have given me and our family.
I acknowledge that, sadly, our journey in marriage has come to an end,
and here our paths diverge.
In the spirit of love, I return the wedding ring you gave me, and with it I release you from the vows we made that day.
You have my blessing, and I hope you find joy on the path before you.

(Pause to acknowledge the moment before having the second partner repeat these words and return their ring. Pause again before continuing.)

Releasing the Relationship

You have released each other from the vows you made. Are you now ready to let go of your relationship as you have known it?

Focus couple: We are.

LEADER: [Name 1] and [Name 2] have chosen [object] to symbolize their relationship. [You might explain why they chose it. Then address the couple again.] Will you please put the [object] in the bowl?

They will now burn the [object].

(Each member of the couple picks up a taper candle and lights either the kindling or the symbolic object itself. After the fire is established, continue.)

As the [object] burns, they release the energy they have invested in the relationship.
Release the expectations they had of one another.
Release the disappointments and frustrations.
Release the daily intimacies and affections.
Release the patterns and routines they created in their marriage together.

(Wait until the flames die down.)

[Name 1] and [Name 2] have separated their physical spaces, they have ended their legal contract through divorce, and today they end their marriage spiritually and symbolically. They close that chapter of their lives and begin to look forward to what is to come.

Although they will, of course, need time apart to reimagine their lives moving forward, they will not need to leave all of their life together to do so.

They are able to stay connected to each of you, their beloved community. They are both deeply committed to parenting [Children's names]. And they are committed to continuing their friendship, which has sustained them through all the stages of their relationship.

Optional Affirmation of Children

Use this section if the couple have children who are willing and able to participate

[Name 1] and [Name 2] are committed to remaining in healthy relationship with one another, honoring their past, and leaving space for their individual futures as their relationship evolves. They are committed to this, not only for their own well-being, but also for the well-being of their beloved children [Children's names], who they know will be affected by this transition.

(Ask the children to come forward.)

Your parents would like to say something to you now.

(The parents may write their own affirmation or use the words below.)

PARTNER 1: I am and always will be so proud of you and so grateful to have you in my life. I know that things will change now that your [name that children use for Partner 2] and I have chosen to separate, and I promise to support you in this transition. I will always love you.

(Repeat for the other partner.)

Affirmation of Community

As they asked you [number] years ago to support their marriage, and you have done so, [Name 1] and [Name 2] now ask you again for your support.

Your support for each of them individually to create new lives,
and your support for them to enter a new phase of being a family:
As friends and coparents committed to each other's well-being
and devoted to their children.

Are you willing to offer this support?

PARTICIPANTS: We are.

LEADER: May it be so!

Before we close this ritual, I invite you to sing "Love Will Guide Us."

Song

"Love Will Guide Us" (Sally Rogers)

(Lead participants in singing.)

Chalice Extinguishing

LEADER: We extinguish our chalice with the words of Lois Van Leer.

Having let go,
Set our intentions,
Named our curiosity,
Committed our energies,
And given ourselves over to lives of balance, purpose, and meaning,
Let us begin again
In love.

(Extinguish the chalice.)

For Separation or Divorce
(for an Individual)
Rev. Heather Concannon

This ritual is for use by one person, alone, after the end of a marriage or other romantic relationship. It is written to be used flexibly at different points after the relationship's end; it has a consistent beginning and closing, but may include different ritual elements intended to address different emotional or spiritual needs. At different points along the journey of separating from a partner and ending a relationship, individuals will need different things, and you may wish to revisit this ritual several times, using different elements as they feel right to you.

Materials
- ☐ Altar space
- ☐ Chalice

For grieving and releasing the relationship:
- ☐ Picture of the person from whom you have separated
- ☐ Journal (paper or digital)

For removing a wedding ring:
- ☐ Your wedding ring
- ☐ Copy of your marriage vows (if you made them)
- ☐ Two pillar candles or tea lights
- ☐ Journal

For expressing and releasing anger:
- ☐ Paper
- ☐ Fire pit or small fireproof bowl

- ☐ Bowl of water
- ☐ Hand towel

For forgiveness:

- ☐ Dissolving paper cut into small pieces and a pen (or regular paper and a water-soluble marker)
- ☐ Bowl of water
- ☐ Spoon

For imagining a new and different future:

- ☐ Plant pot and soil
- ☐ Seeds
- ☐ Strips of paper
- ☐ Water

Setup

The journey of processing, healing, and finding closure will be different for every person experiencing the end of a significant relationship. Each separation is as unique and personal as the relationship itself. Even so, most people will face several important emotional and spiritual tasks. Depending on where you are in your own journey of separation, you may choose any of the following ritual elements for your ritual. It is recommended to do only one or two ritual elements at a time, not all of them at once. You may want to repeat different versions of this ritual over a period of time after a major separation, breakup, or divorce to give yourself multiple opportunities to facilitate letting go, forgiveness, acceptance, or whatever it is you need.

This ritual is meant to be done at home or in another quiet, comfortable place. Before you begin, clear your schedule and turn off your phone. You may wish to set up a small altar with items that represent the relationship, such as pictures or your wedding ring, to help mark the intention of the space and time you have created for yourself.

Script

Chalice Lighting

(As you enter into the space, take a few grounding breaths and light your chalice.)

My life looks different than I expected it to.
It is okay to have all of the feelings I am having.
I am loved and lovable.

For Grieving and Releasing the Relationship

(For some people it is difficult to accept that a relationship has ended; for others its end may bring feelings of relief and empowerment. Whatever you feel about the end of the relationship, this ritual element is designed to help you reflect on the relationship as a whole, to mark your transition out of it, and to help you release what it has been, so that you may begin to step into a new reality, one in which you are no longer partnered with the other person.)

(Write a letter to the person with whom the relationship has ended, using the prompts below. Each one might spark a single sentence or a longer passage.)

- *Dear _____,*
- *Since we met, you have been* [name all the roles the person has played in your life].
- *The things you, and our relationship, meant to me are _____.*
- *The circumstances that affected our relationship are _____.*
- *I am grateful to you and to our relationship for _____.*
- *The things I wish to hold on to from our relationship are _____.*
- *The things I will miss about our relationship are _____.*
- *The things I will not miss about our relationship are _____.*
- *The expectations or hopes for our relationship that I am letting go of are _____.*
- *The feelings I wish to release about you and our relationship are _____.*
- *When I think of you or see you in the future, I hope to feel _____.*

(When you have finished writing the letter, read it over. You may wish to read it out loud, imagining reading it to the other person.)

For Removing a Wedding Ring

(For many people who have used rings as a symbol of their relationship, it can be hard to know when and how to take the ring off, and the idea of doing so may bring up many feelings. This ritual element is intended to help facilitate that moment. Before beginning this ritual, consider what you plan to do with the ring after you have taken it off.)

(Light two candles.)

(If you made vows or other commitments with your former partner and can obtain copies of them, take them out now and read them. Consider: how does it feel to reread your vows? Which parts of them do you feel that you kept well? Which parts bring up feelings of regret, hurt, or tenderness? You may wish to journal on these reflections for several minutes.)

(Take off your wedding ring and place it in front of one of the candles.)

I release you from these vows.

(Extinguish the candle behind the ring.)

(As the second candle remains lit, take some time to journal about the following prompts:

- *What promises do you wish to make to yourself in the coming weeks and months?*
- *What intentions do you hold around caring for yourself, self-talk, or making time and space for things that are important to you?*)

(After you are done journaling, read over these new commitments. When you are ready, extinguish the second candle.)

For Expressing and Releasing Anger

(After a separation, you may find yourself angry at the other person, at yourself, at circumstances that influenced the end of the relationship, or at others who may impose their feelings or reactions onto your separation. This is an opportunity to express anger and then release it.)

(Take some time to express your anger on paper. You might do this in narrative form, by journaling, or by drawing, scribbling, writing down disparate words, folding, ripping, or tearing the paper, or in any other way you want to express your anger. You can use as many pieces of paper as you need.)

(When you are ready, burn the paper in the fire pit or bowl.)

(Take several slow, thoughtful breaths, waiting until the paper is completely burned.)

I release this anger.

(Dip your hands into the bowl of water and gently wash any soot, drawing materials, etc. from your hands, along with your anger. Dry your hands.)

For Forgiveness

(Forgiving another person is a gift to ourselves, even more than it is a gift to the other person. Forgiveness does not condone behaviors, nor is it the same as reconciliation, but it can be a powerful way to loosen the hold that resentment, regret, anger, and hurt can have on us.)

(Call to mind a specific regret or hurt related to the end of your relationship that you would like to let go of. You may want to forgive the other person for words they said or for actions they took or failed to take, or you may want to forgive yourself for something. Try to be as specific as possible. Write out a description of the hurt on one of the pieces of dissolving paper.)

(Take a cleansing breath.)

(Consider for a moment how it would feel to have the burden of this regret or hurt lightened—not entirely lifted, but lighter. Notice how it feels in your body to imagine letting that go, forgiving yourself or the other person for this hurt.)

(Once you are ready, gently drop the piece of paper into the bowl of water. You may wish to stir it into the water as you watch it disappear. Imagine your regret or hurt dissolving—not disappearing, but transforming—as the paper dissolves.)

(Repeat with any other things you would like to forgive yourself or the other person for.)

For Imagining a New and Different Future

(The end of a major relationship means the end of a future that you had imagined or expected. You may have needed time to grieve this lost future, or you may have been ready for a new one for a long time. This ritual element is designed to come at a time when you feel ready to mark your openness to a new and different future.)

(Fill a pot with soil. As you do so, think about all of the things in your life that have had to pass away and decompose, as compost does, to make space for and nourish new life.)

(On strips of paper, write down some intentions, imaginings, or affirmations you wish to hold in the next chapter of your life.)

(Roll up the pieces of paper into small coils. Make a small hole in the soil. Gently place one of your rolled-up intentions and three or four seeds in the hole and cover it with soil.)

May you have what you need to thrive.

(Repeat until you have planted all of your intentions. Plant them with hope and courage, knowing that some may grow and some may not. Water them.)

Chalice Extinguishing

(Once you have done one or two of the above elements and feel ready to end the ritual you have created for yourself, choose a way to close the space. You may wish to sit in silence or meditate for five or ten minutes, sing a simple song a few times, or offer a short prayer.)

(Extinguish the chalice, and transition out of the ritual by doing a quiet and calm activity, such as making tea, taking a shower or a bath, petting an animal, or listening to soothing music.)

For a Partner Near the End of Life

Rev. theresa rohlck

Dedicated with love to Victor Hola and Scott Ferguson

This is a blessing to offer when someone in a partnership is nearing end of life or has begun hospice or palliative care, as a way to help process anticipatory grief. The ritual is very intimate; it can be for just the partners and a leader, or for a small group of close friends or family. This ritual was created after a conversation with partners who were searching for ways to both honor their life together and imagine life for one partner after the decease of the other; it could be adapted for a relationship of more than two partners.

Materials

- ☐ Small altar table or space
- ☐ Chalice
- ☐ Small stones, one for each participant plus a few extra
- ☐ Small bowl to hold the stones
- ☐ Small drawstring bag to hold the stones (ideally something beautiful and appropriate for the partners)
- ☐ Water in a small bottle that can be tightly closed
- ☐ Towel
- ☐ Optional: Music that is significant to the partners

Setup

Put the bowl on the altar table or in the altar space such that it can be seen by all present. Put one stone in it for each person present, including the partners and the leader.

Script

Chalice Lighting

We light this chalice today in celebration of [Name 1] and [Name 2]'s partnership. May the light remind us that love is what burns brightest here.

(Light the chalice.)

Today, this intimate yet public recognition of these partners' love for each other is important as a moment where we can create space for, and give voice to, the complex emotions we all are holding, knowing that this union, in the shape we know it now, will soon come to an end.

Optional Reflection on the Partnership

(You might continue with a short reflection on partnership, personalized to fit the partners' story.)

Blessing

I invite us into a ritual to bless this partnership.

Please, each, take a stone.

(Offer the bowl of stones first to the partners, then to the other participants.)

If you would, hold the stone, feel the weight in your palm.
The stone is solid, unwavering, as is our support for [Name 1] and [Name 2].
Take a moment in silence to imbue that stone with all the love you possibly can.
Breathe a message into the stone for these partners.
When they need to be reminded that they are not alone, they each can hold any one or all of these stones.

(Allow sufficient time for this. Do not rush.)

When you are ready, place your stone in this bowl.

(Offer the bowl to participants and have them gently set their stones in it. End by having the partners place their stones in it as well.

If the partners wear wedding rings and are willing to remove them [Name 1], [Name 2], you may now place your wedding rings on top of these stones.

[Name 1], [Name 2], I have brought you water. [Name any significance the water's source has.] This water symbolizes the unbroken line of support our community has to offer you both, right now and into the future.

(Pour some of the water slowly over the stones, then ask the partners to pour the rest of it together. The stones and rings do not have to be completely submerged, just wet.)

May you feel the love and care of our community surrounding you and holding you in this moment and in the days to come.

(Remove the stones one by one, dry them off, and put them in the small bag. Give the bag of stones to the partners. If the partners put their rings in the bowl, dry them off and return them. The partners may then put them on each other's fingers as they did during their marriage or commitment ceremony. You might play, or have people sing or hum, an appropriate piece of music during these actions.)

Closing Words

I would like to close with a poem by the poet David Whyte.

Much Has Been Said

Much has been said about the eternal
and untouchable nature of love,
its tidal ungovernable forces
and its emergence from far beyond
the ordinary, but love may find
its fullest, most imagined
and most courageous form

when it leaves the abstractions
and safety of the timeless
and the untrammeled
to make its promises
amidst the fears, vulnerabilities,
and disappearances of our difficult,
touchable and time bound world.

To love and to witness love
in the face of possible loss
and to find the mystery of love's
promise in the shadow of that loss,
in the shadow of the ordinary
and in the shadow of our own inevitable
disappearance may be where the eternal
source of all our origins stands
in awe of the full consequences
of everything it has set in motion.

Chalice Extinguishing

[Name 1] and [Name 2], you have loved each other well. You have experienced love, as the poet says, in "its fullest, most imagined and most courageous form / when it leaves the abstractions / and safety of the timeless . . . to make its promises / amidst the fears, vulnerabilities, / and disappearances of our difficult, touchable and time bound world."

Your partnership has witnessed love in many forms. And now that love is expanding to include an anticipated loss. But even in the shadow of that loss, you have chosen to continue to share your lives fully with each other, and with so many others, including these dear friends right here. And that is nothing short of miraculous.

As we extinguish the chalice, know that the light of love remains burning brightly in your lives.

(Extinguish the chalice.)

Go now, with that love in your hearts, surrounded by peace.

Amen. May it be so.

(After the ritual has ended, pour the water from the bowl back into the bottle and give it to the partners.)

Creating Home

For Blessing a New Home
Rev. Karen G. Johnston

This ritual serves the purpose of marking and making a new home, wherever it is, whether the focus people rent or own it, whether they inhabit it alone or share it with others, and whatever form it takes: apartment, house, houseboat, co-op, group house, assisted living facility, etc. It is designed for individuals, couples, families, and groups committed to living together. The author developed this ritual through crowd-sourcing and in conversation with a family in her congregation.

Materials

- ☐ Chalice
- ☐ Small containers of water, one for each participant
- ☐ Stones (3–8 inches long, preferably flat and smooth), one for each participant
- ☐ Permanent markers in colors that contrast with those of the stones
- ☐ Potted plant or two (if the ritual is taking place entirely indoors)
- ☐ Optional: Fans (handheld, not electric)

Setup

Review the script ahead of time with the focus people and personalize it as appropriate. They may want to gather or choose the stones that will be used. Encourage them to consider inviting family members, friends, neighbors (the ritual could be a way to meet them!), coworkers, and anyone who brings them delight. The stone ritual invites participants to move freely around, choosing a place for their stone; the focus people might want to communicate if there are areas that are off limits.

This ritual can take place indoors, outdoors, or both, and you might want to invoke the four elements in the same place or in different rooms, corners of the yard, etc. Decide ahead of time which elements will be invoked in which spaces, and set up the materials needed in each space. Carry the lit chalice with you as you move around; you may prefer to use a hurricane lantern or a battery-operated candle.

Script

Opening Words

(Sing or recite, alone or in unison with all participants, this excerpt adapted from "May Nothing Evil Cross This Door," by Louis Untermeyer.)

May nothing evil cross this door,
and may ill fortune never pry about
these windows; may the roar and rain go by.

With laughter drown the raucous shout,
and, though these sheltering walls are thin,
may they be strong to keep hate out
and hold love in.

Let us begin in gratitude:
for being together;
for this body and this breath;
for the joy of health in all its forms;
for community that sustains us;
for opportunities to be of service.

To make a home is one of the most elemental acts
we humans—and not only we humans—do.
It is essential to our survival in both body and spirit.

A shelter protects us from the elements.
Yet when a shelter becomes a home
it is a place where roots may hold us close
and wings may set us free.

[Names] have invited us
into this sacred act of recognition and ritual
to intentionally mark the process of making this their home

[optionally add "and accepting responsibility for this land whose stewards they
have become"].

Their inclusion of us affirms that it is in community
we rise above mere existence or pure survival
and find ourselves able to dance and dawdle,
dazzle and dream,
delight and dwell in Love.

We live our lives
in the midst of the four great elements.
It is among these elements that
[Names] make their home.
Fire. Air. Earth. Water.
We welcome them and invite
gentle versions of them
into our shared ritual today.

Fire

The Fire Element.

(Light the chalice.)

We kindle this chalice:
a symbol of hope in hard times,
a beacon of light in dark times,
a sign of resistance against evil.

We respect the element of fire
not only for its power of light and life,
but also for its power of destruction.

May only flame
that soothes, heals, regenerates,
cooks, and illuminates,
be known in this home.

(Move to the next element's location.)

Air

The Air Element.

As our bodies allow,
let us take in a comfortable breath.
This element reminds us that
we do not escape our dependence
upon the air that we and other living beings breathe.
It is not just dependence, but interdependence:
the very essence of this planet, our shared home.

Using our hands [or the fans provided],
let us create the movement of air in our midst,
directing it toward others and ourselves,
a form of blessing to affirm
that in making this place a home,
we celebrate not self-reliance,
but our unavoidable, luscious, generative
interdependence.

(Pause while participants bless the space with air.)

(Move to the next element's location.)

Earth

The Earth Element.

These stones [name the focus people who collected them, if relevant]

are our earth element.
Forged through forces beyond our knowing
and beyond our capacity to survive,
they remind us of two truths:

First: the making of a home,
like the living of a life, can be rocky.
The living of a life and the making of a home
bring trial and tribulation, the texture of lives lived.
And we encounter people and moments
that make the journey smoother,
reminders of our blessings,
such as these stones aspire to be.

Second: we long for, and to a large degree
need, a solid foundation beneath us, and
the opportunity to ground ourselves and each other.
There is something powerful about touching the earth
to remind us of whence we came;
to help us connect with humility;
to affirm our utter interconnectedness.

Come up and take a stone and a pen.
Answer this question in one word:
What do you hope [Names] will find in their new home?
Write the blessing on your stone.
Once you have written your word on it,
Find a place in this [home, yard] where it might reside,
perhaps out in the open,
perhaps hidden away as a future surprise.

(Pause while participants write their blessings on the stones and place them.)

(When everyone returns, move to the next element's location.)

Water

The Water Element.

(Invite participants to take a container of water.)

These containers hold water, source of life,
conveyor of blessing in many traditions.

It is already holy in its essence,
and we shall make it even more so,
speaking aloud or silently
an intention over or into it.
What do you hope [Names] will create in their new home?

Please now speak your intention into the water.

(Pause while participants speak their blessings into the water.)

Now take your container of water.
Find a place to water the ground [or "Water one of these plants"],
knowing that as you do so,
you are adding your intention
to this house to make it a home.

(When everyone returns, move to the chalice.)

Chalice Extinguishing

Let us gather back together to bring this ritual to a close.

"Though these sheltering walls are thin,
may they be strong to keep hate out
and hold love in."

Lyrics, once again,
from the hymn with which

we lit the chalice.
As we started, so we end.

With the words to a song
that we offer as a prayer
for this [family, person, group],
this home, this nation, this world.

And with gratitude:
may it be in our hearts, on our minds, in our bodies
as we move through space and as we rest,
as we offer our gifts to the world.

(Extinguish the chalice.)

For Bidding Farewell to a Home
Rev. Elizabeth Carrier-Ladd

We move from home to home throughout our lives. We often offer rituals to bless new homes. But saying goodbye is just as important as saying hello. When we leave homes in which we have made significant memories, it is especially important to honor the transition and thank the home for holding us through those memorable times. The focus people of this ritual are the family members or housemates—as broadly defined as you wish—who have lived in the home. They should choose one or two of their group to lead it.

Materials
- ☐ Small altar table, or cloth to designate altar space
- ☐ Chalice
- ☐ Candle(s)
- ☐ Small pieces of paper
- ☐ Optional: Music

Setup
The ideal time to do this ritual is in the empty home, right before leaving. If this is not logistically possible, it can be done in the home any time before moving out. Set up a chalice on an altar. Decorate the altar with any sacred objects that have meaning to you and your family or housemates.

Four versions of the central element are offered; it can be verbal, written, or both, and short, medium length, or long. Choose the one that suits everyone's preferences, available time, stress levels, etc., or mix and match parts of several.

Script

Chalice Lighting

We live lives of transition. We do not stay anywhere forever. We are in motion: from place to place, from learning to learning, from moment to moment.

And yet we find and create places of meaning as we journey. We put down roots in those places and cultivate growth in our lives through them. Where we live matters.

As we prepare to leave this place, let us light this chalice in the spirit of transition, knowing that this flame will light this sacred space for but a short time before we extinguish it, and that our time here draws quickly to a close.

We light this chalice with joy for what is before us and sorrow for what we have to leave behind in order to journey on.

(Light the chalice.)

Sharing Memories with Gratitude

Option 1: Short and verbal

This house has held so much over the years that we have lived here. It has been a part of our lives. We have laughed and cried here. We have hugged and argued here. We have made important decisions for ourselves here. We have returned here after long days to process and reconnect to what matters most. This house has held us. It has been our home.

So much has happened in this space. Let us remember and honor together all that holds us in this time. You might remember a specific moment, or a habit or tradition you had here; it might be something you felt or did alone, or it might be something that some or all of us shared together. As you're moved, please say, "I remember" and tell us what you're thinking of. If you'd like to honor an experience but keep it private, you can just say, "I remember something that happened here."

After each memory, we will respond together: Thank you for being our home.

We remember…

(Pause to let everyone share. Don't forget to do so yourself! After each memory is offered, lead participants in saying, "Thank you for being our home." Once everyone has said everything they want to say, continue.)

Thank you for being our home. For holding us and sheltering us. For giving us warmth and light and safety. Thank you for the gifts of these many memories, which we take with us on to our next resting place. We will remember all that has been shared and honor those memories held privately in our hearts. Our time here has passed, but we take so much with us from the time we have had. Our hearts overflow with gratitude.

Option 2: Medium length and written

(This option gives participants a way to honor their memories of the home without sharing them publicly. After the ritual, participants can choose to keep their writing or let it go, such as by burning the paper.)

This house has held so much over the years that we have lived here. It has been a part of our lives. We have laughed and cried here. We have hugged and argued here. We have made important decisions for ourselves here. We have returned here after long days to process and reconnect to what matters most. This house has held us. It has been our home.

We have made many memories here. Let us take some time to honor what has happened in this space.

Let us write down some of the memories that we take with us from this home. They could be of specific moments, such as [name one or two events you all remember], or they could be habits or traditions, like [name one or two familiar practices, such as shared dinners or children's bath time]. You might remember things we shared together, or things you felt or did alone. All of these are worthy of honoring.

These memories are only for you. Once we're done here, you may choose to keep them or let them go.

(Allow time for writing memories together. Play some instrumental music, if it would be helpful.)

So much has happened in this home. We thank you, home, for being our home. Will you join me in saying: Thank you for being our home!

PARTICIPANTS: Thank you for being our home.

LEADER: Thank you for being our home. For holding us and sheltering us. For giving us warmth and light and safety. Thank you for the gifts of these many memories, which we take with us on to our next resting place. Our time here has passed, but we take so much with us from the time we have had. Our hearts overflow with gratitude.

(You may conclude by walking around the home and together thanking each room. Or you may hold hands in a circle in a central or important place and thank the whole home.)

Option 3: Medium length and verbal

(This option gives participants time to share memories associated with different rooms and spaces in the home. You can bring the lit chalice with you as you move around, or leave it behind and return to it at the end of the ritual. If you prefer not to move around as the script directs, you could stay in one place and simply say, "When we think of the kitchen, we remember," "When we think of the porch, we remember," and so on. In this case, you might consider taking a stroll through the home after the ritual is complete to say farewell to each room. Perhaps place a hand on a wall or sit down in each room to say a proper goodbye.)

This house has held so much over the years that we have lived here. It has been a part of our lives. We have laughed and cried here. We have hugged and argued here. We have made important decisions for ourselves here. We have returned here after long days to process and reconnect to what matters most. This house has held us. It has been our home.

We have made many memories here. Let us take some time to honor what has happened in this space. So much has happened in this home. As we move through each room, let us share our memories with each other and with all that holds us in this time. The memory could be of a specific moment, such as [name one or two events you all remember], or it could be a habit or tradition, like [name one or two familiar practices, such as shared dinners or children's bath time].

After each memory, we will respond together: Thank you for being our home.

LEADER: In the [name the room you are in], we remember . . .

(Pause to let everyone share. Don't forget to do so yourself! After each memory is offered, lead participants in saying, "Thank you for being our home." Once everyone has said everything they want to say, move to the next room, name it, and invite memories in the same way. Continue until you have visited every room or other space you want to.)

Thank you for being our home. For holding us and sheltering us. For giving us warmth and light and safety. Thank you for the gifts of these many memories, which we take with us on to our next resting place. We will remember all that has been shared, and honor those memories held privately in our hearts. Our time here has passed, but we take so much with us from the time we have had. Our hearts overflow with gratitude.

Option 4: Longer, both written and verbal

(Giving participants the chance to write down memories and then share the ones that feel right to share allows them to process their memories and feelings in multiple ways. While this takes the most time, it is worth it if your group has the time and energy for it. This option has participants stay in one place while remembering different rooms and spaces in the home, so you might consider taking a stroll through the home after the ritual is complete to say farewell to each. Perhaps place a hand on a wall or sit down in each room to say a proper goodbye. Alternatively, you could move from place to place in the home as you share the memories associated with each. You can bring the lit chalice with you as you move around, or leave it behind and return to it at the end of the ritual.)

This house has held so much over the years that we have lived here. It has been a part of our lives. We have laughed and cried here. We have hugged and argued here. We have made important decisions for ourselves here. We have returned here after long days to process and reconnect to what matters most. This house has held us. It has been our home.

We have made many memories here. Let us take some time to honor what has happened in this home.

Let us write down some of the memories that we take with us from this home. They could be of specific moments, such as [name one or two events you all remember], or they could be habits or traditions, like [name one or two familiar practices, such as shared dinners or children's bath time]. You might remember things we shared together, or things you felt or did alone. They might be associated with specific rooms or spaces, or with the home as a whole.

(Allow time for writing memories together. Play some instrumental music, if it would be helpful.)

So much has happened in this home. Let us share our memories with each other and with all that holds us in this time. We will go through memories we associate with particular rooms first, and then ones of the whole home. Of course, you don't have to share anything you don't want to. If you'd like to honor an experience but keep it private, you can just say, "I remember something that happened here." After each memory, we will respond together: Thank you for being our home.

LEADER: When we think of [name a room or space], we remember . . .

(Pause to let everyone share. Don't forget to do so yourself! After each memory is offered, lead participants in saying, "Thank you for being our home." Once everyone has said everything they want to say, name the next room or space and invite memories in the same way. Continue until you have named every room or other space you want to.)

Thank you for being our home. For holding us and sheltering us. For giving us warmth and light and safety. Thank you for the gifts of these many memories, which we take with us on to our next resting place. We will remember all that has been shared and honor those memories held privately in our hearts. Our time here has passed, but we take so much with us from the time we have had. Our hearts overflow with gratitude.

Chalice Extinguishing

Our time here is over. We have said goodbye. We are thankful for so much of what has happened here. We are grateful for the presence of the holy in this home today and each day we lived here. We ask that this space continue to hold our love as it welcomes new people into its rooms. Our time here is over. This light is released.

(Extinguish the chalice.)

May it be so. Blessed be. Amen.

For Blessing a Temporary Home after a Disaster

Kate Wilkinson

This is a home blessing for temporary housing after a disaster or relocation. It is written for families with children, but it can also be used with minor adaptations by other households or individuals. This ritual was originally created for a family whose house had burned down, to help the children feel more at home in their temporary housing.

Materials

- ☐ Optional: Water to bless each part of the home. (If this ritual is being done in a Unitarian Universalist setting, Water Communion water would be appropriate to use.)
- ☐ Optional: A phone or camera to take a picture

Setup

Review the script with the focus people ahead of time and personalize it as needed. It is written to begin in the living room, but if the family mostly spends time in a different room, you may want to begin there. If you are using water to bless the home, make sure it is in a portable container that has a wide enough mouth to dip fingers into.

Script

(Gather in the living room.)

Today we are gathered to bless our temporary home.

Dear couch,

You're not the couch we are used to, but we are glad to have you in our home.

We look forward to collapsing on you at the end of a long day.

We look forward to snuggling up on you to watch movies together.

We look forward to lying under a blanket on you when we don't feel well.

Thank you for holding our family with your cushions!

(Optional: Invite family members to dip their fingers into the water and sprinkle it over the couch)

(Move to the kitchen.)

Dear kitchen,

You're not the kitchen we are used to, but we are glad to have you in our home.

We look forward to making meals to feed our family here.

We look forward to nourishing our bodies with food prepared here.

We look forward to telling each other about our day at the dinner table here.

We look forward to late night cups of tea here.

Thank you for being the center of our new home.

(Optional: Invite family members to dip their fingers into the water and sprinkle it over the kitchen.)

(Move to a bedroom.)

Dear bedrooms,

You're not the bedrooms we are used to, but we are glad to have a place to sleep.

We look forward to having good dreams here.

We look forward to getting rest here to recharge our bodies.

We look forward to whispered conversations on pillows.

We look forward to quiet hours of playing within your walls.

Thank you for sheltering us at night.

(Optional: Invite family members to dip their fingers into the water and sprinkle it over the bedrooms.)

(Move to the bathroom.)

Dear bathroom,
You are not the bathroom that we are used to, but we are glad to have a place to wash up.
We look forward to refreshing showers here.
We look forward to giggling while we brush our teeth.
We look forward to having a private moment to ourselves in here.
We look forward to looking in this mirror each day to see how we have grown.
Thank you for the convenience of running water and a flushing toilet!

(Optional: Invite family members to dip their fingers into the water and sprinkle it over the bathroom.)

(You can add any additional blessings you'd like as is relevant to the space you are blessing.)

(After blessing the individual parts of the house, gather in the space that you consider the heart of the home.)

Dear new home,
You are not the home we are used to, and we don't plan to be here forever.
But for the next [period of time], you are our home.
The place where we gather at the end of each day.
The place where we dream for the future.
The place where we do our homework.
The place where we come together as a family.
Thank you for being here for us in our time of need.
Within your walls we will laugh and play and grow.
You are not our forever home,
But we know that home is where we are together.

(Optional: Invite family members to dip their fingers into the water and sprinkle it over each other.)

(Optional: Take a family photo in the heart of your temporary home and frame it.)

Blessing
Our Bodies

For Assisted Conception

Rev. Jennifer Gracen

Dedicated to Virginia Gracen and the child we created together

This ritual is designed for the individual(s) hoping to conceive a child through procedures such as intracervical insemination, intrauterine insemination, or in vitro fertilization. Planned conception, however it is achieved, may require many attempts over several months or years. This brief ritual is offered to bring intentionality and spiritual focus to each attempt.

Materials

- ☐ Candle
- ☐ Optional: Seed, such as an acorn, and something to plant it in

Setup

You can do this ritual either at home, before you leave for the place where the conception attempt will happen (if it does not also happen at home), or in the place where it will happen. Medical facilities may not allow you to light a candle; you could use a battery-operated one, use a seed instead, or do the ritual outside the facility before entering. If possible, make the space comfortable and easeful.

Script

(Light the candle or hold the seed. If you are intending to become pregnant alone, you can place a hand on your abdomen. If a partner or support person is with you, they can place their hand on your abdomen. If you are working with a surrogate and they are willing to be touched in this way, you can place a hand on their abdomen. Change "I" to "we" in the script as appropriate for your circumstances.)

Spirit of Life and Love,
I invite you into this moment
As I strive to bring new life
Into this world.
I welcome the miracle of life
Into my life.
May I be open to the possibilities.
May I be open to the questions.
May I be open to the love.
Be with me in this and all moments.
Amen.

(Extinguish the candle and allow the smoke to rise for a moment. If you are using a seed, consider planting it.)

For Abortion

Rev. Susan Chorley

This is a ritual to follow an abortion. It includes options to cover abortion of an unexpected or unplanned pregnancy, abortion of a wanted pregnancy, abortion chosen by a person already parenting children, and abortion connected with violence or abuse; you can choose and combine the elements relevant to your circumstances. Remember that this ritual, and the experience of abortion, may bring feelings of celebration or relief to some, while to others it may evoke grief; some people will feel multiple and even conflicting emotions. The ritual is designed to recognize an individual's abortion experience, and that of their partner(s) if relevant, in all its complexity.

Materials

- ☐ Altar table
- ☐ Chalice
- ☐ Small taper candles or votives
- ☐ Bowl or tray of sand, to hold candles
- ☐ Oil for anointing
- ☐ Meditation bell or chime
- ☐ Optional: Flowers

Setup

Set up the room to be warm, welcoming, and sacred, perhaps with some candles lit. Invite people to light a candle as they enter. Put the altar table in the middle of the space, with the chalice, candles, bowl or tray of sand, anointing oil, and perhaps some flowers on it. Set up a circle of chairs for the focus person and participants to sit in.

It is important to engage the focus person or people in the ritual's planning, as well as any support people they may want to include, so that the experience will meet their specific needs. Ask them to think about what they would like to share in the ritual, using the following questions to spark their thoughts:

- What do you want yourself and others to know about your experience?
- What words of compassion can you offer to yourself in this moment?
- What do you need from those who love you? How can we best hold and support you at this time?
- What kind of blessing do you wish to offer to yourself, or your partner, or the soul whom you could not welcome into this living world?
- What is the wisdom of this experience, and how will it carry you forward?
- What is the new shape of light your experience of abortion is offering?

Script

Chalice Lighting

It is with gratitude that I welcome you to this space and this time set apart for acknowledging the multitude of feelings we hold in our minds, hearts, and bodies regarding an abortion decision. Our bodies are sacred. The decisions we make about our bodies and potential life are sacred. They are also full of complexity. And in this space and time we wish only to acknowledge the sacredness of our bodies and our lives. In this time we wish to lift up the holiness inherent in a decision that may be our liberation and that may also feel painful or conflicted. It is in this both/and space that we light our chalice, to remind us of the great light that is glowing in the world and within all beings.

(Light the chalice.)

There are as many stories of abortion as there are people who have experienced abortion. Because of the heightened political and religious tensions surrounding abortion, and because the choice is uniquely private and often stigmatized, we rarely get to hear the detailed and precious story of an individual's decision and experience. And yet all of life's passages are worthy of acknowledgment through ritual. We are grateful for this time set aside to be with [Name(s)] following an abortion experience.

Song

"Stay with Me" (Jacques Berthier)

I invite you now into a time of singing. We will sing together a song from the Taizé Christian monastic community that repeats the words of Jesus as he prayed in the Garden of Gethsemane the night before he was betrayed. The words mirror the experience of all of us facing a challenging experience and wanting the support and care of our community. Following the Taizé tradition, we will sing the chorus through multiple times, until we feel a natural sense of closure. After singing, we will hold a few minutes of silence together.

(Lead participants in singing the song through ten or fifteen times, then hold silence for a few minutes. At the end of the time of silence, ring a meditation bell or chime.)

Sharing

We will now enter into a time of open sharing and community compassion. [Name(s)], we ask you to begin by sharing any reflections you wish on your experience of abortion, and then on how we can best support you at this time.

(The focus person or people share as they wish to.)

We are here surrounding [Name(s)] to offer our support and care. Having heard their story and what they need from us in this moment, I invite those gathered here to reflect back to them words of care and compassion. How can you support them? How are you holding them in this time? [Give instructions about how people should speak up: in order around the circle, popcorn style, etc.] Let us take several moments of silent reflection and meditation, and when the bell rings, you are invited to share your support and care with [Name(s)].

(Hold a few minutes of silence, then ring the bell or chime.)

Support can take many forms, sometimes in words and sometimes not. If you find yourself without words, you can press hand over your heart to quietly offer your support.

Reading

"the mother" (Gwendolyn Brooks)

Abortions will not let you forget.
You remember the children you got that you did not get,
The damp small pulps with a little or with no hair,
The singers and workers that never handled the air.
You will never neglect or beat
Them, or silence or buy with a sweet.
You will never wind up the sucking-thumb
Or scuttle off ghosts that come.
You will never leave them, controlling your luscious sigh,
Return for a snack of them, with gobbling mother-eye.

I have heard in the voices of the wind the voices of my dim killed children.
I have contracted. I have eased
My dim dears at the breasts they could never suck.
I have said, Sweets, if I sinned, if I seized
Your luck
And your lives from your unfinished reach,
If I stole your births and your names,
Your straight baby tears and your games,
Your stilted or lovely loves, your tumults, your marriages, aches, and your deaths,
If I poisoned the beginnings of your breaths,
Believe that even in my deliberateness I was not deliberate.
Though why should I whine,
Whine that the crime was other than mine?—
Since anyhow you are dead.
Or rather, or instead,
You were never made.
But that too, I am afraid,
Is faulty: oh, what shall I say, how is the truth to be said?
You were born, you had body, you died.
It is just that you never giggled or planned or cried.

Believe me, I loved you all.
Believe me, I knew you, though faintly, and I loved, I loved you
All.

We will now enter into a time of quiet meditation, reflecting on these words. Following the quiet together we will sing.

(Allow a few minutes of silence.)

Song

"Find a Stillness" (words: Carl G. Seaburg, music: Transylvanian hymn with harmony by Larry Phillips)

(Lead participants in singing.)

Witnessing

A midrash, a Jewish commentary, on the creation story in the book of Genesis says that when God said, "Let there be light," ten vessels appeared, each filled with light. But they were too fragile to contain the holy light, and they shattered, scattering the light throughout the universe. The midrash reminds us that even in the shattering pain of life, there is light to be found everywhere. The experience of abortion can feel like a breaking open of our hearts, our feelings, our bodies, our spirits. Each of us is full of holy and sacred light—and we continue to shine that forth into the world.

Honoring the light that bursts forth from the brokenness of our world, [Name(s)], we invite you to share with us what kind of blessing you might want to offer to yourselves, or to the soul whom you could not welcome into this living world. What is the wisdom of your experience, and how will you carry it forward? What new shape of light does your abortion experience offer?

(The focus person or people take some time to share.)

Let us remain in silence for a few minutes. You are welcome to light a candle and place it in the [bowl or tray], as a reminder of the light that bursts forth from all of us.

(Participants light candles as they wish.)

Anointing

From ancient times, people have anointed one another as a way of offering healing and comfort. The feel and scent of the oil is a physical reminder of the care and comfort we all deserve and desire. We invite [Name(s)] to enter into the circle for the ritual of anointing.

May this anointing be a blessing to you and a symbol of love for you, your body, your decisions, and the holiness inherent in it all.

(Anointing words for a variety of circumstances are offered below. Choose the ones most appropriate for the focus person or people. You can combine parts of several.)

For an unexpected or unplanned pregnancy

[Name(s)], you are brave and cherished and brilliant and full of grace. You made a decision for yourself, for the world, out of love and full of worth. We are with you in the myriad of feelings you hold in this moment, and that you held in the time leading up to your decision to end your pregnancy, and in any story you wish to share with the world or hold in the depth of your beautiful soul. Most of all, we want you to know you are not alone. Countless people have gone before you on this path, and countless others will follow. And yet your story of abortion is unique, as is each person's. May you cherish yourself and your decision, and know that you are cherished by this community and in this world. Amen and blessed be.

For those already parenting children

[Name(s)], you are a good parent. That has not changed. Sometimes a decision for abortion is the best parenting decision you can make. Breathe in the blessing of your sacredness and the sacredness of this decision. Breathe out any place where you cannot celebrate your goodness or might hold yourself back from full life and full love. Amen and blessed be.

For a survivor of abuse or violence

[Name(s)], your body is precious, holy, and sacred. Abuse and violence were a violation of the sanctity of your body and spirit. Though we live in a world that is broken by oppression and an ongoing lack of compassion and care, this reality was never meant to be and is always to be condemned. No human deserves violence or abuse. You did nothing to deserve to be treated as less than the holy, precious, amazing person you are. Sometimes the termination of a pregnancy can be the best, safest, and most caring decision you can make for your body and for the future body and soul of a little one. Even so, the decision can be painful, and we want you to know you are not alone. We surround you now and will surround you in the future with love, acceptance, and deep care. Amen and blessed be.

For a wanted pregnancy

[Name(s)], we are with you in your grief and in the painful decision you had to make. Know that the pain of this loss will never completely leave you, and that you are forever deeply loved, respected, and inherently good. Allow the jagged edges of the pain surrounding the end of this pregnancy to be slowly sanded down by the care, compassion, and respect your family and community hold out for you. The soul that you could not welcome at this time wishes you well. You will have a soul connection forever in liminal space between this life and the next. Amen and blessed be.

Song

"Courage, My Friend" (South African call and response song)

(Lead participants in singing.)

Chalice Extinguishing

As we close this sacred time together, let us rise in body or spirit and hold hands. Hear these words by the poet Leah Lakshmi Piepzna-Samarasinha, from her poem "Femme Futures."

Where does the future live in your body?
Touch it.

When I hear us dream our futures,
believe we will make it to one,
We will make one.

The future lives in our bodies.

(Extinguish the chalice.)

May we go from this place blessed by the future that is in our bodies, the future
we dreamed of and co-created in this time, and the future we are building for all
people—full of love, acceptance, compassion, and deep joy.

For Planned Hospitalization
Rev. Liz Weber

For the children and youth at the Massachusetts General Hospital for Children

This is a ritual of creating a chalice for someone to bring with them to a hospital stay as a reminder that they are held in love. It can be used by a family or small group. The ritual is adapted from one that the author created for pediatric patients at the hospital where she was a chaplain resident. As one child put it, "The candle can hold the happy and the sad and the love."

Materials

- ☐ Large battery-operated candle (pillar size is best; a drawing of a chalice or candle could be used instead)
- ☐ Tissue paper in a variety of colors
- ☐ Scissors
- ☐ Glue
- ☐ Permanent markers
- ☐ Saucer or dish to set the candle in, if desired
- ☐ Optional: Scrap paper and pens
- ☐ Optional: Music
- ☐ Optional: Notepaper

Setup

Make a small test mark on the candle to verify that the permanent marker will not rub off. If it does, write or draw on light-colored tissue paper instead of the candle itself. Permanent markers should still be used to prevent the marks from bleeding when the paper is glued to the candle.

Set chairs around a table. The focus person can hold the candle or set it in the center of the space. Spread the other supplies across the tabletop.

For safety reasons, open flames are not allowed in hospital settings. If a battery-operated candle is not available, use a drawing of a chalice or candle instead. A large drawing could be taped to the wall where it will be visible from the focus person's bed. Draw just the chalice or candle in advance, not the flame.

If the focus person is blind or low vision, work with them to choose adaptations that will work well for them. One possibility is to use a variety of papers and fabrics with different textures, rather than only tissue paper.

The focus person should consider whether they would rather lead this ritual themselves, ask someone else to lead it, or share leadership with another. Leading it oneself can be empowering. Asking someone else to lead it can add to the feeling of being well cared for. The script here is written with someone else as leader; if you are leading it for yourself, change it as needed: "help me prepare for my hospitalization," and so on.

Script

Opening Words

Thank you for being here today to help [Name] prepare for their hospitalization. Together, we will create a chalice that [Name] will bring with them to the hospital to serve as a reminder of our love and support while they are there. We will also have time to speak to [Name]. Begin to let a blessing, prayer, or caring message come to mind. We will share that blessing while decorating the chalice. The decorations represent our community, and the chalice flame represents [Name]'s inner strength or spark. It will be lit for the first time during our ritual.

Throughout our lives,
each of us experiences moments
when we are called to offer our support to another
and moments when we ask for support for ourselves.
It is good to be together in times of challenge,
finding hope and strength for the path ahead.

And so we gather in community now
to offer care and blessings to one among us.

Grateful for our interconnected lives,
let us be agents of sustenance, hope, and healing
this hour and in the days to come.

Creating the Chalice

We are ready to create our chalice.

The chalice is made by gluing tissue paper onto the candle and writing words of encouragement on it. We will do this one by one, as we share our blessing, prayer, or caring words with [Name].

Look around at the paper and see which colors or patterns call to you. Get creative! The tissue paper will look good bunched up, layered in different colors, or extending above the top of the candle. You can cut it into specific shapes, or tear it for a more organic form. If you'd like, use the markers to draw on it before you glue it to the candle. You can decide how best to represent your blessing.

As you think about what you want to say, these questions can guide you:

- What hopes do you have for [Name]?
- What strengths or qualities does [Name] have that you think will sustain them in the hospital?
- How do you want to help [Name] feel supported and loved throughout this time?

Let's take some quiet time now to choose our words and design. Go ahead and get your paper and words ready to go onto the candle.

(Participants should be choosing paper and working with it. Some background music here can be nice. You may also want to have some notepaper on hand for people to jot down thoughts about what they want to say.)

(Resume when each person is ready to offer a blessing. The focus person can choose to abstain or to add the first or last piece.)

Let's decorate the candle and offer our blessings, prayers, and caring words now.

Take the candle, say what you would like to say to [Name], and then glue your tissue paper onto the candle. If you wish, you can also write a few words on the candle itself.

Who would like to begin?

(Pass the candle from person to person until everyone has participated. Later, if desired, the candle can be coated with Mod Podge or a similar clear sealant for protection.)

Lighting the Chalice

(If possible, the focus person should read these words and turn the candle on. If not, someone else can read or light for them. If someone else will read, change the words to "We light this chalice knowing that [Name] is not alone. Each time they hold it in their hands," etc.)

I light this chalice
knowing that I am not alone.
Each time I hold it in my hands,
I will remember the community that surrounds me.

I light this chalice
warmed by your blessings and prayers.
Each time I see its pillar,
I will remember your support and love.

I light this chalice
strengthened by my own determination and hope.
Each time I kindle its flame,
I will remember my inner spark.

(Switch the chalice on; if using a drawing, draw in the flame.)

(The person who had facilitated the first parts of the ritual should resume leadership here.)

LEADER: Let us pause here for a moment,
taking in the beauty of this chalice and its flame
and the supportive power of this gathered community.

(Take a few moments to observe and enjoy the lit chalice.)

And now let us sing together.

Song

"Where You Go" (Shoshana Jedwab)

(Lead participants through the song three times.)

Closing Words

(You may extinguish the chalice to close the ritual or keep it lit so that the focus person can savor the spirit of the ritual after participants leave.)

We close our time together today
with hope for [Name]'s time in the hospital.
May [Name]'s treatment and recovery go well.
May the nurses, the doctors, and all whom [Name] encounters
be blessed with gentleness and grace.
May [Name] be uplifted by our love and their inner light.
May all of us be sustained by the connections we share
until we are together again.
Amen, and blessed be.

For a Hysterectomy

Rev. Jessica Clay

This ritual is for anyone who is preparing for a hysterectomy. It is designed for a small, intimate circle of no more than a dozen people.

Materials

- ☐ Small altar table
- ☐ Chalice
- ☐ Tea lights, one for each participant and one extra
- ☐ Small starter candle
- ☐ Small bell or singing bowl
- ☐ Music
- ☐ Small pieces of colored card stock and pens

Setup

Review the script with the focus person beforehand to personalize it to their situation. Ask about how they would like you to describe their relationship with their body, including their uterus and ovaries, and (if relevant) their reproductive hopes or history. Some people may need the ritual to center on grief, while others might be celebrating rather than mourning; choose words and songs appropriate to their feelings. Find out if they are comfortable with being touched in a laying on of hands; if not, adapt the ritual by inviting participants instead to rub their palms together and hold their warmed hands up toward the focus person.

This ritual is designed to be gender inclusive; if the focus person is not a cisgender woman, it is especially important to ask them how you should speak of their experiences and anatomy.

Give participants the ritual prompts ahead of time so they can think about what they would like to share.

This ritual includes three songs, all of which are simple enough to be sung without accompaniment. You may want to line up a song leader ahead of time. If the group isn't comfortable singing, you can either have one person sing or skip the music and instead opt for more silence.

This ritual should be held in a quiet, comfortable setting, ideally in someone's home. Tea and finger food afterward might be nice.

Set up chairs in a circle, with the small altar table in the middle. Place the chalice and the bell on the table, and arrange the tea lights around the chalice. Place a pen and one piece of cardstock under each person's chair. Seat participants with limited mobility next to the focus person so that they can easily join in the laying on of hands.

Script

Opening Words

Welcome to all who have come here today to honor and bless [Name] as they prepare for their hysterectomy. We gather today to honor this loss and bless a new beginning, [Name]'s new relationship with their body. All who gather in this sacred circle are called to hold [Name] in love and care during this time. [Name], we gather to remind you that we are your community, that you are beloved to us, and that you are held in love as you undergo this. We gather to support you, mourn with you, and bless you during this time.

Chalice Lighting

We light this chalice for [Name]'s body.
This body that has held [Name] and now prepares for a transition, a loss, and a new possibility.
We light this chalice for all of the feelings that [Name] is feeling.
Loss, pain, relief, fear, hope, possibility, and many more.
We light this chalice for this community gathered here,
Sacred witnesses to this transition.
We light this chalice for this moment together.

(Light the chalice and then ring the bell.)

Moment of Silence

(Pause for a brief moment of silence.)

Song

"I Know This Rose Will Open" (Mary E. Grigolia)

(Lead participants in singing.)

Naming

We gather in this moment to acknowledge the significance of this hysterectomy.

(Speak here about the focus person's experiences, reproductive history, or reasons for the hysterectomy, in accordance with your conversations with them ahead of time. Depending on their circumstances and preferences, you might say something like one or more of the following.)

- We name that [Name]'s uterus held life and gave birth to [number] children. We give thanks for this.
- We name that [Name]'s uterus held life that ended too soon. We acknowledge the pain and grief of this loss.
- Societal messages of what it means to be a woman inform the way we relate to our bodies. Many people feel a complex mix of emotions around hysterectomy, including loss of identity.
- [Name] wanted to give birth, but has never had that opportunity. This procedure takes that possibility away. For this we grieve with them.
- [Name] had an incredible amount of [pain, disease, complications] leading up to this moment. We acknowledge this suffering and the hopes for its release. [Name] has sometimes felt that their body was betraying them, and we honor this feeling and acknowledge their physical, mental, and emotional pain.
- [Name] never wanted a uterus and ovaries; all they have represented is a betrayal by their body. We honor this feeling in this moment and rejoice with them as their body becomes more true to their soul.

(If the focus person wants to speak as well, they can do so now. Please let there be silence between things that are said. This is not a ritual to be rushed.)

(Ring the bell.)

Sharing Blessings

With this change we also name the opportunity for new possibilities. We wish for you to reconnect with your body, to be free from pain and disease, and to be open to and curious about what's next. Our hearts are big enough to hold grief, loss, and hopes for possibilities all at the same time.

There are cards and pens under your chairs. Please pick them up and think of your blessings, your hopes for [Name]. What are your wishes for them as they undergo this procedure and move forward in their recovery? What do you want them to remember? What blessings do you want to give them? Please write them on your card now. [Name], you are invited to write on your card your own blessings and hopes for yourself.

(Play quiet music in the background as people write. Wait until everyone has finished before continuing.)

I invite you to come to the table, read your card, and light a candle. Please give the card to [Name] after you light your candle. After each person speaks we will sing one verse of "Comfort Me" by Mimi Bornstein-Doble.

(Alternatively, hold silence for a few moments after each person reads their card. After all participants have read, invite the focus person to read their own card aloud.)

Laying On of Hands

Please come in and surround [Name] with our love as we sing another round of "Comfort Me." I invite you all to touch [Name] for this laying on of hands.

(Lead the singing as people gather around the focus person. Sing as many verses as feels right.)

[Name], you have received the blessings of this community. Hold them in your hands, hold them against your body. Know the care that is wrapped up within each word. Remember these blessings in the days and weeks ahead. Return to them to be reminded of the love and hopes held in this community for you. I light the last tea light now for the unexpected blessings that haven't been named in this space, but will come to you nonetheless. This is a reminder to be open to the unexpected as you move through this journey.

Please be seated.

Prayer

Spirit of Life and Love, we pray for [Name] on this day.

We lift up the ["grief and loss" or "relief and joy"] they are feeling, the path that brought them to this moment.

We pray for their body as it prepares to undergo this procedure; we pray for the healing of [Name]'s body and heart with this.

We pray for their doctors, nurses, medical staff, all of the people who will be caring for our dear [Name].

May they know theirs is a sacred task.

We pray that as [Name] heads into surgery, they may remember the blessings of this community and hold them against their heart.

May they feel held in this community after this circle has ended and know that they are beloved.

We pray for each member of this circle today; may they remember to check in with [Name] and offer care and support in the days and weeks ahead.

Holy One, we ask that you hold [Name] in deep care and remind them that they are not alone, especially in those moments when they are frightened.

Remind them of the hope within these blessings, remind them of new possibilities, remind them of the unexpected blessings that will come along just as they need them.

For all of these things we pray.

Amen.

Song

"There Is More Love Somewhere" (African American spiritual)

(Lead participants in singing.)

Chalice Extinguishing

We extinguish this chalice, but not its light. May [Name] take that light with them in the days and weeks ahead with our blessings. This light lives on in you, you who are so beloved to us. May this light within you provide comfort and remind you of this circle of care which holds you. So may it be.

(Extinguish the chalice.)

For Beginning Gender-Affirming Hormone Therapy

Rev. Bran Lennox

This is a ritual of blessing for a transgender individual as they take their first dose(s) of gender-affirming hormones. It is recommended as a stand-alone ritual for a small group of supporters, but can be adapted to serve as part of a congregational worship service.

Materials

- ☐ Altar table
- ☐ Hormone medication
- ☐ Blessing card
- ☐ Bowl with a little water
- ☐ Hand towel

Setup

This ritual uses the focus person's hormone medication. If for any reason the focus person can't bring their actual hormones with them, you can substitute something else. For example, the focus person could bring the paper prescription with them, or a box of mints that they will eat alongside their first few doses, or a sacred object that they will store with their hormones or have at hand as they take them.

Consult with the focus person in advance to learn how they want you to identify and describe them and their journey to this point. Work with them to ensure that the script suits them. The ritual includes an opportunity for the focus person to share a reflection about their transition journey, their beliefs, and their pains and hopes; it could be only a few sentences, or up to eight minutes long. (Giving people an eight minute time limit tends to produce a ten minute reflection, which we recommend as an upper limit to keep things moving.) Give them ample time to decide if they want to do this, and offer support in preparing it if they do.

Additionally, the ritual calls on the focus person's loved ones to provide active support, as a strong support network is an important part of an individual's well-being during transition. Many transgender people are not accepted by their family of origin. It is important to affirm that the gathered community fully recognizes chosen family as family. The ritual also offers some community education, which can make it beneficial in a congregational setting. If it is used in a worship service, it should be a single continuous element of the service.

Prepare a small card containing the four-line blessing from the script below.

Place the altar table front and center in the ritual space, with chairs or stools in front of it if you or the focus person want them. The lit chalice, water bowl, and hand towel may all be placed on the altar table for convenience. The focus person should keep their hormones (or alternative object) on their person.

Script

Opening Words

Here we have gathered to bless and offer our wholehearted support to [Name] on this next stage of their journey of transition. We are gathering to affirm without reservation that [Name] is a [woman, man, nonbinary person, agender person, or other term as preferred by the focus person]. We are here to hold space for the heartbreaks felt along this path, and the many fears which may accompany each stage of a gender transition. And yet we are also here to celebrate and magnify those special gifts which only a transgender person gets to experience—the moments of euphoria and magic, the discoveries of community and self which unfold.

[Name] has considered deeply and made the courageous decision about the next stage of their pursuit of expressing the most genuine form of their self. Before today, [Name] has [describe previous gender-affirming decisions, such as "revealed their name," "come out to their community," "changed their wardrobe," "aligned their body more with their image of self," or anything else the focus person wants you to share]. Now, [Name] is beginning the transformative process of hormone therapy, as they prepare to take their first doses of [name of hormone].

Handwashing

[Name], before you move forward, there's a sacred part of this process that we have to honor so that what comes next can be greeted with full joy. We know that our own expectations about what our lives should be can be the biggest barrier to appreciating what they actually are. I want to give you the gift of a beginning blessed by curiosity and exploration. So that you may be free of any nagging worries and cloying expectations, I offer you this cleansing water. Please wash your hands with it now, knowing that in so doing you are freeing yourself of these obstacles.

(The focus person washes their hands and dries them with the towel. You may want to hold the bowl for them, or hand them the towel.)

Blessing

(If a symbolic object is being used rather than the hormone themselves, first explain what it is and then change the wording below accordingly.)

Now that we are open to what lies ahead, I'm going to invite you, [Name], to take the bottle of hormones in your hands. Hold it close, close your eyes, and we will hold a circle of silence for you as you silently place your hopes, intentions, and good will into it.

(Allow thirty seconds to one minute of silence.)

Now open your eyes, but continue to hold on to that bottle. Hug it to your chest. Look out at these loving people who have gathered in support of you today. I'm going to ask everyone present to offer their silent hopes, intentions, and good will to you.

(Turn toward the gathered participants.)

Please offer [Name] your open hands; if it's comfortable for you, lift them up like this. (Put your open hands up, with your palms facing the focus person.) You may also keep your hands in your lap with palms up, or simply visualize. Allow your breath to fill you up with light as you send it through your hands to [Name] and their hormones.

(Hold position in silence for a few moments before continuing.)

[Name], we're offering you all the love and support in the room today. Will [Name]'s loved ones join me in naming aloud into this space, in a word or two, what gifts you are offering?

(Offer one or two words yourself as a starting point, such as "listening" or "stability.")

We'll lower our hands now, but the connection in our hearts remains.

I will now offer you a blessing, which I will read aloud and then give to you to take home. Whenever you take a dose of your hormones, take the opportunity for a quiet moment of gratitude to reflect and feel the sacred nature of this transition. I recommend keeping this blessing by your hormones, along with a few items which inspire or comfort you. Let it be a reminder of all the support and love present in this room today.

[Name],
In body, as it was, is, and will be, you are complete.
In knowing and learning of self, you are a beacon.
In community, family, and friends, you are held.
In the unfolding of your sacred life, you are a miracle.

(Give the blessing card to the focus person.)

I'll ask you to put this with your hormones in a safe place.

Reflection

[Name] has prepared a reflection for us. We are ready to receive what they wish to share, and listen with open minds and hearts.

(The focus person shares their reflection, if they wish to. If not, move on to the closing words.)

Closing Words

In gratitude for all that we have shared here today, we once more open our hands toward [Name] and reaffirm our blessing for their journey.

(Lift your hands, palms out, toward the focus person again, and silently invite participants to do the same. Hold position for around ten quiet seconds.)

May you find exactly what you need in this time of transformation. In those moments when fear and pain are with you, may you remember this circle of support and care. May you follow your joy, and continue to make courageous decisions in the service of living your most liberated life.

For Gender Affirmation Surgery

Li Kynvi

In memory of our trans ancestors for whom surgery was never an option

This is a ritual to support and help prepare someone before they undergo gender affirmation surgery. It is designed for the focus person plus one to six people, one of whom is the leader. The ritual has five main elements, each followed by a song; it can be simplified and shortened by abbreviating or omitting one or more elements. The author underwent gender affirmation surgery in June 2021, and this ritual emerged from what they needed at the time and their reflections on the experience since.

Materials

- ☐ Altar table
- ☐ Chalice
- ☐ Massage oil, hand lotion, or similar (chosen by the focus person)
- ☐ Bowl to hold gathered water
- ☐ Backup cups of water (in case they're needed)
- ☐ Any meaningful objects the focus person would like to add to the altar
- ☐ Optional: Music to supplement or replace live singing

Setup

Go through the script carefully with the focus person, adapting it as necessary to suit their circumstances and the language they prefer to use. Ask how they want you to describe their upcoming surgery, including what anatomical terms you should use. If they are not comfortable having their hands massaged or their body touched, choose alternative ways for participants and you to interact with them. Give them time to think about what pains and barriers they may want to name aloud in the ritual, in single words or short phrases; possibilities include transphobic insurance companies, racism, isolation, hostility from coworkers or employers, rejection by friends or family, financial worries, and many more. Also invite them to develop an image of themselves that they would like their supporters to hold in mind: something like "Picture me surrounded by beautiful light" or "Imagine me wrapped in a thick soft warm fluffy maroon comforter of love."

Tell participants ahead of time that they will be asked to speak briefly about something that has been important in their relationship with the focus person, and to offer a sentence of celebration and joy about the upcoming surgery. Ask them to come prepared for this, and also to bring about a half cup of water. Before the ritual begins, ensure that everyone remembered to do so; give a cup of water to anyone who forgot.

Set a chair for the focus person in the middle of the space, and seat participants around them in a U shape, so that no one is blocked off behind someone else. Put the chalice and bowl on the altar table, directly across from the focus person.

Script

Chalice Lighting

We kindle the flame—transformative energy dancing
Held by the chalice— solid supportive context
Together marking this time of gathering as sacred.
May every beautiful, beloved trans and nonbinary sibling
have full access to the medical care and loving support they need.

(Light the chalice.)

Opening Words

As people move through gender transition, we [or "they" if you have not done so yourself] are presented with the intimately personal question "Have I gone far enough with my transition to feel basically whole and at ease in the world?" This question presents itself again and again, and each time there is only one person who can answer it. Sometimes the response is "Yes" or "Yes, for now." Other times we [or "they"] need to move forward with another aspect of our [or "their"] evolving.

We gather today because when you, [Name], have asked that question, your answers have led you to your upcoming surgery on [date]. We celebrate the persistence that brought us to this day, and offer our gratitude for you, for each other, and for living in a place and time in which gender-affirming surgery is a possibility. Being able to decide how you move in the world is a beautiful gift, so important for our thriving.

Naming Challenges, Pain, and Oppression

First we name the pain you have arrived here with, [Name]. We name the structures of oppression that operate within you, within others, and within our society, and how they have affected you. And we acknowledge your pain as a part of your history, part of our history. Knowing that all of us here are committed to working to dismantle those oppressive systems wherever we recognize them. Knowing we are committed also to turning toward ourselves and each other in compassion. We hope that in this place there is the possibility of healing within ourselves, between each other, and with the wider world.

[Name] is going to be sharing some words and gestures. Our role is to pay close attention, and—as a way of holding their expression with them—after each phrase and gesture, to repeat just what they said and did. We don't add our own spin, or something we want for them. We mirror back just what [Name] says and does, including their tone and energy.

[Name], you'll be naming the pain, challenges, and oppressions you bring to this important moment. You're welcome to accompany your words with any sounds or gestures that feel right.

(If the focus person needs a place to start, suggest that they inhale as they bring their arms up and close to their body, close their fists tightly for a moment, and then exhale while opening their fists and lowering or shaking out their hands.)

Participants, remember our job is to offer our full attention and to mirror back what [Name] says and does, including their energy and tone.

[Name], take all the space and time you need, and continue until you feel done.

(Continue when the focus person has said everything they want to, but do not rush; allow a beat of silence at the end.)

Let's take a cleansing breath together. Feel the weight of your body, your connection to the earth.

Song

"Gentle Heart" (Jen Myzel)

(Lead participants in singing or invite them to listen to the recording.)

Acknowledging Relationship

We are honored to be by your side, [Name], and we are here today to offer our blessings and to pledge our loving support as you heal.

(If it is part of the focus person's tradition to name important ancestors, do so now, using the language most appropriate to their tradition. Then turn to address the participants.)

One at a time we'll move forward and, using the lotion [Name] chose, we will massage, anoint, or just hold their hands. We'll each take a couple minutes to briefly share something that has been important to us in our relationship with them, and offer them some words of celebration and joy about their upcoming surgery, before returning to the circle.

(Guide participants in this; you may need to gently keep people moving if they have a great deal they want to say.)

Song

"Sweet Love" (Taya Mâ Shere and Oscar Maynard)

(Lead participants in singing or invite them to listen to the recording. If you are singing, sing the song through once as written, then a few times more using the focus person's name.)

[Name], do not play it small
The world depends on your greatness (2x)
May you be blessed as you go forward (4x)

Preparing for Surgery

Sweet [Name], it is time for us to offer messages of love and information to your body. So wiggle around until you are as comfortable as possible. In fact, everyone can do this; all of us are invited to participate in this body scan. You are all welcome to move in any way you are called to move.

(Pause for a moment as everyone gets comfortable.)

Beginning with your scalp, become aware of any tension there
And in the area between your hairline and your neck
Behind the ears
Through the forehead and temples
Around the eyes, becoming aware of the little tiny muscles there
So many exquisite muscles around the eyes and nose, the mouth and jaw—able to move precisely and with such nuance
Becoming aware of these, maybe letting them know they're welcome to take some time off

Feeling into the muscles of the neck, free to move your head
Moving down, feeling the muscles across your shoulders and upper back
Invite meditative breaths into this area, being aware of your inhaling and exhaling
Bringing your awareness into your arms, elbows, wrists, hands, fingers

Bringing your breath and awareness more fully into your chest and belly area, your middle and lower back
Breathing
And down into your butt muscles and further to the large muscles of the thighs
Inviting awareness to the area of the knees, backs of knees, calves, ankles, feet, toes, and soles of the feet

Then one more breath into the whole, exactly as it is.

Let us take this time to prepare your body to receive the surgical procedures it will undergo in [number] days.

We acknowledge that part of the body's job is to protect you and to resist any physical invasion, to fight against anything that could seem like harm. Sacred attention and deep trust in your healing powers underscore everything we say and do here.

[Name], I invite you to place your hands on your heart (or on the area of the body where the surgery will occur, if the focus person prefers). We will now come forward and each place one hand on you.

(Pause while people surround and touch the focus person. Ensure that the focus person is comfortable with how they are being touched; ask if they would like to adjust the placement of anyone's hands.)

You have invited Dr. [Doctor's name] to perform a very important operation on you on [day]. In the hour before surgery, your beloveds will be holding you in [prayer, light, love, mind], and you will be preparing by relaxing as deeply and fully as possible. Many medical professionals will be around, asking you questions and taking care of you. Your focus can quietly remain on your internal state, on relaxing, and on opening your body to receive this so wanted and joyous surgery.

Your medical team will take excellent care of you, making sure you are safe and that you will feel no pain. You have invited your surgeon to [briefly explain the upcoming surgery]. They will do exactly what you have asked, no more and no less.

This surgery is so important and so welcome. We ask that your body, [Name], open to this surgery and the incisions it involves; that it welcome this needed change in your physical being; that it do everything within its power to work with the surgery, support it, and heal from it quickly and fully.

On surgery day, about an hour before the scheduled time, we will begin to hold you and the image you have chosen. Can you describe that now with as much sensory detail as you can?

[The focus person describes the image they want people to hold of them.)

We will hold you and this image in love, and you will hold yourself and this image in love. Your body will remember to work with the surgery, supporting it and healing quickly.

In that spirit, let's sing together "There Is a Love."

Song

"There Is a Love" (text by Rebecca Parker, music by Elizabeth Norton)

(Lead participants in singing or invite them to listen to the recording.)

Offering Blessings

We have each arrived here, at this deep well of community, bearing water. We are here to pour our love, respect, blessings, hopes, prayers, and support for you, [Name], into this common bowl. I invite everyone gathered to pour the water they have brought into this bowl, symbolizing the community that surrounds [Name].

(Each person pours water into the bowl.)

(Invite the focus person to hold their hands over the bowl. Take some water in your palms or a cup and pour it onto their palms. Then immerse your hands and place your wet palms gently on the focus person's head.)

From these shared waters and this gathered community, we offer these blessings:

May your surgeon, anesthesiologist, and entire medical team perform to the best of their abilities, and freely offer you their respect, care, and expertise.

May your strong body open and receive this joyful, affirming surgery, healing and renewing at its own pace, deeply integrating its new reality.

May you know how loved and affirmed you are—before surgery, during surgery, and after it. May you feel our presence, our strength, and our love all along the way, and be steadied by them.

May you open to the ways this operation will change you, both those you have anticipated and those you have not: the ways it will invite you further into your fullness.

And may you know you are deeply held in the grace of a larger love that will not let us go, and will not let us let each other go.

Song

"I Am Light" (India.Arie)

(Lead participants in singing or invite them to listen to the recording.)

Exchanging Gratitude

Our care does not end with this ritual. [Describe here some arrangements that have been made for the focus person's care, such as "One of us will check in with you this evening, and will be in touch between now and surgery day. [Friend's name] will pick you up after surgery, bring you home, and stay that first week, and meals will be provided by the folks who signed up."]

The final piece of our ritual is an exchange of gratitude for each other. It is an honor and a blessing to be able to show up for one another.

We will [sing, hear] a final song. It is four lines long, and we will repeat it once for each person here. For each repetition, come toward one of us and express and receive the gratitude that flows between you. Then move to the next person as [we sing, it plays] again. When you have exchanged gratitude with all of us, we will [sing it through, hear it] one final time.

Song

"I Am Saying Thank You" (Judy Fjell)

(Lead participants in singing or invite them to listen to the recording.)

Chalice Extinguishing

As we end, we extinguish the chalice,

and carry with us how moving it has been to be a part of this ritual.

What a blessing to share this transformative time.

May you know, [Name], how very loved you are,

and may you feel deep in your bones that supporting you is an honor and a blessing.

May the Spirit of Persistent Life and Love stay with you from now through your surgery and healing,

and may the blessings of this day resonate long in your heart,

ringing a song of deepest affirmation and joy.

(Extinguish the chalice.)

For a Service Dog Partnership

Rev. Joanna Lubkin

Dedicated to Sully and the staff and volunteers of NEADS World Class Service Dogs

The partnership between a disability service dog, guide dog, or hearing assistance dog and their human is a sacred relationship. Service animals are not pets; they are working dogs specifically trained to assist a person with a disability. However, there is a great deal of love and trust between the human and their dog, who is their constant companion and an integral part of them living as full and independent a life as possible. Many people wait years and fundraise extensively before being partnered with a service dog, and the match is an occasion for excitement, relief, and joy. This ritual is meant to celebrate the partnership, offer the human a chance to express their commitment to the dog, and offer a community a chance to bless the partnership. The author was matched with Service Dog Sully from NEADS in September 2021.

Materials

- ☐ New dog toy
- ☐ Dog treat or small amount of dog food
- ☐ Service dog gear (e.g., vest, harness, or leash) or a ribbon

Setup

This ritual can be an element within a congregational worship service or a separate ritual attended by guests of the focus person. Either way, consult with the focus person (and their caregivers, if appropriate) about their needs and preferences for the ritual rather than making assumptions. Ensure that the vows they will make reflect the circumstances and responsibilities of the specific partnership between them and their service dog.

Place the service dog and focus person somewhere that the assembled community can see well, either up front or in the center of a circle. The focus person may want a chair or need space for mobility devices, as well as the dog and any family or aides who will be centered with them. Ask about the best way to keep the dog centered and calm during the ritual. It may be easiest to have it in a sit-stay or a down-stay, but that may make it hard for the community to see it.

The ritual calls for the service dog's gear to be passed around, which may confuse some dogs to whom having their gear off signals that they're "off duty." If the focus person prefers to keep the dog dressed in its gear, you can pass around a ribbon for the community to bless, which can then be tied to the harness or leash. You may want to recruit a helper to track the gear or ribbon, keep it moving, and bring it to you when needed.

If the focus person is unable to read or sign the vows or is uncomfortable doing so, a friend or family member can read the script while the focus person holds the ritual item. If the focus person is blind or low vision, take special care to describe what's happening in the room (e.g., "We're passing the vest around from person to person," or "Your dog is looking at you so intently right now!"). If the focus person is Deaf or hard of hearing, make sure you have an ASL interpreter or other language assistance ready for the day of the ritual.

Toward the end of the ritual, you will offer the community some guidelines on how to interact respectfully with the service dog and the focus person. Familiarize yourself in advance with best practices for this, including "approach the handler and not the dog," "never offer food to a service dog," and "keep your own dog away from working service dogs." (Some reputable sources of guidelines include Guide Dogs of America, NEADS World Class Service Dogs, and Canine Companions.) In addition, ask the focus person what they want the community to know about how to interact with their dog in particular. You may want to prepare a handout.

Script

Opening Words

We gather today to bless the partnership between [Name] and Service Dog [Dog]. [Name] is here to express their gratitude for and commitment to [Dog], and we are here to witness, bless, and offer our ongoing support to this partnership. The partnership between a service dog and their human is a sacred thing. [Dog] [has been trained, is in training] specifically to learn tasks that assist [Name] with daily life, to help [Name] live a full and thriving life with their disability. It is a relationship of trust: the human trusting the dog to assist them skillfully, the dog trusting the human to care for its needs and well-being. It is a relationship of steadfast devotion, love, and joy.

Blessing the Gear

Today, [Name] will make vows to [Dog], and we will bless some of the symbols of their partnership. The most identifiable of these symbols is the [vest, harness, leash] that [Dog] wears when they are working.

(Hold up the dog's gear for people to see.)

When the dog is wearing this, it's a sign that it is working and we should not touch or pet it. But we have an opportunity now to imbue it with our blessings. We will pass it around, and as each of you hold it, I invite you to take a moment with it. You may want to hold it gently, and silently offer your best wishes for this partnership—you may even picture these blessings and warm wishes flowing through your hands and into the [vest, harness, leash]. When you're ready, pass it to the next person, and it will make its way around the room.

(Give the gear to the first participant, or have a helper do so. Continue the ritual as it is passed around.)

Vows

[Name], your partnership with [Dog] is both a solemn responsibility and a joyous blessing. Will you offer your vows to [Dog], your promises about how you will be in this partnership?

(The focus person holds up a few pieces of food or a dog treat.)

FOCUS PERSON: [Dog], I'm grateful for all the ways you will help me and take care of me. I promise to take care of you to the best of my ability, tending to your health and well-being. I promise to always make sure you have shade on hot days, plenty of water, visits to a kind vet when you need them, and, of course, the best of food.

(The focus person feeds the treat to the dog. They may want to have the dog follow some command to "earn" the treat, such as lying down or giving their paw to shake.)

LEADER: May you both be nourished and cared for, and may you be well.

FOCUS PERSON: [Dog], you are such an example of love and service. [They name a few things that they love and appreciate about the dog, e.g., "I love how your eyes express such soulful attention" or "I love the way you cuddle up to me when I'm having a bad pain day."] I promise to offer you love, affection, and appreciation in return.

(The focus person pets the dog or offers them other physical affection.)

LEADER: May you both know yourself surrounded by love.

(The focus person holds up a tennis ball or new dog toy, if the dog won't be fixated on it. If offering a toy and then taking it away would upset the dog or derail the ritual, have it gift-wrapped.)

FOCUS PERSON: [Dog], you are so focused and dedicated when you're working. I promise to always make sure you have plenty of time to play! I'm grateful for all the ways you remind me to be playful and experience joy. [They name some examples, e.g., "I love when you're outside and you pause to sniff the breeze; it reminds me to slow down and appreciate the world too" or "I love how happy you are to meet any new doggie playmate; it reminds me to greet others with joy and openness too."] I promise to make sure you get lots of exercise and daily time for play.

(The focus person gives the toy to the dog, or holds up the wrapped gift and says, "This is a new toy for us to play with later.")

LEADER: May you both make time for joy and play.

(Return the dog's gear to the focus person so they can hold it up to be seen.)

FOCUS PERSON: And finally, [Dog], I thank you for all your hard work to help me every day. [They name some of the dog's tasks, e.g., "I'm grateful for your careful guidance as we cross busy streets" or "I'm grateful for each time you pick up something I've dropped."] I promise to keep up with our training, so I can be the best partner for you I can be, and to trust you as we travel together through life.

(The focus person puts the gear on the dog.)

LEADER: [Dog], may you wear this [vest, harness, leash], blessed by these people who love and support you, and may you and [Name] know yourselves surrounded by the blessings and best wishes of this gathered community.

[Name] and [Dog], we are so delighted to support this partnership. We, this gathered community, offer our love and our commitment to continued learning about the best ways to be in community with a service dog partnership.

(Either describe the ground rules you prepared or provide a handout of them. You may want to do both.)

To celebrate your partnership, we'll close with a special song.

The song "Where You Go, I Will Go, Beloved" was written by Shoshana Jedwab. Its lyrics come from the biblical book of Ruth, and they express a promise to journey together in love. [Name], maybe you want to sing it to [Dog], and know they express that same commitment every time they put their vest on. And this gathered community sings it to both of you, as we promise to journey alongside you.

Let's sing together.

Song

"Where You Go" (Shoshana Jedwab)

(Lead participants in singing.)

Closing Words

[Name] and [Dog], we're so glad the two of you have found your way to each other. May you go forth with the love and blessings of this community. Congratulations!

For an Assistive Device

Rev. Bran Lennox

This ritual honors the use of a mobility device, assistive device, medical aid, or similar ability companion: a cane, wheelchair, scooter, rollator, splint, limb brace, prosthetic, hearing aid, cochlear implant, pair of glasses, screen reader, mobile AAC system, adaptive utensil, insulin pen or pump, or anything else. It is designed as a stand-alone ritual, but could be adapted for use in a congregational worship service.

Materials

- ☐ Altar table
- ☐ Chalice
- ☐ Long spool of thin ribbon (or a ball of yarn for larger groups)
- ☐ Scissors
- ☐ Optional: Music

Setup

Review the ritual with the focus person beforehand. Find out what terminology they want you to use and how you should describe the function or purpose of the device. They may not want you to say anything. Ask whether it's okay for you to touch the device.

The ritual includes an opportunity for the focus person to share a reflection if they wish to. Give them ample time and support to prepare it. It should ideally be no more than five minutes long. They may wish to describe their own journey or they may wish to speak more generally, on a topic like disability justice or the theology of embodiment. They could offer the reflection themselves or have it read by someone else if they prefer.

Recruit a helper ahead of time to assist with passing the ribbon.

This ritual contains some community education, which may be beneficial in a congregational worship service. If it is used in a worship service, separate the ritual elements and intersperse them throughout the service—using the chalice lighting at the opening, the songs for hymns, the prayer for the pastoral prayer, etc.—rather than retaining the ritual as a single unit.

Script

Chalice Lighting

We light this flame,
Embraced within a chalice.
This light casts a circle of warmth
Which longs to hold us all in our entirety
And grows ever wider,
Shimmering with unending possibility.

Song

"Glorious" (MaMuse)

(Lead participants in singing. You could substitute another uplifting song, prerecorded or live, that resonates for the focus person.)

Opening Words

It is said that the use of tools is part of what makes us human. Certainly as a species we demonstrate a drive to develop ever more intricate technologies, and when we are at our best, we devote our energy to creating tools which help people be the selves they wish to be. Assistive devices are a symbol of the beauty of both human ingenuity and human compassion.

This is a sacred moment. One among us has come to a time in their life when it is easier for them to access parts of the world with an assistive device. It is a sacred moment, and it can also be a vulnerable one. Many people have misconceptions about such devices and the people who use them, and from those misconceptions can arise misinformed actions. A person with an assistive device may be subjected to stares that exhaust, comments that wound, and even touch that dehumanizes. It takes courage to claim space as a disabled person in an ableist world.

The support of our chosen community, the people nearest and dearest to our lives, can affirm and sustain us in times when living authentically is painful and challenging. Our community can affirm that, yes, we deserve to be in as little pain as possible. Yes, we deserve to exist in public spaces. Yes, we deserve to live and to thrive to the maximum extent achievable. And yes, it can feel glorious when we embrace a new tool that makes such thriving possible.

And so we gather today, to affirm [Name] and their use of this [device]. [Name] wants to share some information about this with us. [Describe the device and its purpose however the focus person wishes you to, or say something like "Though they are happy to celebrate their use of [device] today, they ask that everyone respect their privacy regarding their reasons for using it."]

Reflection

I'd like to invite [Name] to share more about their journey in their own words.

(If the focus person wants to offer a reflection, they may do so here, or have a helper deliver it for them.)

Blessing

This [device] is now a part of what connects [Name] with this community. We accept it wholeheartedly as a tool of that connection, and commit ourselves to respect and honor its place in [Name]'s life. For however long this item continues to be of help, whether just today or every day of [Name]'s life, we offer our blessing.

(Tie one end of the ribbon loosely around your wrist, and then hold up the spool of ribbon for all to see.)

I'm going to pass this ribbon around the room now. When it reaches you, please wrap it gently once or twice around your wrist, and then pass it to the next person. Take your time with this, and allow yourself to put intention into this symbol of our connection. [Helper] is available to help as necessary.

(Begin to pass the ribbon around the room. If there are more than a few people present, some instrumental background music will help create an appropriate mood.)

(When everyone else is connected by the ribbon, pass the spool to the focus person, who will also wrap their wrist. If you have permission to do so, tie the remaining ribbon to the assistive device, and cover the knot with your hands in a moment of silence before continuing. If the focus person does not want you to touch the device, they can tie the ribbon themselves, or just lay it over or hold it against the device if tying a knot would be difficult.)

While we are all still connected by this ribbon, let's engage our hearts and feel the power of what it means to be whole in our togetherness. Please repeat after me.

(Read the following text line by line, pausing after each to let participants repeat what you have said.)

[Name], we love you for all that you are.
We commit ourselves to honoring your wholeness.
We pledge to respect your agency and your privacy.
We will broaden the paths of accessibility for you and for all.
We embrace all the struggles and joys of embodiment.
May this [device] be part of your story of thriving.

(Cut the ribbon so that it remains adorning the device. Be careful not to touch the device if you do not have permission to.)

May you carry this with you however you choose, as a symbol of our commitment to you.

As we now unwind our wrists, let's sing together.

(The helper collects the ribbon during the song.)

Song

"From You I Receive" (Joseph Segal and Nathan Segal)

Prayer

Spirit that weaves divinity through all mundane things,

Give us the strength to overcome our attraction to binaries and dualisms.

When we relegate experiences to the realm of the body or the mind,

Whisper to us with your inescapable gentleness

That we are fully body and fully spirit.

When we wonder if we are healed or wounded,

Sigh to us with the patience of a presence beyond time

That we are all broken and infinitely whole.

When we imagine that there is a perfect way to be embodied,

When we suspect that we or someone else could take a better form,

When we are tempted to define anyone's body as an inconvenience,

Shake us with the truth:

That everything we are is moving and flowing within every living cell,

That to know the soul is to know the shape,

And to embrace this is liberation.

Spirit, reveal to us the self of the self of the self,

And the ever-unfolding realness of each companion around us,

And hold us in our sacredness of entirety.

Amen.

Song

"There's a River Flowin' in My Soul" (Faya Ora Rose Touré)

Chalice Extinguishing

As we extinguish our chalice, let's go forth in our human wholeness and celebrate all the blessings we have shared today.

(Extinguish the chalice.)

For Head Shaving during Chemotherapy

Rev. Emily Conger and
Rev. Rebecca C. "Beckett" Coppola

This head shaving ritual offers a rite of passage to patients and to their circle of support. It can be used to mark a moment in chemotherapy treatment, or in any illness or treatment causing hair loss. There is space for lament and mourning, holding and being with, and there is movement toward reclaiming and celebration, honoring the healing journey being traversed. It is best used by no more than a dozen people.

The authors created the original ritual for Beckett's head shaving during cancer treatment; it embodied healing, transformation, and community connections. They have adapted it here to be appropriate for a larger audience.

Materials

- ☐ Altar table
- ☐ Chalice
- ☐ Tray for ritual supplies
- ☐ Small hair ties, or ribbons cut to about 18 inches
- ☐ Body or face paint
- ☐ Hair scissors or other very sharp scissors
- ☐ Clippers
- ☐ Bowl or tray
- ☐ Music
- ☐ Three towels or sheets
- ☐ Tissues (for tears and paint)
- ☐ Optional: Bags for cut hair

Setup

This script assumes that the focus person is undergoing chemotherapy for cancer; if that is not the case, adapt the language accordingly.

Give the focus person time in advance to think about what expectations they want to name and let go of in the ritual. Possibilities include their perceptions of their own appearance and how they present themselves in the world, their certainty about what the next months or years will bring, their financial security, or their privacy or independence; whatever comes to mind for them can be honored.

If the focus person's hair can be gathered into locks that are then cut off, discuss in advance with them the best way for this to be done. Choose hair ties or ribbons that suit their hair's texture. Note that if locks are tied off too close to the scalp, cutting them can be difficult for the participants and painful for the focus person. Depending on the texture, amount, and length of the focus person's hair and the skill you expect participants to have in handling it, you may want to have participants tie off only small, symbolic locks and, when the time comes, cut them off yourself.

Choose soothing and centering music and decor that resonates for the focus person; you can play the music throughout, or let the space be held by silence. Lay a sheet down on the floor in a central location and place the altar table and a comfortable chair on it. Allow space to move around the chair. Put a sheet over the chair and have another one available for the focus person to wear on their shoulders. Gather ritual items and other sacred objects and place them on the altar table. Set up other chairs in a semicircle around it, and put out tissues around the space.

Choose a helper to handle the clippers.

Let participants know ahead of time that they will be invited to say a few words, share a short poem, or otherwise express their thoughts about being part of a communal healing journey, and also to say a few words of prayer or blessing for the focus person.

Script

Opening Words

Welcome to each of you who has gathered today for this important ritual head shaving.

There are many with us in spirit as well—those who live near, those who live far, those who have died—they are all with us, and we feel their loving presence.

We are coming with our hearts full of emotion: sadness, loss, fear, anticipation, joy, love, and any others in your heart. All emotions are welcome here.

We know that we need loving people to help us honor sacred moments and powerful transitions. You are among the circle of people who have journeyed and will continue to journey with [Name], so it is fitting that you are here today.

Chalice Lighting

Selection from "Determined Seed" (Laura Wallace)

As frozen earth holds the determined seed,
this sacred space holds our weariness, our worry,
our laughter and our celebration.
Let us bring seed and soul into the light of thought,
the warmth of community,
and the hope of love.

(Light the chalice, or have the focus person light it.)

Naming the Challenge

Evolution and transformation are always a part of our lives, and that is the frame to hold close during this rite of passage.

As you all know, [Name]'s doctors have discovered that there are cancer cells in their body which are incompatible with a healthy life. They have determined together that the best path toward healing at this point is through chemotherapy.

Chemotherapy can be seen as an injection of the Spirit of Life into the body, in order to transform those cells that have fallen out of harmony with life. The dead cells are broken down and their components are recycled into the body, returning them to be the building blocks of future health.

This is a physical and spiritual transformation, worthy of sacred recognition. During our ritual, we will move through five phases, honoring the challenges and possibilities of a healing journey.

- First, Invocation. We will gather the community and center ourselves in this moment.
- Second, Gathering of the Locks. We will gather locks of [Name]'s hair in order to share some of their burden.
- Third, Cutting the Locks. We will cut locks of hair and grieve the path [Name] had planned, which has been diverted.
- Fourth, Shaving the Head. We will shave their head to prepare for something new.
- And Fifth, Adorning. We will decorate their head in celebration of beauty and possibility.

Song

"Spirit of Life" (Carolyn McDade)

As we recognize the metaphorical injection of the Spirit of Life on this healing journey, let us call that spirit into this moment by singing "Spirit of Life," by Carolyn McDade.

(Lead participants in singing.)

Invocation

We begin by inviting all who are here to connect to their inner wisdom, to [Name], to the community, and to the Spirit of Life and Love.

The laying on of hands has been used in healing rituals for centuries. I invite you to please come up and place your hand on [Name], or on someone who is touching them.

(Allow time for participants to do this.)

I invite you into a moment of prayer.

Let us take three smooth breaths together, balancing the breath in and the breath out, releasing any muscles that are holding excess tension.

Spirit of life and love and all that is holy,
known by many names,
Be with us this day as we recognize
this sacred time of transformation
in [Name]'s life
and the life of their community.

Help us to stay connected
to the power of love present here
as we support [Name].

And guide us gently forward
as we journey—
in community,
in connection,
in release,
and in healing.

I invite you to silently offer your own prayer or intention for our time together.

(Pause for a period of silence.)

Amen.

Gathering of the Locks

As the gathered community, you are a part of [Name]'s journey toward healing.

Each person is invited to symbolically take ownership and lift a small part of this weight. Through this practice, [Name] has the embodied knowledge that they are not alone.

If the focus person's hair can be gathered into locks

The community will participate in gathering and cutting locks of hair. By doing so, we lift some of the burdens and griefs of this journey.

I invite each of you to come up and gather a small lock of [Name]'s hair. Tie off the gathered lock and say, "I am with you." Then share the words you have brought about healing and community.

(Add any further instructions that may be needed; if locks are to be saved, for instance, you might ask participants to braid them. Smaller locks are easier to cut. If you are using ribbons or something else without elastic, wrap them twice around the lock of hair and then tie them off tightly. You might go first in this step, to model it for participants, or last to mark its end.)

If the focus person's hair cannot be gathered into locks

Each of you is invited now to come into the center, to connect with [Name] in a manner that resonates for you, and say, "I am with you" to them. Then share the words you have brought about healing and community.

(Participants might hold the focus person's hands, look into their eyes, touch or caress their hair, or anything else that is comfortable for the focus person. You might go first in this step, to model it for participants, or last to mark its end.)

Scissors

In her poem "Sangha," in her book *Go In and In: Poems from the Heart of Yoga*, Danna Faulds writes,

May we be
reminders, each for the other, that
the path of transformation passes
through the flames.

Chemotherapy can be seen as a process of going into a fire so that anything not serving life can be burned away.

In this path of fiery transformation, let us honor the shift in expectations of life that is a part of this process.

[Name], I want you to think about what expectations have had to change because of this illness. Maybe they are things you envisioned about your vocation, housing, family, priorities, spirituality, or identity. Maybe they had to do with something else entirely. As each lock of your hair is cut, please name one expectation you have had to let go of, and then say to it, "I release you in love."

(Participants take turns coming forward, cutting a lock or portion of hair, and placing it on the bowl or tray. You might go first in this step, to model it for participants, or last to mark its end; or you might do all the cutting yourself if that seems advisable. With each cut the focus person names an expectation: for example, "Privacy, I release you in love." If they prefer not to name one aloud, they can say something like "I release another thing in love.")

Letting go of expectations and moving forward even the smallest bit takes courage and grace.

Later in her poem "Sangha," Faulds writes,

to stay on the path day after day,
choosing the unknown and facing
yet another fear, that is nothing
short of grace.

Clippers

We are now heading into the fallow time of the healing journey, a time when things will need to pause. Shaving the head metaphorically clears the field so it can rest for winter. We prepare well, in hopes that the seeds that will be planted in the spring can grow and thrive.

As [Name]'s head is shaved with clippers, I invite you to sing "There Is a Love," a meditative hymn which connects us to the core of our being in this universe.

Song

"There Is a Love" (words by Rebecca Parker, music by Elizabeth Norton)

(Lead participants in singing while the helper cuts the focus person's hair very short, about a quarter inch.)

Adorning

(If you are playing background music, shift it now to something more upbeat and celebratory.)

We will now take some time to adorn [Name]. By doing so, we bless them with possibility, love, and the power of our collective community. We do this creative practice to celebrate the beauty and resilience in this moment and the moments to come.

Let us now collectively adorn the newly shaven head of our beloved [Name] with colors and patterns. If you feel called to do so, you can say a few words of prayer or offer words of blessing to [Name] as you paint.

(Give any necessary instructions about using the face or body paint, and either have participants take turns or invite two or three up at once, depending on how crowded the space will get.)

(As the adornment is nearing completion, offer the following reading. Read it slowly, pausing after each stanza.)

Let go of the idea that you know
what breathing
should feel like.
Just notice the breath as it moves
in and out
of the body.

Let go of certainty.

Be with the breath as it is.
Allow openness.
Allow curiosity.

Notice the mind.
Each thought that arises.
Allow openness.
Don't judge your mind.
Or your experience.
Be loving in your curiosity about each thought.

Let go of certainty.

Let go of any idea about what
you should be thinking,
accepting your thoughts exactly as they are.

Be with yourself
as you are.
Be curious
about who you are.
Love
how you are in the world.

Gently and intentionally take a breath,
maybe even give a big sigh,
reenter the present moment
and the stream of your life.

Please join me now in singing "I Know This Rose Will Open," by Mary Grigolia.
As you sing, notice what has unfurled for you in this time of community, what
has opened for you, and what has been burned away by the power of love.

Song

"I Know This Rose Will Open" (Mary Grigolia)

(Lead participants in singing.)

Chalice Extinguishing

Let us gather our collective energy once again, joining in a circle as we admire [Name]'s beauty, strength, and resilience.

(Have everyone, including the focus person, join hands.)

[Name], may you feel the strength of this community through each part of the journey toward physical and spiritual harmony and health. May you know that you are not alone and that you are held in love.

Let us extinguish our chalice with these words by an anonymous author:

May we be reminded here of our highest aspirations,
and inspired to bring our gifts of love and service to the altar of humanity.

May we know once again that we are not isolated beings
but connected, in mystery and miracle, to the universe,
to this community, and to each other.

Amen.

(Extinguish the chalice.)

For a Loved One with Dementia or Cognitive Decline

Rev. McKinley L. Sims

This is a blessing for a person living with dementia or cognitive decline. It could be done with just a leader and the focus person, or with a small circle of loved ones. Adapt and personalize it to suit the focus person's preferences in music, textures, smells, and so on, how they like to be touched or not touched, and their ability to understand what is happening.

Materials

- ☐ Chalice or candle
- ☐ Sensory object, such as a cut flower or piece of soft cloth
- ☐ Perfume, incense, essential oil, or something else aromatic
- ☐ Small bowl or cup of water
- ☐ Music

Setup

Put a chalice or candle in the space and have materials readily accessible. Include something to play the music with, such as a record player or speaker.

Script

(If the focus person may not recognize you or fully track what is happening, always explain what you are about to do. It's usually best to ask permission before touching them.)

Chalice Lighting

[Name], we're here to love you with a blessing today. Are you okay if I do that? I'd be holding your hand, blessing you with this [flower, cloth, or other sensory object], and then we are going to sing a song I think you know. Is that okay with you?

Okay, let's breathe together for a few moments. Take a nice easy breath in . . . and out. In . . . and out.

(You can hold the focus person's hand, or place your hand on their arm or shoulder. If possible, make eye contact or have both of you close your eyes.)

[Name], you are loved and worthy of love. Your body, mind, and soul are holy, even when they don't feel entirely whole. May your time be filled with sacred moments of rest, laughter, connection, music, and love.

(Light the chalice or candle.)

We light this chalice for you, [Name]. Your light burns bright like this flame, and we are warmed by your spirit and your memories. Your memories are sacred, and we will cherish them and hold as many of them for you as we can.

(If you like, dip the sensory object in water or dab it with something that smells good. Touch it to the focus person's hands.)

[Name], we bless your body, your tool for building bridges and making memories with family and friends. It is a tool that can be used for healing or harm, and we are so grateful for the healing your body has helped to create. The world has been changed for the better by your presence in it. We are grateful together.

(Touch the sensory object to their head.)

[Name], we bless your mind, your fragile and wonderful brain and its neural pathways that hold all the images and sounds and wonder of a life lived in full complexity. Although our brains can hold so much, they can also hide so much from us over time. We are so grateful for your mind that has thought and pondered, reasoned and rationalized, guided your way and helped you to recognize our faces with love and care. We grieve your mind's changing, and yet life is change. We change together.

(Touch the sensory object to their heart.)

[Name], we bless your heart, your center of gravity and anchor in this world. For your fierce love and spirit, for your care for and commitment to us and to [name causes or engagements that were meaningful to the focus person]. As your body changes, and your mind changes, your heart remains constant in connection with our hearts. We are here together, grieving and loving you through your changes, our changes. You, [Name], are loved and worthy of love, no matter how long it takes you to remember a name or a word, no matter how long it takes you to find your way. You love us and we love you. We love together.

(Hand the sensory object to the focus person to hold.)

[Name], may you be at peace, may you feel safe, may you be surrounded by love. Amen. Blessed be.

Song
(Choose from the following options or pick one you know the focus person enjoys.)

"Comfort Me" (Mimi Bornstein-Doble)
"Amazing Grace"
"You Are My Sunshine"

Chalice Extinguishing
Come, Spirit of Life,

Be in this space that holds so much love and sorrow and change. May this space be a continued blessing for [Name], and may love resound through the halls often and fully. As the Love that never lets go and never lets us down reminds us:

"Love is patient, love is kind, it is not jealous; love does not brag, it is not arrogant. It does not act disgracefully, it does not seek its own benefit; it is not provoked, does not keep an account of a wrong suffered, it does not rejoice in unrighteousness, but rejoices with the truth; it keeps every confidence, it believes all things, hopes all things, endures all things. Love never fails." (1 Corinthians 13:4–8)

Our bodies and minds may fail, but we are grateful love does not. We are grateful for you, [Name]. You are loved for all time. Amen.

(Extinguish the chalice or candle.)

Grief and Memory

For Losing a Wanted Pregnancy
Rev. Caitlin Cotter Coillberg

This ritual is intended for individuals or families who have suffered (or are suffering) a miscarriage, or have discovered that their wanted pregnancy (fetus) is nonviable and are undergoing treatment (such as a D&C procedure) to end the pregnancy.

Materials
- ☐ Chalice

Setup

This ritual is intended to be used after a miscarriage, while the focus person is miscarrying, or on the day of the procedure that will end the pregnancy and is designed to be led by a support person (such as a minister, chaplain, or trusted friend). It can also be done shortly after a miscarriage or procedure. Most hospitals have chaplains on call who can help you with this if you ask.

This ritual was written for the end of a pregnancy involving a single fetus. Adapt the language if the situation involves multiples.

If the focus person is heading to the hospital for a procedure, you may wish to lead this ritual in a living room or similar space before you go, to include as many loved ones as desired.

Script

Chalice Lighting

> We light this chalice
> for the fierce spark of devotion
> the unquenchable ember of tender hope
> the deep bright fire of compassionate connection.

(Light the chalice.)

Together we journey through the blazing pain of this day,
sure in the knowledge that we are held in the unending warmth of love.

Prayer

(This is a good moment to invite all present to hold hands, and perhaps to close their eyes.)

Spirit of Life and Love,
be with us today in our pain and sorrow
as we grieve the end of this pregnancy,
as we honor this life that will not be lived,
as we release the dreams that are now ended.

We grieve the longed-for spark that was so joyfully carried,
the possibility of a life that never got to breathe,
never got to shine out into this beautiful hurting world.

We grieve the child this fetus might have been,
all the moments that might have happened,
the possibilities that live on in our hearts.

We honor the beauty of [Name]'s pregnancy
and the anguish of this moment of ending,
the tenderness of these hurting hearts.

We affirm that this is not a moment of finding fault or shame,
but of care and grief and release,
of presence with these hurting hearts.

[If the focus person is about to undergo a procedure] May the hands of the doctors and nurses be steady.

May [Name]'s recovery be swift,
even as we know that grief may be long.

[Names of family members], may you be met with compassion and understanding, today and in the days to come.

Saying Goodbye

(If you are doing this ritual during an active miscarriage or before a procedure, you may wish to place your hands on the stomach of the pregnant person, if they consent to this. You could instead invite them to place their hands on their own stomach, and—again, only if they consent—invite participants to touch their shoulders. If you doing this ritual after a miscarriage or procedure, you may wish to invite participants to place their hands on their hearts.)

Together in grief, we now say farewell.
Tiny one, sweet small beginning, we had so hoped to meet you,
so longed for you to grow and thrive.
We are so sad that we will never get the chance to say hello—
never get to hold the child you might have become.

Goodbye, sweet small beginning, tiny one.

Does anyone else have words of farewell, or anything you would like to say?

(Take a moment of quiet here, allowing for whatever may or may not be spoken.)

Chalice Extinguishing

We extinguish this chalice,
but not the love that holds these tender grieving hearts.
Today is not the end of dreaming, nor of grieving,
and we hold each other gently in the ache of this day,
in this moment of ending.

(Extinguish the chalice.)

[Focus person and names of family members], blessings on your grieving, and your loving.

May you know in every moment that you are loved, and you are not alone—
not alone in loving, in grieving, in traveling through this pain.

You are so, so loved.

For a Baby Who Has Died or Will Soon Die

Rev. Rose Maldonado Schwab

This is a ritual to use when a baby has died or is soon to die. It requires minimal materials or setup so that it can be used in the moment when it is needed.

Materials

- ☐ Optional: Water or oil
- ☐ Optional: Swaddling cloth

Setup

If you are in a medical setting, make sure the nurses know that you are starting to do a ritual, and create a private, protected space however you can: close the door, dim the lighting, etc.

Prepare the water or oil and the cloth if you are planning to use them.

If the baby cannot be present (for instance, if it is in the morgue, or is not in a condition to be seen or held), you can still do the ritual, asking participants to hold the image of the baby in their minds and hearts.

Script

Opening Words

Sweet one, you have fought hard to stay with us. Listen to the fervent wishes for your well-being that fill our hearts. As we prepare ourselves to bless you, hear this prayer from your [parent, parents] who [has, have] loved you with such love, the nurses and doctors who did everything in their power to care for you [your siblings who waited expectantly for your arrival], and this world itself which needed you to witness it and needed the blessing of your presence.

Naming

We name this child today, so that we will remember them coming among us. What name do you give this child?

Parent(s): [I, We] name them [Name].

Leader: Oh, child whom we have barely known, we call you [Name]. Receive this name as a sign of your uniqueness to us and to this world. By this name you are known, and will be remembered.

Blessing of the Body

Great love, you lift us up throughout our life's journey. Send your love to us and into this [oil, water] as we bless [Name].

(Invite participants to anoint each part of the baby's body as you name it.)

We bless your face, [Name], for the color your eyes would be, for their lashes, and for the light and spark of spirit that will not shine within. For the voices that echoed around you in the womb, for the sounds of watery noises, and music and thunder. We bless your face, that you might somehow have known the love we sang to you.

We bless your mind, [Name], that you might know how much we wanted to teach you. That you might know the wonders of the universe. We wish we had been able to be the ones helping you learn the important lessons you need to know.

We bless your heart, [Name], that you might know how much we love you. That you will always be carried in our hearts.

We bless your arms and legs, [Name], for their little toes and little bones, your precious body that would let you move in your own way, and we grieve for the earth they will not move upon.

We bless your hands, [Name], for the skill and grace they could have possessed. We wish we had been able to hold hands with you as you grew and learned to use them in the way that best suited you.

We grieve for all that you will not sense, the ground you will not walk, the tools you will not wield, the love you will not know. Let us mourn, weep, and sit in silence with this precious babe, one last time.

(Allow several moments of silence.)

Closing Prayer

Compassionate and loving one, give strength and comfort to this family and all those who grieve the loss of this child. In their sorrow and pain may they experience a healing presence. May they know that they are surrounded by unending love. Amen, and blessed be.

For Blessing a Body after Death
Rev. Jami Yandle

This ritual is for anyone wishing to bless a loved one who has recently died. It can be done before or after postmortem care, before the body is removed.

Materials

☐ Oil, water, or a favorite lotion of the deceased person

If you want to use essential oils, or anything with a scent, be sure no one with scent sensitivities will be present.

Setup

Set up chairs for participants where they will be able to see you and the body of the deceased person. Allow enough space for you to move around the person and for everyone to gather beside them.

Adapt and expand the blessing to reflect the particulars of the person's life. You could name specific things they did with the different parts of their body: danced with their feet, sang with their hands or voice, etc. You could also bless items that were intimate and intrinsic parts of how they lived in and used their body, such as a wheelchair, communication board, or insulin pump.

Script

(Move to the deceased person's feet and lightly dab them with oil, water, or lotion.)

We bless [Name]'s feet, which made traveling, journeying, and so many important life passages possible.

(Anoint their hands in the same way.)

We bless [Name]'s hands, which touched and held loved ones, and were touched and held by them. We honor [Name]'s hands and the lives and communities touched by them.

(Anoint their forehead.)

We bless [Name]'s mind, the electric spark which held their creativity, thoughts, and dreams, and which made sense of the world. We honor [Name]'s mind and the ways their mind made our lives brighter, better, and more joyful. Their thoughtfulness made the world a better place.

(Anoint their throat or lips.)

We bless [Name]'s voice, the breath of humanity, the individual ways that we convey our dreams and desires. We honor [Name]'s communication style and voice, easily recognized by those who loved them.

(Anoint their chest.)

We bless [Name]'s heart, which held their deepest sorrows, hurt, and pain and their greatest joy, peace, and love.

[Name], we honor your entire life and your corporeal body. We are grateful for your spirit and your physical presence that traveled through this life and created so much love and care in this world.

I invite all those gathered to extend their hands, as they are willing and able, in blessing for our final prayer.

Spirit of Life and Love,
While our hearts feel broken in this moment,
We remain grateful as we honor the joy, life, and love that we shared with [Name].
We offer blessings upon [Name]'s heart, mind, body, and soul

As they become our ancestor.
In this moment, we say farewell to [Name]'s body.
We thank you, Spirit of Life and Love,
For the breath of life you breathed into [Name]'s body.
And now their breath is stilled.
We ask for tenderness and softness in our grief journey,
Knowing that [Name]'s spirit and love are with us still.
Amen.

For Blessing a Space Where a Loved One Has Died

Rev. McKinley L. Sims

This is a ritual of restoring the space in which someone has died and honoring participants' love of them. It is designed to be used at whatever stage of grief feels appropriate to the participants. If you are working with a group of more than four or five, provide several flowers or pieces of cloth so that several people can bless the space at a time.

Materials

- ☐ Chalice
- ☐ Cut flower or piece of soft cloth
- ☐ Perfume, incense, or essential oil
- ☐ Small bowl of water
- ☐ Optional: Music

If you are using essential oils or anything else with a scent, be sure no one with scent sensitivities will be present. You could use unscented candles instead of the perfume, incense, or essential oil. You will want enough candles to place throughout the space; you can set them out in advance, or place them as you light them.

Setup

You may need to adapt the ritual ahead of time, especially for circumstances where the death was unexpected or traumatic, such as by accident or suicide. Do this in consultation with the participants and with sensitivity to the complex feelings they may have around their loss.

Script

Chalice Lighting

> In Holy Mystery we are born.
> In Holy Mystery we live.
> In Holy Mystery we die.
> For those who are no longer here, and for those who remain,
> We light this holy flame.

(Light the chalice.)

Please join in singing "Meditation on Breathing."

Song

"Meditation on Breathing" (Sarah Dan Jones)

(Lead participants in singing.)

Naming

(Take perfume, incense, or oil and disperse it around the space, moving slowly and carefully. Let the air fill with a light smell. If you are using candles instead, light them. As you do this, repeat the following as many times as feels right.)

[Name],
we remember you.
We honor you.
We love you.

[If participants agree that it is appropriate, add "Even when you were hard to love."]

We let you go into the Mystery.

(When the room is filled with scent or candlelight, continue.)

Cleansing

(Dip the flower or cloth into the water.)

From the waters of the womb you came, through the stormy waters of life you lived, and across the waters of death you sailed. We bless your memory in this space and lovingly release you from its bounds.

I invite you to take the [flower, cloth] and, one by one, cleanse this space. Touch and bless each part of it, each item of furniture, that holds a memory, a grief, or a tender joy. Take the time you need, and as we do this, we will sing together "Comfort Me" by Mimi Bornstein-Doble.

Song

"Comfort Me" (Mimi Bornstein-Doble)

(Lead participants in singing. As they sing, participants gently move around the space, touching and blessing with drops of water the important features of the space: bedposts, desks, tables, doorframes, and windows.)

(Repeat or improvise verses as needed until everyone has had a chance to bless the space, then continue.)

This space has been witness to so much of life: the living, the loving, the healing, and the dying. May it continue to be a sanctuary of living, loving, and healing. May this place be filled with love once more and provide support and care to any who need it. May those gathered here find joy amidst the sorrow and take solace in the blessing of sheltering walls and rafters, windows and hearths. Where there has been death, may there be new life.

Let's sing one more verse of "Comfort Me."

(Lead participants in singing.)

Reclaiming

Come, Spirit of Life,

Be with us in this space that has held both joy and sorrow, life and death.

Help us to honor and remember [Name] and live out the precious gift of life in recognition of them.

May this space be a continued blessing, and may its walls and doorway, ceiling and floor be reclaimed as a place not only where death came, but where life also happened.

As the Love that never lets go and never lets us down reminds us:

All things can be made new, for those who are willing to brave the mystery and reclaim them. Help us to bless this space in honor of [Name] and in honor of those of us who remain here, in this space, on this side of the Holy Mystery.

May it be so, and amen.

Let us close by blessing the space with a song. Please join in singing "May Nothing Evil Cross This Door."

Song

"May Nothing Evil Cross This Door" (Louis Untermeyer)

(Lead participants in singing.)

Chalice Extinguishing

We extinguish this flame

And bless this space to the continued use and care of

any who dwell here.

We release its past to the Mystery, and we welcome

the future. May it be filled with love.

Amen.

(Extinguish the chalice.)

For the Dedication of a Memorial Bench or Tree

Rev. Elizabeth A. Harding

Dedicated to my hospice patients and their families

This ritual is intended to help an individual or family who have experienced the death of a loved one to memorialize them by planting a tree and/or installing a memorial bench. It could be combined with a scattering of ashes near the bench or tree. The author created it while working as a hospice chaplain and bereavement counselor.

Materials

- ☐ Small altar table
- ☐ Chalice
- ☐ Photo of the deceased

For dedicating a memorial bench:

- ☐ Small bowl of diluted lavender oil
- ☐ Handkerchiefs or tissues
- ☐ Feathers or wands

For planting or dedicating a tree:

- ☐ Small cups of water, one for each participant
- ☐ String or ribbon, if the tree is already planted
- ☐ Soil, if the tree will be planted during the ritual

Setup

Put the altar table close by the bench or tree, and arrange the photo and ritual items on it. Some people are very sensitive to essential oils, and others may simply not wish to get oil on their hands. When you hold the ritual, invite participants to dip a wand or feather rather than their finger if they prefer. You can also substitute an unscented oil, cut flowers, or something else that is safe for all.

If you are planting or dedicating a tree, mark off its space with ribbon or string, especially if it is already planted and needs to be distinguished from others around it. If you will be planting the tree during the ritual, dig the hole ahead of time and designate participants to do the physical labor of planting it. Make sure you have any other tools you may need, such as a knife to cut twine or burlap.

If any participants have limited mobility, make sure they have easy access to the tree or bench. If it will be impossible for them to access it, ask them ahead of time how they would prefer to participate. You may want to have a small tray of the ritual items to bring to participants with limited mobility.

Script

Opening Words

Our opening words come from Marge Piercy.

Connections are made slowly, sometimes they grow underground.
You cannot always tell by looking what is happening.
More than half a tree is spread out in the soil under your feet.
Penetrate quietly as the earthworm that blows no trumpet.
Fight persistently as the creeper that brings down the tree.
Spread like the squash plant that overruns the garden.
Gnaw in the dark and use the sun to make sugar.

Weave real connections, create real nodes, build real houses.
Live a life you can endure: make life that is loving.
Keep tangling and interweaving and taking more in,
a thicket and bramble wilderness to the outside but to us
interconnected with rabbit runs and burrows and lairs.

. . . .

This is how we are going to live for a long time: not always,
For every gardener knows that after the digging, after the planting,
after the long season of tending and growth, the harvest comes.

Chalice Lighting

We light this chalice today to celebrate the life and grieve the death of [Name].

Each of us, at the end of our lives, returns to the center, at rest, body and spirit returned to the Great Love, the Great Love that surrounds us and is a part of every human journey.

Throughout our lives we experience sorrow and struggle, joy and celebration, accomplishment and failure. Each moment, holy and sacred, making up the whole that is the light we shine in the world.

While today we note the loss of [Name] and know that their individual light has gone out and returned to the Sacred, we know that the love we share today, in our stories and memories and ritual, is all part of that Great Love, that sacred energy that is part of life and part of death.

As we light this chalice, may we be held in the light we share with [Name] and the light that we will take with us throughout our lives. Our lights, when combined, create such brilliance.

(Light the chalice.)

We come together today to dedicate this [bench and/or tree] to [Name]. A place of rest. A place where people can gather and remember them.

Sharing

In order to bring [Name]'s spirit into this time and this space, I invite you to say a word or a phrase [or "share a memory or story"] that sums up [Name] for you, that brings their energy, their light, here.

(Participants share.)

Option 1: Bench Dedication

At this time, we will dedicate this bench. Our lives are often busy. To have a place of rest when we are moving back and forth taking care of loved ones is a gift.

This bench will become a place for those of us gathered here to rest our spirits and remember [Name]. There will be tough days, when it is difficult to think about anything but our loss; and there will be days of joy, when [Name]'s energy will permeate each moment, and we will feel as if they are with us. And they are, always, tied to us and tied, now, to this bench as we make it our sacred space.

The history of anointing can be traced back to the ancient Greeks. The word *consecration* means *making sacred*. To consecrate this bench means to make it a sacred space where we can go to remember [Name] and feel connected to them and to the Great Love that holds us throughout our lives, through joys and sorrows, struggles and celebrations.

The Greeks used oils partly to cleanse, partly to perfume, partly to set apart that which was important to them. Today, we do all those things for [Name]'s bench. We use lavender oil because it helps people find a sense of calm and rest.

I invite you, family and friends of [Name], to line up and each take a fingertip or a feather and dip it into this little bowl of lavender oil. Then spread it or touch it to the bench.

(Participants dip their fingertips or feathers and put the oil on the bench, then wipe their fingers with handkerchiefs or tissues and return to their places. When all who wish to have done so, wipe any excess oil off the bench so that animals will not lick it up and be harmed.)

Option 2: Tree Dedication

Reading

"Becoming, Always" (Elizabeth Harding)

First.

A seed burrows deep underground.

Water comes.

Sun shines.

Air moves here and there and everywhere.

The seed grows.

Roots begin twining their paths, finding connections among their fellow trees-to-be.

The trunk emerges.

The tree begins to seek water, air and sunlight, connection among the other trees, and the earth.

Reaching out.

Standing strong.

Growing.

Reminding us of all the ways we are connected to each other.

Growth allows us to deepen and expand those connections as leaves sprout, flowers grow, and fruit may flourish.

Let us plant this tree so that we may join together.

Remembering our loved ones.

Moving onward while holding all that went before us close.

Becoming. Always.

At this time, we [plant, dedicate] the tree, this place of memory for [Name] and their family and friends.

(If the tree is being planted, the designated participants place it in the hole and add soil.)

I invite you to take a cup of water. As you feel moved, please water the tree with your cup of water. Like sharing memories, watering this tree will help us keep [Name]'s spirit with us.

(Participants water the tree.)

Song

Having dedicated this beautiful place of memory for [Name], let us sing together "For the Beauty of the Earth."

(Lead participants in singing.)

Closing Words

May we be grateful for all that is given and grateful for all that is shared, especially in sharing the life of [Name]. Let us remember that the stories, phrases, words, and song shared today are sparks of light. They are part of the light we kindled today as we began our service together. They will continue to shine within us as we remember [Name] and their life with us. May [Name] live on in each of us.

["May the bench be a place to gather our thoughts, and to find rest in this busy world" and/or "May the tree shade us as it grows."] May we keep [Name] present in our memories to keep the gift of their presence always with us.

Chalice Extinguishing

May we take the opportunities that come to create those connections, share those stories, and light those lights within us even as we extinguish this chalice. May that light join our lights and keep that sacred flame burning, day after day, month after month, year after year, helping us to know that we are deeply connected to each other, both in life and in death. Blessed be and amen.

(Extinguish the chalice.)

For the First Anniversary of a Death

Rev. Heather Concannon and Rev. Allison Palm

In honor of Katie Tyson

This ritual is written for the first anniversary of a loved one's death. It can be used by any group small enough to allow time for each person to share, generally up to about twenty-five participants.

Materials

- ☐ Altar table
- ☐ Chalice
- ☐ Tea lights, at least two for each participant
- ☐ Small stones, at least one for each participant
- ☐ Basket for stones
- ☐ Two bowls of water
- ☐ Tray

Setup

Ask participants ahead of time to bring pictures or small mementos of the deceased to build a shared altar together. Set up chairs in a circle with an altar table in the center. You could put tea lights on the altar in advance, or have them in a basket or on a tray for participants to take and light. If you place them on the altar, set out at least one for each participant, according to your best guess of how many will be needed; do not overload or clutter the table (it's unfortunate if too many remain visibly unlit) but be prepared to set out more before they run out (so that no one will feel bad about lighting more than one).

A small portable altar (with a bowl of water and candles) can be created on a tray and carried to any participants who are not able to move to the center of the circle. Place it on the central altar at the end of each time of sharing.

Script

Chalice Lighting

With remembrance and love for [Name]
And love and care for one another
We light this chalice.
It is good to be together.

(Light the chalice.)

Opening Words

Welcome, and thank you all for coming. As you know, [Name] died a year ago today, and we are here to honor this anniversary and to be together.

This day brings forth many feelings. Some of us may be feeling celebration and joy for [Name]'s life, others of us may be feeling sorrow for their death and isolation around the turns that grief has taken over the past year. Some of us may be feeling all of these, or other emotions that are unnamed and perhaps unnameable. All our emotions are welcome here.

We are here to both remember [Name] and share with one another the ways that we have experienced [Name]'s death. We are here to laugh together and to cry together—to be together on this day. Thank you for bringing your spirit and your heart to this gathering of memory and love.

Please join in singing "Meditation on Breathing" to open our time together.

Song

"Meditation on Breathing" (Sarah Dan Jones)

(Lead participants in singing.)

Releasing

The loss of a friend or loved one can take a very long time to heal, and the loss looks different for each of us throughout our lifetimes. While we will never forget [Name], there may be parts of our grief or loss that we wish to release. We will now release some of the pain of this loss: regrets, unresolved conflicts, anger, the despair of grief, loneliness, or questions that cannot be answered.

(Pass around the basket of stones.)

As we pass around these stones, please choose one. Once you have your stone, I invite each of you to think of the ways in which this loss has burdened you in the last year that you wish to release. As you hold the stone in your hands, imagine those burdens becoming one with the stone.

(Give participants a few moments to meditate quietly with their stone.)

I now invite each of you to come to the altar and drop your stone into this bowl of water. Water literally makes these stones less heavy, just as our burdens are lightened when they are shared with others. If you wish, you can tell us what burden you wish to release, or you may place your stone in the bowl in silence. If you prefer to have a bowl of water brought to you, just raise your hand.

(After all who wish to have participated, continue.)

We release these feelings that this loss has brought us, but not the memory of [Name]. May the pain and grief that we have released make space for celebration, memories, and love. Let us pray.

Prayer

Eternal spirit,

Moving through our lives in unseen ways,

    Be present to us now.

We gather with such a wide range of emotions.

    Some of us may be celebrating [Name]'s life,

    Others of us are still bewildered, longing for answers and connection.

It is good to be together.

    It is good to gather to honor [Name].

Today, on the anniversary of [Name]'s death, we celebrate, laugh, affirm, cry, mourn.

We pray that our love for [Name] allows us to always remain connected in memory to them.

We pray for healing for ourselves, that over time, those moments of sorrow and grief may become easier burdens to carry.

We are grateful for the time we had with [Name], though we may wish that we had had the gift of more years together.

May we remain open to love, and connected to life.

    May we celebrate [Name], and give thanks for their life.

    May we know that we are held in the love of those gathered here.

And may we know that we are held, together, by a Love that is beyond our understanding, but never beyond our reach.

May it be so, and amen.

Song

"There Is a Love" (words by Rebecca Parker, music by Elizabeth Norton)

(Lead participants in singing.)

Remembering

Today we gather to remember [Name], and to share the blessings they brought to our lives. Now we have a time to share our memories of [Name], our favorite stories about [Name], or the things we most miss about [Name] with one another. Our memories can bring us comfort and joy, and they are so often bittersweet, as we know that [Name] is no longer with us.

I invite each of you to come forward and light a candle on the altar in honor of [Name]. You may light a candle silently, or you may share a memory, a story, or something you miss about [Name]. Feel free to light more than one candle or share more than one memory. If you prefer to have the candles brought to you to light, just raise your hand.

(After all who wish to have shared in the ritual of remembering, continue.)

May our memories of [Name] bring us some comfort and joy in our sorrow. We are blessed by these memories in their death, just as we were blessed by [Name] in their life.

Song

"Spirit of Life" (Carolyn McDade)

(Lead participants in singing.)

Chalice Extinguishing

We extinguish these flames,
but the light of [Name]'s life burns bright
in our hearts.
May we be comforted by our memories
And held by our time together.
Go in peace.

(Extinguish the chalice and the candles of remembrance on the altar.)

For Burying or Scattering the Ashes of a Pet

Rev. Caitlin Cotter Coillberg

This is a ritual for burying or scattering the ashes of an animal companion.

Materials

If burying:

- ☐ Shovel
- ☐ Loose dirt to fill the grave
- ☐ Shroud or small box holding the body
- ☐ Optional: Stones or flowers
- ☐ Optional: Craft supplies, such as markers, paint and brushes, plain stones or small plaques, etc.

If scattering ashes:

- ☐ Container of ashes
- ☐ Water for rinsing hands
- ☐ Towel

Setup

Your vet can help you with arranging cremation or storage of an animal's body until you are ready.

This is an outdoor ritual. Choose a location that is beautiful or meaningful to you, perhaps one connected to your life with this animal companion: a park or trail where you walked your dog, someplace with lots of birds your cat would have loved to watch or chase, a spot in your yard where you let your turtle or guinea pig run around, etc. If you need permission to bury an animal or scatter the ashes there, get it in advance. Make sure all participants will be able to access the location; think about issues like road access and, if someone will be attending by video, the strength of your phone or Wi-Fi signal.

This ritual is intended to be done with at least two people; even small children can take part, though they may need help. If you wish, it can be modified for you to do on your own. You may want to call a friend or family member who knew your animal companion and ask them to be present with you as you move through the ritual.

You could decorate the box, shroud, or container of ashes as part of this ritual. Use any nicknames your animal companion had, as well as its official name; remember it by everything you called it. Think of specific memories, images, and gratitudes you want to name and honor.

If you will be burying a body, dig the hole in advance; it always takes longer than expected. You may want to look for pet cemeteries in your area. If you will be scattering ashes, check the weather forecast; you want some wind, but not rain or snow.

Script

FOR BURYING AN ANIMAL'S BODY

Opening Words

(Gather all those who wish to take part in this ritual around the grave.)

Today we have gathered to bury our beloved [Name], and to remember what we loved about them, and all that we experienced together. We are so sad not to have them as a living companion on our journey through life anymore, and we treasure all the joy and comfort and laughter they brought us.

[Name], today we are taking you on one last outing, and remembering you.

Words of Grief and Gratitude

[Name], we are so grateful we got to have you in our lives. We are grateful for the times you made us laugh, and all the times we could not help but pause to take in how wonderful and beautiful you were. We are so grateful for all of the ways you made us smile, and we miss you. [Name], we are so sad you died.

We will remember you. We will remember how you looked when you slept, when you ate your favorite treats, when you looked back at us with your sweet, beautiful eyes. We will remember the sounds you made, and the way you felt under our fingertips when we petted you, and how you made us feel. We loved you.

Today we release you into the earth, but you will not be forgotten. We hold our memories of you close, as we wish we could still hold you close.

Burial

(Carefully place the body in the grave.)

I invite each of you to take a small amount of dirt in your hands and think about what you are most grateful for about [Name]'s time in your life. When you are ready, sprinkle the dirt on [Name]'s grave and, if you wish, say aloud what you are remembering about them.

(Participants take turns sprinkling dirt on the grave. When everyone who wishes to has done so, sprinkle some dirt yourself.)

[Name], thank you for [specific gratitude]. In grief and in gratitude, we release you.

In grief and gratitude we came here today. May our tears and our laughter fill our hearts as [Name] once did. May we leave this place today knowing we are not alone in our grieving or our remembering, and that life is better because we have loved.

(Fill in the grave. Once the animal is completely buried, move on to a time of sharing stories and memories.)

Sharing Stories and Memories

(Gather everyone around the grave again. Alternatively, you could gather everyone around a craft space and invite them to make or decorate items to mark the grave.)

(Invite people to share memories and stories of your animal companion, and perhaps to place stones, flowers, or items they have decorated or made on the grave. You may wish to offer a memory first, to help start off. It is often best to remember a funny moment first: some piece of mischief your animal companion was prone to, or a time they got stuck somewhere amusing, or the holiday costume you put them into, for example.)

Closing Words

[Name], you are now beneath the earth but you remain in our hearts and memories. We are so grateful for all that you brought to our lives.

FOR SCATTERING ASHES

On the Way There

(Gather participants together before going as a group to the spot where you will spread the ashes. This might mean gathering at the car before driving to an overlook, in a living room before moving together to the backyard, at a trailhead before walking to a stream bank, etc. Hold up the container of ashes for a moment.)

Today we have gathered to release the ashes of our beloved [Name], and to remember what we loved about them, and all that we experienced together. We are so sad not to have them as a living companion on our journey through life anymore, and we treasure all the joy and comfort and laughter they brought us. As we head out to release these ashes, let us take time to share stories.

[Name], today we are taking you on one last outing, and remembering you.

Who has a story to share?

(As you move toward the location you have selected, invite people to share stories about your animal companion. You may wish to offer one first, to help start off. It is often best to remember a funny moment first: some piece of mischief your animal companion was prone to, or a time they got stuck somewhere amusing, or the holiday costume you put them into, for example.)

At the Site

(Once you reach the site where you wish to spread ashes, test the wind by tossing something light into the air, like small dry leaves or dandelion fluff, or by holding out something like a small ribbon. It is very important to ensure the ashes will blow away from you and others. Once you have determined this, you can gather participants around the container of ashes, on its upwind side.)

Words of Grief and Gratitude

[Name], we are so grateful we got to have you in our lives. We are grateful for the times you made us laugh, and all the times we could not help but pause to take in how wonderful and beautiful you were. We are so grateful for all of the ways you made us smile, and we miss you. [Name], we are so sad you died.

We will remember you. We will remember how you looked when you slept, when you ate your favorite treats, when you looked back at us with your sweet beautiful eyes. We will remember the sounds you made, and the way you felt under our fingertips when we petted you, and how you made us feel. We loved you.

Today we release you into the [wind, water], but you will not be forgotten. We hold our memories of you close, as we wish we could still hold you close.

Ritual of Release for Ashes

I invite each of you to take a small amount of ashes in your hands, and think about what you are most grateful for about [Name]'s time in your life. When you are ready, release the ashes into the [wind, water].

(Participants take turns selecting and releasing small handfuls of ashes. When everyone who wishes to has done so, scatter the rest of the ashes yourself.

[Name], thank you for [specific gratitude]. In grief and in gratitude, we release you.

(Pour water over each person's hands as you continue speaking.)

In grief and gratitude we came here today. May our tears and our laughter fill our hearts as [Name] once did. May we leave this place today knowing we are not alone in our grieving or our remembering, and that life is better because we have loved.

Closing Words

[Name], you are now released to the [wind, water], but you remain in our hearts and memories. We are so grateful for all that you brought to our lives.

Rituals for Congregations and Communities

Healing, Hope, and Blessing

For Mending a Broken Covenant

Rev. Elizabeth Carrier-Ladd

When a community or group of people have made a covenant together, agreeing on how they will treat each other and the work or play they do together, they must also bear in mind that the covenant may at some point be broken. People make mistakes, they have bad days, they behave poorly sometimes, they hurt each other. But the breaking need not be a total destruction. When a covenant is broken, we may be called to come back together, to mend it and start again. This ritual creates a container for a community to work through a breaking of their covenant, so that they can recommit themselves to it and to each other. It is grounded in restorative justice and the human possibility for transformation and redemption.

Unitarian Universalism is a covenantal faith; rather than requiring members to hold a particular belief, it calls them into covenantal relationship with one another and the world. This ritual was created for a congregation's youth group. It works best in smaller groups of five to fifteen people. The group must have a covenant that is explicit and shared, and it must have been clearly broken in a way that the group agrees has harmed the community.

Materials

- ☐ Chalice
- ☐ Covenant, either posted for all to see or printed for each participant
- ☐ Easel, whiteboard, or chalkboard
- ☐ Extra chair that can be easily lifted and moved

Setup

The most important thing to do in preparing for this ritual is to talk with the person or people who have broken the covenant and invite them to apologize. The ritual is not a space to surprise someone with an accusation that they have broken the covenant; it presupposes that they have acknowledged doing so and have accepted the community's call back into covenant. Encourage them to write out their apology in advance and help them to do so, as appropriate. Remember that a true apology includes four parts: the person must admit responsibility for what they did, express remorse for it, make amends as best they can, and plan how they will avoid making the same mistake again.

You may wish to recruit helpers to read different parts of this ritual, so that it isn't all in one voice.

Arrange participants in a circle so that they can all see one another. Leave enough space in the middle for someone to stand or sit there, but do not place a chair there yet.

Script

Chalice Lighting

Come, come.

Be among us.

Come, spirit of possibility.

Come, human power for change.

Come, accountability.

Come, forgiveness.

Come, kindreds, into this circle of care.

All of us are welcome.

All of us are beloved.

All of us have fallen short, fallen flat on our faces, fallen into someone we care about and harmed them.

Come, come, whoever you are.

(Light the chalice.)

Opening Words

Covenants are not contracts. Covenants transcend agreements. They are made with the understanding that they will be broken. They are lofty ideals: vows we commit to do our absolute best to stay true to. And as humans, we accept the reality that we will not always be able to live up to all of them. And when we fall short of our goals, we do not give up. Because being in a covenantal community means being willing to keep trying. It means coming back and recommitting.

Song

"Come, Come, Whoever You Are" (Rumi and Lynn Adair Ungar)

(Lead participants in singing. Ideally, use the descant "Though you've broken your vows a thousand times.")

Reading

"I Want to Be with People" (Dana Worsnop)

Often people say that they love coming to a place with so many like-minded people.

I know just what they are getting at – and I know that they aren't getting it quite right.

I want to be in a community where I *don't* have to think like everyone else to be eligible for salvation.
I want to be with people who value compassion, justice, love, and truth,
     though they have different opinions about all sorts of things.
I want to be with people of good heart,
     people who have many names and no name at all for God,
          who see in me goodness and dignity,
          who also see my failings and foibles, and who still love me.

I want to be with people who feel their interconnection with all existence and let it guide their footfalls upon the earth,
     people who see life as a paradox and don't rush to resolve it.
          who are willing to balance upon the tightrope that is life,
          who will help steady me when I wobble.
          who give of themselves, who share their hearts and minds and gifts.

I want to be with people who let church call them into a different way of being in the world,
     people who support, encourage, and even challenge each other to more ethical living,

who are willing to be uncomfortable trying to get there.

who inspire one another to follow the call of the spirit,

who covenant to be honest, engaged, and kind,

who strive to keep their promises and hold me to the promises I make.

I want to be with people who know that human community is usually warm and generous,

often challenging and almost always a grand adventure.

In short, I want to be with people like you.

Naming of Impact

Together, let us name the impact of our broken covenant. Each of us will have a moment to share from our own perspective, if we wish. Please focus on your feelings and experiences, using "I" statements.

(You may want to speak first, to model appropriate sharing of impact. Be ready to help participants call one another back if they venture into generalizations or speaking for others. Allow time for all who wish to speak to do so.)

Apology

Covenants are aspirational. When we break them, we are called back in. We are called to return again. To take responsibility. To say we are sorry and that we will do better. We are all on a journey of growth and change—and we all make mistakes along the way.

[If one or a few people clearly broke the covenant] [Names] have come to us prepared to make a statement to this community. May we listen with our hearts open. May the spirit of redemption and transformation be among us in this space.

[If no individual or group is clearly responsible for the broken covenant] We have gathered to discuss and work through [describe the untenable dynamic or conflict]. We agree that this is harming the community. We will go around the circle and share any regrets or apologies that we may have about our part in the situation. One by one, as much as we can, we will name whatever we are responsible for that has contributed to this problem harming all of us. This naming does not have to be exhaustive. It does have to be genuine. May we all listen deeply to one another with our hearts open. May the spirit of redemption and transformation be among us in this space.

(Invite someone to begin, and then go around the circle. Participants may pass if they choose.)

Returning to Covenant

As we return to this covenant, let us hear its words together. Let us read it aloud, in a circle, one line at a time.

(Have participants read the written covenant. Allow them to pass if they choose.)

And now, given what has transpired, let us consider what is needed for our covenant moving forward. Is there anything we need to add? Or change?

(Take notes, or have a helper do so while you facilitate the conversation, on the posted covenant text and/or on the easel, whiteboard, or chalkboard, so that everyone can see what is being discussed and proposed. Move toward a new covenant through consensus. This may take time. Give it the time it needs. If you come to feel that consensus cannot be found in the time available, shift the topic and guide the group toward planning how and when to return to the work of building consensus.)

If the group has succeeded in developing a revised covenant

(Write out a clear copy of the revised text where everyone can see it.)

What good work we have done! Let us read this new covenant together as a means of adopting it!

(Have participants read the new covenant, going around the circle with each person reading one line as before. Allow them to pass if they choose.)

If the group has not succeeded in developing a revised covenant

(Write out, where everyone can see it, a clear copy of the plan that has been developed for how the group will continue the work.)

Creating covenants takes time, and thought, and the willingness to work together. We haven't finished crafting our new covenant—but we have covenanted to keep working on it. Let us all affirm our commitment to doing so.

(Have participants affirm their commitment. You could have them repeat a line like "We will keep working together in good faith" after you, or you could state any concrete plans that have been made, such as "We will meet again on Wednesday night," and have them agree aloud.)

Affirmation Circle

We have done good work today—let's celebrate!

(Lead some cheering.)

We are all loved, precious beings. Whether we have been harmed directly or indirectly, and whether or not we have caused harm, we are all loved, precious beings. We are all deserving of care. We know that each of us holds real value in this community. We know that we are better together and that rebuilding trust will feel risky for us all.

In a moment, I'll invite each of you, one at a time, to come into the center of the circle. Friends on the outside of the circle, you will be invited to share words of affirmation with this beloved in our center.

When you are in the center of the circle, please do your best to receive. Resist the urge to argue or second-guess the ways in which you have value. Just listen to the ways in which you have been a gift to this community. You can sit or stand, whatever you like. If you are comfortable with it, you can close your eyes when you're there to focus on the words.

(Move the extra chair into the center of the circle. Invite one person into the center at a time, and have the rest of the group share what they value and appreciate about them. Continue until everyone who wishes to has had a turn in the center.)

Closing Words

We are fragile humans. Being in relationship means that we will be hurt. Engaging in a community is a risk. No one can assure you that you will be completely safe when you interact with others. I assure you that if you truly engage with those around you, you will often be uncomfortable. We will all be hurt. We will be disappointed. We will push each other too far. We will misunderstand and be misunderstood. We will get angry. We will make mistakes and harm people we care about. This is part of what is so special and beautiful and hard about life in community.

And it is so worth it. Belonging to a community who will support us in our joys and sorrows is priceless. By practicing our values together, we are becoming our best selves and strengthening this community that we hold so dear. By practicing accountability and forgiveness, by living into our covenant, we are living lives of transformation that transform the world.

May it be so. Blessed be, and amen.

Song

"How Could Anyone" (Libby Roderick)

(Lead participants in singing.)

Chalice Extinguishing

We extinguish this flame
And we hold the light it represents in our hearts.
We honor the spark of the divine in each one of us
And we aspire to work toward a world where each spark is cherished.

(Extinguish the chalice.)

For Honoring Grief and Gratitude
Rev. Rachael Hayes

This ritual of grief and gratitude is designed for a congregational worship service but could be adapted for individuals, families, or small groups. It is suitable for all ages. Honoring many types of grief and gratitude, it helps participants recognize that we may be holding many types of grief at once and that grief and gratitude are interrelated.

Materials

- ☐ Altar table
- ☐ Sliced bread, one slice for each participant
- ☐ Trays for bread
- ☐ Cups of water
- ☐ Chime or bell
- ☐ Music

Setup

There should be a visual focal point, which can be an altar containing a chalice and other service elements. If you are not doing this ritual as part of a congregational worship service, you may want to open with a chalice lighting. The ritual is well suited for celebration in the round, but it may work in any space where people gather to hold grief in community. Since eating bread may make participants thirsty, it is helpful to have water available.

The script can be divided for multiple leaders. Recruit helpers ahead of time to pass out the bread.

Unless you are certain that no one will need them, provide gluten-free and allergen-free bread options. This ritual may also be performed by taking sips of water.

Decide whether you will have live instrumental music or recorded music, and arrange for it.

Script

Opening Words

There is so much grief. We lose loved ones. Injustice is everywhere. The planet struggles to hold us. This grief is here with us, whether we acknowledge it or not. Francis Weller, in his book *The Wild Edge of Sorrow*, writes of five gates of grief, five ways we encounter the grief that moves us individually and brings us into community with everyone who grieves in a communal hall of grief. Each individual grief is a passageway into this larger experience of communal grief.

Let us journey through these gates, these passages, together, to be together in our grief. On the way back from this communal hall of grief we will turn toward the gratitude that is intertwined with these griefs.

Just as our grief and gratitude become part of us, we will mark our experience of grief and gratitude by eating bread together, and the bread we eat will become part of the strength we take from this day. Everyone will get a slice.

(Explain any allergens and describe the alternative breads available.)

And if you prefer not to eat bread, we invite you to take a small sip of water instead.

The helpers will make sure everyone gets a slice of bread or a cup of water, or both if you wish. Please wait to eat and drink until we are all called to do so together.

(Helpers pass out bread and water.)

There will be ten times in the service where you are invited to take a bite. Which means ten bites—or sips of water, if you prefer. The chime will ring, and as you hear the chime, then eat or drink.

There is a silence that is more than waiting to speak.

Together, let us build a holy silence where our hearts can listen to their own beating.

Breathe in. Breathe out.

Feel your weight in your chair. Trust it to hold you.

Pour your silence into our larger silence.

(After a short silence, play some instrumental music.)

The First Gate of Grief

The first gate of grief, the one we acknowledge most often, is the loss of someone or something we love. Those who have loved us, those who have inspired us, those who have comforted us. The love continues on, even though we no longer know how to reach the beloved. This grief becomes so clear in the seats left empty in holiday gatherings, those we wish we could have one more conversation, meal, or adventure with, those whose presence meant so much, those whose existence meant the world to us. There will never be another like them. We love them, and we have lost them.

For all we have lost, we mourn.

To mark your grief for those you have loved and lost, you are invited to take a bite of bread.

(Sound the chime or bell.)

The Second Gate of Grief

The second gate of grief is the places within us that have not known love. For every time we could not be who we truly are, had to cover up a part of ourselves, we feel grief. For the times we have been rejected. For the times we could not be known and for the times we were unloved because of who we are. We mourn for LGBTQ+ youth kicked out of their homes or harmed by those who claim to love them. We mourn for those who found abuse where they should have found love. We mourn for those who are afraid to be themselves or to love whom they love. We mourn for those who died of hate or cruelty, and for those who fear persecution and abandonment, and for the places within us that have not known the love that we need.

To mark your grief for the places within you that have not known love, to dedicate yourself to offering that love to others, you are invited to take a bite of bread.

(Sound the chime or bell.)

The Third Gate of Grief

The third gate of grief is the sorrows of the world. What is my personal grief when faced with pandemic, fire, famine, war, and genocide? It is still grief. There are many passages into this hall of grief, and we can meet each other at the common altar. The sorrows of the world connect us to each other and bring us together to mourn. We mourn wildfires, hurricanes, earthquakes, and the sorrows of our beloved earth. We mourn the systems of violence in our culture. We mourn white supremacy. We mourn poverty and hunger and war. This too is grief, with us in every moment.

To mark your grief for the sorrows of the world, you are invited to take a bite of bread.

(Sound the chime or bell.)

The Fourth Gate of Grief

The fourth gate of grief is what we expected and did not receive. Not so much a thing we had and lost, but a disappointment. A depth of community we don't know how to find. An emptiness or hollowness we don't know how to fill. A relationship that did not last. A child we wished for but did not have. A chance that didn't come. For the times when belonging did not come or was not enough, for the times when community was not deep enough to fill our need, we mourn.

To mark your grief for all you expected and did not receive, you are invited to take a bite of bread.

(Sound the chime or bell.)

The Fifth Gate of Grief

The fifth gate is ancestral grief, the losses of those who came before us.

Each of us has ancestors who lost their homeland: some when they chose to move to this continent, some when they fled their homes as refugees, some when they were abducted and enslaved, some when they were forced from their land by violence. Each of us has ancestors who lived this story, or we lived it ourselves. Each of these stories bears its own trauma and loss.

We acknowledge that for many of us, our ancestors not only suffered but caused others to suffer. We therefore carry not only their own grief, but also grief for the harm they did. We mourn for the trauma our ancestors experienced, and for the trauma our ancestors caused. We mourn the ways this trauma is passed down into the present day, in the continued oppression of Black, Indigenous, and other People of Color. We mourn for what all of us have lost in a culture that values the idea of whiteness over what any of us actually are. For the many ancestral griefs, coming to us from our ancestors of blood and our ancestors of spirit, we mourn.

To mark the ancestral grief that lives inside you, you are invited to take a bite of bread.

(Sound the chime or bell. Wait until people have finished eating before continuing.)

Moving to Gratitude

Those were the five gates of grief. Breathe in. Breathe out. I won't ask you to eat any more grief today.

Let us return to the holy silence we found before.
Breathe in. Breathe out.
Let your heart listen to its own beating.
Feel your weight in your chair. Feel the earth holding you tight with gravity.
In this silence, you are known and loved beyond all words.

(After a short silence, play some instrumental music.)

For each of Weller's gates of grief, there is a corresponding gate of gratitude that leads us back into that great hall of meaning and worth, back to our common altar. There is no need to mourn the things that do not matter. We mourn things, people, and events of worth and meaning. For the chance to hold this meaning, to say, "yes, this matters, there is goodness as well as sadness," we may find ourselves grateful. Gratitude may also help us hold our grief, connect us to goodness when there is so much to mourn.

The First Gate of Gratitude

For the love we share with others, we give thanks. There is so much to love in this life. For the freedom to love as we will. For beloved family members and friends. For all those who touch our lives and inspire us, we give thanks.

To mark your gratitude for those you love, you are invited to take a bite of bread.

(Sound the chime or bell.)

The Second Gate of Gratitude

For the love we have received, the love that has nurtured us to this very moment, we give thanks. Love has carried us through so many moments to be here now. For compassion, nurture, and companionship. For the love that has met us along the way, for the love that has journeyed with us, we give thanks.

To mark your gratitude for the love you have received, you are invited to take a bite of bread.

(Sound the chime or bell.)

The Third Gate of Gratitude

For the goodness in the world, for that which is beautiful, for that which inspires wonder and joy, we give thanks. The goodness of the world comes to us in nature, in the earth's cycle of seasons, rest and growth and rest, in the delight of experience, and in our fellow human beings. For the goodness that we have met in ourselves and in our many experiences of this life, we give thanks.

To mark your gratitude for the goodness in the world, you are invited to take a bite of bread.

(Sound the chime or bell.)

The Fourth Gate of Gratitude

For the community we have found, for all the places where we are known and loved and can be ourselves. For the times when we know we have enough and the times when we know we are enough. For the sense of belonging to a place, to a community of love, we give thanks.

To mark your gratitude for community, you are invited to take a bite of bread.

(Sound the chime or bell.)

The Fifth Gate of Gratitude

For the joy of our ancestors. Our very presence in this moment is the triumph of our ancestors. That their blood and spirit has carried forward in you and through you to this day is their joy, just as you will find joy in those who by blood or spirit descend from you. For this joy we give thanks.

To mark your ancestors' joy alive in you, you are invited to take a bite of bread.

(Sound the chime or bell.)

(After a short silence, play some instrumental music.)

Closing Words

Breathe in. Breathe out.
Our grief is holy. Our gratitude is holy.
The earth is holy. We are whole.
We live deeper into humanity,
into our connection with earth, with each other,
with the past, and with the future,
when we remember the sacred.
We bless our grief and our gratitude, because love has many faces.
Blessed be. Amen.

For Letting Go

Rev. Kimberley Debus

This is a ritual of healing, of releasing negative attachments to thoughts, regrets, disappointments, etc. It is suitable for groups of any size. It may be used with a particular focus, such as conflict, judgment, or grief, or with a more general theme of healing.

Materials

- ☐ Altar table
- ☐ Dissolving paper
- ☐ Markers, at least one for each participant (water-soluble markers will tint the water, which you may or may not want)
- ☐ Large, clear vessel of water
- ☐ Long spoon for stirring
- ☐ Baskets for papers and markers
- ☐ Music

Setup

Decide how you will phrase the opening words. What concern, event, or theme is the ritual focusing on, what kinds of emotions around it are your participants holding, and what action do you want to move them toward?

Cut the paper into slips. If you would like participants to write only a word or phrase, cut it into two-inch squares; if you want to invite more in-depth reflections, cut larger pieces. Make at least one slip for each participant.

Put the paper slips and markers into baskets. You can recruit helpers to pass them during the ritual or have participants pass them hand to hand.

Place the vessel of water and the spoon on the altar table.

Decide which parts of Coco Love Alcorn's "The River" you and participants will sing. Provide lyrics if participants are singing the whole song.

Script

Opening Words

We hear the phrase "letting go" all the time. Let go of anxiety, anger, disappointment, frustration, regret. But it's not always easy, and so we focus on them, fixating on our longing to destroy those negative thoughts and feelings. We repeat positive affirmations to dispel them, we imagine balls of energy consuming them, we use fire to burn them.

And still we don't let them go. Indeed, by striving to destroy them in these ways, we're actually focusing our attention on them.

What happens when we decide to relax and let them dissolve away?

We are all carrying [thoughts, feelings] because of [issue or event]. And while one ritual will not remove the problem, letting go of our [thoughts, feelings] will help us [action]. When we relax and let those concerns dissolve away, we are more able to [action] with love, grace, and patience.

Take a moment and think about the [thoughts, feelings] you long to let dissolve away, as we prepare to undertake our ritual of letting go.

(Allow a moment or two of quiet. Then begin passing out the baskets with the paper and markers.)

The baskets now being passed contain small slips of paper and markers; please take one of each and write or draw the thing you wish to let go of.

(Allow time for the passing and the writing.)

Now that we've written these things down, it's time to let them go. Many cultures use water to carry away troubles, from the floating flowers placed at the shore for the Santeria goddess Yemaya to take away to the Christian ritual of baptism, meant to wash away sin. Water is cleansing and releasing.

You are now invited to dissolve your anxiety, anger, disappointment, frustration, and regret into the cool water in this vessel. Let go, allow your troubles to be dissolved away. As you drop the slip of paper into the water and give it a stir, you may wish to say, "I release my attachment to this."

(While people are coming up, offer some gentle instrumental music. When everyone has stirred their paper into the water, invite participants to sing with you.)

Song

"The River" (Coco Love Alcorn)

(Lead participants in singing.)

Responsive Prayer

(Place a hand on the vessel of water or lift it up.)

Please join me in prayer, responding with "We give thanks for this healing water."

Spirit of Compassion and Release, we give thanks to the earth for its life-giving, healing, sustaining gift of water, and give thanks for this container in which our burdens can be held, dissolved, and removed. We open our hearts and minds to offer gratitude, saying—

PARTICIPANTS: We give thanks for this healing water.

LEADER: We can now start to free our minds, and turn to curiosity and wonder. For this we say—

PARTICIPANTS: We give thanks for this healing water.

LEADER: We can now start to feel lighter, and turn to possibility. For this we say—

PARTICIPANTS: We give thanks for this healing water.

LEADER: We can now start to feel freer, and turn to passion and strength. For this we say—

PARTICIPANTS: We give thanks for this healing water.

LEADER: We can now start to feel energized, and turn to love and commitment. For this we say—

PARTICIPANTS: We give thanks for this healing water.

LEADER: For all this and more, we say amen.

PARTICIPANTS: Amen.

LEADER: Let us close by singing "There's a River Flowin' in My Soul."

Song

"There's a River Flowin' in My Soul" (Faya Ora Rose Touré)

(Lead participants in singing.)

For Those Living on the Threshold of Significant Change

Rev. Karen Hering

Blessings are especially important when we find ourselves on the thresholds of new roles, identities, and experiences. Whether we wanted the change or are facing it unwillingly, whether we planned for and expected the change or have been taken by surprise, a blessing offers us safe passage by assuring us we are witnessed and supported.

While serving as associate minister at Unity Church-Unitarian in St. Paul, Minnesota, the author led the congregation in offering this blessing every year to members on the cusp of significant personal change. It is designed to be part of a congregational worship service, but can be adapted for anyone living through great change. For a more in-depth perspective on the theology of this blessing, see the author's book *Trusting Change: Finding Our Way through Personal and Global Transformation.*

Materials

- ☐ Flat cords or ribbons, one to span each aisle or path that the focus people will move along
- ☐ Copies and/or projected script of the responsive blessing

Setup

Choose cords or ribbons that will be visible against the floor, but that are easy to step or roll over and will not present tripping hazards. Have them rolled up at the front of the ritual space, and designate helpers to unroll them at the appropriate time.

Announce ahead of time that this ritual will be happening and invite focus people to sign up. Make clear that while they will be named and blessed in the ritual, the particulars of their threshold moments will not be shared. Tell them that they will be invited to the front of the sanctuary but that they may also receive the blessing without coming forward.

Alternatively, you can adapt the ritual so as not to name or mark out individuals at all, but instead to bless a community in general.

Script

Opening Words

Today, we as a community will bless those among us who are living on the sometimes terrifying, sometimes exhilarating threshold of significant change. We know that all of us are living in threshold times—collectively or individually—to some degree, but those we name and bless today have specifically requested our blessing of their passage.

Some of their thresholds are desired and chosen; many are not. Their particulars are unique, and each person must determine how best to cross their threshold, where to find the wisdom, courage, and guidance they need. Crossing thresholds is often daunting and difficult. It can be frightening, overwhelming, and confusing. There are losses and there is grief, as well as gifts and excitement. Always, there will be portions of the journey that can only be made alone. But always, there will also be companions whose presence and witness, whose kindness and wisdom, will mean that even the solitary path need not be lonely and need not bring despair. These are characteristics of life on the threshold, which, in addition to all of that, is sacred, alive with new possibilities, a chance to practice letting go, mustering courage and curiosity, finding wisdom, and fostering a larger Love that abides even and especially in the midst of loss and change. This is the sacred and significant work of living on the threshold. This is the work I ask you to now join me in blessing.

Calling Forth Those on a Threshold

I will read the names. You may not know the particulars of their thresholds—and you don't need to in order to bless them and uphold them through this passage in their life. For those being named, please come forward when your name is called, or stand, or wave to us from your seat. Here are the names of this year's thresholders.

(Speak the names and gather the focus people who come forward at the front of the space, facing the participants.)

Responsive Blessing

Will the community please rise in body or spirit and read with me responsively the words of blessing? And if you have not been named but are yourself on a threshold, please feel free to silently receive this blessing, listening as others around you speak it to you.

For all those pausing on a threshold, about to move into the unknown, we are present with you.

PARTICIPANTS: Although we may not know the particulars of your threshold, which is uniquely yours, we offer you our supportive presence for steadiness on your path, our compassionate and understanding minds to hear your hopes and fears, and our open hearts to share the joys and sorrows of your passage, spoken and unspoken.

LEADER: As you move toward the uncertainty of all that is unfolding, we remind you of the Love that holds you, certain and true.

PARTICIPANTS: May your heart remain open to grieve what you are leaving and to receive the gifts that will come your way in this crossing.

LEADER: May your own inner light guide you and may you learn to trust it, even when it does not shine far down the road.

PARTICIPANTS: If your light begins to flicker and fade, we will offer sparks to reignite it.

LEADER: May you be blessed by courage to keep moving into the life that awaits you.

PARTICIPANTS: May you be blessed by compassion, especially for yourself.

Leader: May this passage bring you new discoveries and renewed faith, and offer you a gateway to ancient wisdom and healing wholeness.

Participants: May you always remember the pledge of this community, extending hand and heart, open to you in all that is to come.

Please be seated and turn your attention to the aisle as those we have blessed will now cross this symbolic threshold on the floor and pass through your midst, receiving the blessing of your presence in addition to the words you have spoken. And if you are on a threshold and have received this blessing from wherever you are, please take this time of silence, as other thresholders cross the symbolic threshold and return to their seats, to fully absorb this blessing given to you as well.

(Have helpers unroll the ribbons or cords across the heads of the aisles or paths the focus people will go back down. The focus people cross over the ribbon or cord thresholds, moving from the front of the space to the back. After they have reached the back, have the focus people return to their seats.)

For Honoring Elders

Rev. Tom Capo and Martha Kirby Capo

This ritual is written to honor our elders and is designed to be used as part of a congregational worship service. It was designed after one of the authors spent two years leading a Conscious Aging group, in which he actively listened and learned about the experiences of aging in a youth-oriented society. He collaborated with his wife, an established writer and author, to create this ritual.

Materials

- ☐ Altar table
- ☐ Roses in full bloom, one for each focus person
- ☐ Vase large enough to hold roses
- ☐ Scarves, one for each focus person
- ☐ Copies of the statement of intention, statement of losses, and statement of gains, one of each for each focus person
- ☐ Optional: Copies of the unison responses

Setup

Announce this ritual to the congregation several weeks in advance so that those who wish to be honored can let the leader know. Elders will self-identify. Let them know that they will be invited to share one legacy they wish to pass on. Ask them to prepare this ahead of time and to keep it to one or two sentences.

Although it is not absolutely necessary, consider pairing this ritual with a half-day retreat ahead of time in which the focus people identify which aspects of their lives becoming an elder means setting down, and which it means taking up. If you do this, present the scarves to them at its close; ask them to put their scarf in a place where they can see it daily and contemplate what they've discerned during the retreat. They should then bring their scarves to the worship service.

It's a good idea to have a few extra scarves and roses on hand for any elders who decide on the spot that they want to be focus people (and any retreat participants who may forget to bring their scarf). Prepare copies of the focus people's statements; use a large font and easily readable design. Decide whether participants will read their unison responses or repeat them after you, and prepare copies of the responses if necessary; distribute them at the beginning of the worship service.

The ritual is placed in the worship service wherever a child dedication, bridging ceremony, or new member recognition is usually placed.

Place the altar table in front of the congregation, and set the vase filled with roses on it.

Reserve seats for the focus people; if they don't already have scarves, do so by placing the scarves on them. Place some chairs at the front of the space for any focus people who may prefer to sit rather than stand during the ritual.

Script

Opening Words

As we move into this time of honoring and expressing gratitude for our elders, I offer these words from Cathy Carmody, written during a Choosing Conscious Elderhood retreat in British Columbia, in August 2012:

Leaving behind my journey of struggling and racing through
the white water of many rivers, I become the river,
creating my own unique way.
Leaving behind my self-imposed role as a tree upon
which others have leaned, I now become the wind,
with the freedom to blow whenever and wherever I choose.
Leaving behind the boxes I've created in my life, crammed with
roles, responsibilities, rules and fears,
I become the wild and unpredictable space
within which flowers sprout and grow.
Leaving behind the years of yearning for others
to see me as somebody,

I soften into becoming my future,
with permission from SELF to
continually unfold as I choose, without concern
for how others may see me.
Leaving behind years of telling and teaching,
I become instead a mirror
into which others can peer and
view reflections of themselves to consider.
Leaving behind the urge to provide answers for others,
I become—in the silence of this forest retreat
—the question.
Leaving behind the rigor of my intellect,
I become a single candle in the
darkness, offering myself as a beacon for others
to create their own path.
I become an elder.

I invite you now to honor our elders with me.

Invitation to Elders

I invite the people who think of themselves as elders in our community to please identify yourselves so that we may have the privilege of honoring you. Please come forward with the scarf from your seat, or stay in your seat and wave your scarf at us.

(Elders assemble at the front as they are able and willing, holding their scarves.)

Responsive Reading

(Distribute the statement of intention to the focus people; have a helper deliver copies to any who have stayed in their seats.)

Beloved elders, you have come before us this morning so that we, as a congregation, may honor you. I ask you to read aloud the following statement of intention.

ELDERS: I realize that I have attained a new stage of life and growth, that of a senior adult, an elder. I want to celebrate this, and I ask that you share this celebration with me.

LEADER: If you are willing to share in this celebration with our elders, I invite you to respond, "We are willing."

PARTICIPANTS: We are willing.

LEADER: Even in the earliest days, our ancestors knew that living meant changing. They gazed upon the skies and saw the moon rise, first as new, then as full, then drawing down into the dark. They marked with circles the path of the sun, and crossed the unmarked deserts and seas guided by the sparkling stars. As above, so below. They honored with rites of passage those among their kin who passed the mileposts of this life, with rites to honor birthing, coming of age, marriage, and elderhood.

Honored were the elders, those who held the wisdom of the people. They were the teachers, the healers, the diplomats, the sages, the wise ones, the interpreters of the mysteries. It was they who cared for and blessed the dying. It was they who showed in their living and their dying that all life continues, and that death is not to be feared.

Much of the power, recognition, and honor once given to older persons has been lost over time, and today many elders are almost invisible in our society. We will not allow that to happen to you, our own beloved elders. And so we acknowledge that we honor and respect all of our elders, and recognize their many gifts to us.

I ask each of our elders to now share your name and, if you wish, one legacy you wish to pass on.

(Elders speak in turn. Don't forget to invite any who have remained in their seats to speak as well; have a helper bring them a microphone.)

Everyone please join me in thanking them.

(You can either have participants read the unison responses in this section aloud or have them repeat each one line by line after you.)

PARTICIPANTS: Thank you for sharing your wisdom with us. We are honored to celebrate this stage of life with you. By your sharing, may we come to better understand our own lives.

LEADER [ADDRESSING ELDERS]: Entering this stage of life requires that you acknowledge the aspects of your life that are diminishing, the losses that age imposes. Each of you has been given a scarf. As you hold your scarf, take a few moments to consider what has impacted your life as you have grown older. Let your scarf be a tangible symbol of the losses imposed on you through aging. When you have all done this, I invite you to honor your losses together.

(Pause for a few moments, then invite the elders to recite.)

ELDERS: I lay down the appearance of youth, for gray hair and wrinkles are fast overtaking me. I lay down the energy and strength I once had and enjoyed, for the aches and pains of my age are making themselves felt now. I lay down the privilege I have enjoyed of thinking far into the future, dreaming of what I might become, for the days to come are fewer for me now, and I must seize what the present has to offer me.

(Elders lay their scarves on the table.)

PARTICIPANTS: We honor your strength, your wisdom, and your envisioning. By your sharing, may we come to better understand our own lives.

LEADER [ADDRESSING ELDERS]: As we honor your losses, so too we honor the new seeds you are yet planting for future harvest. And so I ask, what do you take up at this stage in your life? Please pick up a rose as you honor the things you gain.

(Each elder picks up a rose.)

ELDERS: I take up confidence, knowing that I have overcome many obstacles and survived many trials in my lifetime. Though none may know the measure of their days, I will move forward and be of help to others in my life. I take up optimism, knowing that there are many good days and good times to come, and I can make my corner of the world brighter and better for those whose lives I touch. I take up the wisdom that I have gained through the many life experiences that have influenced who I have become.

PARTICIPANTS: We honor your strength, your wisdom, and your envisioning. By your sharing, may we come to better understand our own lives.

LEADER [ADDRESSING CONGREGATION]: [If appropriate, begin with "When children are dedicated in this congregation we offer them a rose, as a symbol of their unfolding life and beauty."] You who are elders are now in full and glorious bloom. May this rose, symbol of the richness of your life experiences, remind you that every day you live, you leave a legacy. You have become the wild and unpredictable space within which flowers sprout and grow. We are honored to journey with you.

PARTICIPANTS: We will journey beside you in these elder years. We will offer you our support as you face your losses. We will rejoice in your wisdom. And we thank you for what you offer us through your presence in this community.

LEADER [ADDRESSING ELDERS]: You have chosen the meaning you will make of your aging. May you taste its sweetness in the coming years. We celebrate you today and honor you as elders of [name of congregation].

(Congregation applauds and elders go back to their seats.)

For Carrying Hope after Collective Loss

Heather Petit

There are times when holding hope for ourselves can feel impossibly difficult, and yet we can still hold hope for someone else. This may be especially true when a community has undergone a trauma—such as significant layoffs, a tragedy or injustice tied to an identity shared by many community members, or something else—that affects some community members in ways they prefer to keep private. This ritual allows us to offer our hopes for others to hold without naming them, and to collectively carry the hopes of each individual. It is not appropriate for communities that are experiencing significant issues of misconduct or breach of covenant.

Materials

- ☐ Altar table
- ☐ Chalice
- ☐ Small stones or other objects, at least one for each participant
- ☐ Bowl to hold the ritual objects
- ☐ Small fabric bags, baskets, or other containers for people who have difficulty holding small objects in their hands

Setup

The script is written assuming that you are using stones, but you can use any variety of small objects that all participants will be able to hold and touch: sea glass, crystals, large seeds, etc. Do not use objects that are all identical.

Arrange seats in a circle, with the altar table in the center where it can be accessed by all attendees. Put the bowl of stones on the altar. If accessing the altar may be difficult for some participants, recruit a helper to deliver stones as needed, and give them a smaller bowl to carry stones in.

Decide who will take the extra stones at the end of the ritual, to hold the hopes of those who contributed those stones. This might be you or another community leader or group.

Script

Chalice Lighting

Blessed Universe, Spirit of Life and Love and Hope,

May we know ourselves and each other as we are. We are beings with minds and hearts and spirits, with histories and relationships and senses. We all arrived here as ourselves, with every aspect of our being present, every identity, every bit of our humanity, with every concern and hope embodied.

Here in this beloved community, we are not just each ourselves—together we recognize our shared identity as members of this [community, congregation]. [If offering this ritual in a religious context, add "and we know that we are part of the living tradition of our faith that extends far beyond these walls."]

Today we each come bearing burdens and cares that are only ours to bear, and yet together we can take up the weight of these things for each other. We can as a community transform burdens into hope.

May it be so. Blessed be.

(Light the chalice.)

Opening Words

Today we will be holding hope for each other and sharing that hope collectively. We will not be speaking any of these hopes aloud, and yet some things may be too tender to be offered to collective care, even silently. Today may not be the day to offer a particular hope, but another hope may do. Likewise, today may not be the day for one or another of us to pick up a hope to carry for someone else. We may not have the focus or energy to offer to the task. The ebb and flow of each of those acts, for each of us, is unique. Feel free to participate in any part of this ritual as you are moved, knowing that you are welcome and included however you participate, in whatever ways you choose to be present.

Let us take a moment to enter this space.

(Allow several moments of quiet for people to settle in.)

Sharing Stones

Here in this bowl, there are smooth stones. We will each place a hope into one of these stones, and then each of us will take away a different stone, bearing the hope of another of us. Since some people may choose not to return their stones to the bowl, and some people may choose not to take away someone else's stone, any remaining stones will be taken by [Name] to be held—no hope will be left untended.

I invite each of you to come up and pick a stone from the bowl. If you prefer, we will bring some to you for you to choose. Just raise your hand, and a helper will come to you.

(Each person takes a stone.)

Hold in your heart something that is troubling you, or that is difficult or worrisome or simply is too much to deal with right now.

(Pause for several moments.)

Now think of a hope that would lift that burden, something that would ease the weight, resolve the problem, tend the heartache, begin to bring you fully into yourself with joy and satisfaction and courage once again. If you have no words, no names, no way to formulate this in your mind or heart, then just feel the longing, the yearning to be more at ease in the ongoing work of being human, alive, and present to all that is our lives.

(Pause for several moments.)

I now invite you to place this newly formed hope or longing into the stone. Let it soak in, until it is held fully in the shape of the stone.

(Indicate by gesture the stones left in the bowl.)

While you place your hope into the stone you hold, I will place hope for myself, this community, and our larger communities in the world into the stones that remain in the bowl. [If you are holding this ritual in response to a particular event, adapt this line to speak specifically about it.]

(Touch the stones, hold your open palms over them, or in some other way show that you are symbolically placing hope into them. Pause again for several moments to give everyone time to finish.)

I now invite you all to return your stones to the bowl, as you choose. If you wish to keep yours to hold for yourself, that is entirely welcome. If you raise your hand, a helper will come collect your stone and bring it to the bowl, or you can come forward to return it yourself.

(Wait until everyone who wishes to has returned their stones.)

Our collective hopes are . . . here.

(Gently stir the stones in the bowl.)

I now invite us each to take a different stone back out, as we choose. You may not feel able to hold someone else's hope today, even if you put yours into the bowl to be held. That is entirely okay. If you do want to take one, you can raise your hand and a helper will bring some stones to you for you to choose, or you can come forward now.

(Each person who wishes to takes a stone.)

If you are holding a stone, look at it now. Feel the shape and weight of it. This represents a hope either in someone else's heart or in your own.

Whether or not you are holding a stone yourself, look around at each of us, at all of us. Whether or not you are holding a stone, you are part of this community that has shared its burdens and hopes with one another. Take a moment to breathe gently. See, hear, feel our collective presence, all of us together, each of us with hopes we have for ourselves, each of us choosing where our hope is best held, each of us choosing to witness or to take up the hopes of others, all of us right where we should be.

The hopes we held alone in our hearts just a few moments ago are now held in community, together.

If you are holding a stone, I invite you to take it home with you. Place it somewhere you can see it throughout the next week, so that you can be reminded to hold up that unknown and unspoken hope for another or for yourself. If you have chosen not to take a stone today, know that your hope will be well tended, and allow yourself the comfort of knowing that all these hopes are well held.

Individually, we all have difficulties.

Together, we are all upheld.

Song

"From You I Receive" (Joseph Segal and Nathan Segal)

(Lead participants in singing.)

Chalice Extinguishing

When we are hurting
In any of the ways we hurt
Brokenhearted or worn down

When that thing that bothers us
Seems like too little to mention
Or far too much to share

Especially when everyone else
has their troubles and cares
And we don't like to be a burden

May we remember that hard things—
Little difficulties and major challenges—
When met with loving community
Transform into hope
And hope is not a burden at all.

(Extinguish the chalice.)

For Honoring Our Connection to Water

Liz James and Kathryn Green

This ritual can be used by a group of any size to acknowledge our spiritual and bodily connection to water and honor the central importance of water to life. It could be part of a congregational worship service on water, e.g., to celebrate World Water Day, an annual United Nations observance day held on March 22. It was created by the authors for such a service in their congregation, the Saskatoon Unitarians, in Saskatchewan, Canada.

Materials

- ☐ Altar table
- ☐ Chalice
- ☐ Several bowls of water, one of them small enough to be carried to participants
- ☐ Tables, one for each of the larger water bowls
- ☐ Recorded water sounds or video

Setup

This ritual can be performed in any indoor space that is suitable for the size of the group, or outdoors. You can use a choir and soloist, a song leader and accompanist, or recorded music.

Place the chalice on the altar table, and one of the larger bowls of water on each of the other tables. You will staff one water station; recruit helpers to staff the others, and another helper to carry the smaller bowl to any participants who prefer not to come forward. (If you have a small group, use only one large water bowl, placing it on the altar table with the chalice.)

Script

Chalice Lighting

We do not fight for the water.

Even when we act as water keepers, we are not brave warriors stepping between the gun and its target, saving something outside ourselves.

We are the water. We are a tiny piece in its journey through this world, and when it breaks we break, and when it sings we sing.

And when we fight for it, we are fighting for ourselves.
When we protect it, we are protecting ourselves.
And when we love it,
when we are filled with an awe so wide that it feels
like a soul gasp that reaches right to our toes,
we are loving ourselves

unfolding in our knowledge that this world is a miracle
and we are miracles
and that we
and it
deserve to be safe.

(Light the chalice.)

Reading

(Adapted from Rev. Anne Barker)

All water is holy water
From the sky or from the sea or from the tap
It is not holy because we bless it
It is not holy because we gather with it in reverence
It is holy because it is the stuff of life
Its movement in our veins is part of a larger stream
That comes from sources that stretch farther back than history

And stretches into a future that reaches farther forward than imagination
And its place in us
Makes us a part of that great story

Song

"The River" (Coco Love Alcorn)

(Lead participants in singing, have the choir sing, or play the recording.)

Opening Words

Most of our planet is covered with water, and most of our body is made up of water. The molecules of water that are in us have already been in and out of countless living things, perhaps in every form of life that has ever lived on earth. Through water we are bound together with everything else that lives, everything that has lived, and everything that will live.

Water's essential role in life has always been understood by human beings, and so it is not surprising that water is a virtually universal element in religious and spiritual traditions. It is used as a metaphor and in narratives and rituals: giving life, blessing, cleansing, and protecting. Indigenous worldviews recognize water as the lifeblood of Mother Earth, with the power to create life and to destroy it. Water is a living spiritual force that we exist in relationship with; it is not just a resource for us to use as we will.

The water blessing that you are invited to take part in today reflects the inherently sacred nature of water. Water does not need our blessing; rather, we are blessed by water's existence in our world, and in our very bodies.

In a moment, you will hear several simple songs. You are welcome to sing along! After we sing for a bit, my helpers and I will go to the water stations.

[Indicate the location of each station.]

If you'd like to receive a water blessing, come to a water station, or raise a hand and we will come to you. We will touch your forehead with a drop of water. If you'd prefer to have your hands blessed, just hold them out like this [demonstrate]—whatever feels right. Then we'll put a hand on your shoulder and speak the blessing. Step back when you are ready. If you don't remember the instructions, don't worry. You can hold back and watch others first.

Music

Three Water Chants

(The choir or song leader sings each of these chants several times, with the congregation invited to join in as they feel comfortable. You may wish to provide lyrics. The singing should continue until everyone has had a chance to participate in the water blessing.)

Water moving through the world
Wetland, stream, and flood
Water moving through me
Breath and bone and blood

Holy water, flowing free
From the mountains to the sea
From the rain clouds to the ground
Holy water, all around

In a dance of air and sky
Rain we fall and waves we rise

Anointing

(After singing for a while, you and your helpers go to the water stations and, with a silent gesture, invite participants to come forward. Another helper watches for people who have raised their hands and brings the smaller bowl of water to them. Anoint each participant's forehead or hands with a drop of water, and then place one hand on their shoulder while you say the blessing.)

With this water, you are blessed.

(Musicians should be invited to participate in the ritual too, timing their participation so that the singing can continue without interruption. After most people have come forward for the blessing, start playing a video or audio recording of moving water, and continue to play it as the singing fades out. Allow everyone to quietly take in the sounds, and perhaps images, of the water for a few moments.)

Chalice Extinguishing

You are blessed
In your stillness

And in your wildness, too
In the rush of current that will carry you
Through the muck and mud puddles of living

You are part of a larger story
You are blessed

(Extinguish the chalice. As the chalice is extinguished, play or have a soloist sing the following excerpt from "The River.")

Water heal my body,
Water heal my soul,
When I go down down to the water
By the water I feel whole.

Three Water Chants

Words by Kathryn L. Green & Liz James, music by Kathryn L. Green

Sing each chant as many times as needed, flowing from one section to the next. To end, you may wish to repeat the last line ("Rain we fall and waves we rise") twice.

For Saying Goodbye to a Sacred Space

Rev. Tricia Brennan

This ritual is designed for congregations who are demolishing a part or all of their building, and it can be adapted for the sale of a building as well. It is appropriate for multigenerational groups.

The author is grateful to Louise Marcoux, former director of religious education at the Unitarian Church of Sharon, Mass., with whom she created a number of rituals, including a version of this one.

Materials

- ☐ Chalice
- ☐ Markers of many colors
- ☐ Newsprint (if the building is being sold)
- ☐ Food and drink
- ☐ Small objects to pass while speaking, such as stones, flowers, or ornaments
- ☐ Music

Setup

Arrange several circles of six to eight chairs each, enough for the number of people you anticipate. Depending on who you expect, you may need small chairs for children, or spaces left open for a wheelchair. Put one of the ritual objects in each circle.

Decide which walls you will invite people to write and draw on. If the building is being sold and shouldn't be marked up, cover those walls with newsprint. Set out some simple food and drink.

Often a building is being sold or massively renovated because it is not accessible. If accessibility is a problem in your space, try to find ways for anyone who cannot physically access the ritual to participate if they want to. They might ask someone else to share their memories for them in the ritual, or draw or write something in advance that can be taped to the wall, or participate virtually.

Script

Chalice Lighting

This building we are in is made of wood and stone, concrete and glass. Its physicality is apparent. Yet what we don't see and can't touch, yet know well, are the countless memories contained here. We light this chalice in gratitude for all that has been in this space and for this time of remembrance we now will share.

(Light the chalice.)

Opening Words

Welcome, everyone. I am so glad you are able to be here as we gather to remember, share, and say goodbye to this [name of building].

Let us begin by recognizing that before there was a church here on this land, and before we were here, the [name of Indigenous people] lived, worked, played, celebrated, worshipped, and died in this region. We and this faith community, [name], came later. [If your community has a standard land acknowledgment, you could use it here instead.]

We gather together knowing that this building, which holds many memories for us, will soon be gone. We let it go so that our congregation's vision of our future can come into being. Sometimes, oftentimes, we can only move forward into our fullness when we let go of things that no longer serve us well. Still, the letting go is a loss. Our time together will make space for that loss, as well as space for gratitude for the many moments of meaning that have occurred within these walls.

Our ritual of remembrance will have time for you to be alone and time to be together. There are three parts to this ritual: moving through the space, writing on the walls, and sharing stories.

Moving through the Space, Moving through Time

First is a quiet journey through the building, letting the building speak to you of what you have experienced here. Go at your own pace, and go wherever you want. You can move through alone or with a friend or family member. If you want to go with others, keep your conversation to a minimum, and speak softly so as not to disturb the remembrances of those nearby. We will gather back here in fifteen minutes. Before journeying, let us sing together "Return Again."

Song

"Return Again" (Shlomo Carlebach)

(Lead participants in singing the song three or four times. Then allow fifteen minutes for people to move through the building. Once everyone has regathered, continue.)

Writing on the Wall

(Adapt these instructions if you have posted newsprint on the walls because the building is being sold and shouldn't be marked up.)

Does the idea of writing on a wall intrigue you? We now will get to do something that usually is forbidden, but today is just right. Choose a marker or two and write or draw whatever you want on this wall that has stood the test of time but soon will be no more. Memories from this place, prayers, names of people you've known in this community, pictures, hopes for the future. All are encouraged. Know that before the building comes down, we will take photos of what is remembered here, as part of the congregation's memory treasure trove. We will have fifteen minutes for this drawing and writing. When you're done, help yourself to something to drink or eat, and take a seat in one of the chairs.

(As people write, have quiet music playing.)

(Once everyone has finished writing, invite them to sing. If people are taking a very long time or their attention has wandered, you could also use the song as a way to gather them.)

Song

"Come Sing a Song with Me" (Carolyn McDade)

(Lead participants in singing.)

Sharing Memories

It is good to remember. It is good to capture those memories in writing and pictures. And it is good to listen to and share memories and feelings. When our stories are heard by another, we are listened into a deeper sense of ourselves. When we listen to another's words, we learn a bit more about the other person, and sometimes find ourselves in their story too. We come to know one another's minds.

We will have thirty minutes to share memories of your time in this building. In each circle of chairs there is a small object—a stone, flower, or ornament—that can be held by each speaker. While that person holds it, the others in the circle should just listen, deeply and caringly. Someone can start, and then pass the object to the person beside them when they're finished. No one needs to speak if they don't want to. I will let you know when there are ten minutes left.

(Allow thirty minutes for sharing, giving participants a signal when there are ten minutes left and again when it is time to wrap up.)

Closing Words

I invite you all to gather in a large circle, standing or seated, as you prefer.

This has been a rich time of remembering and sharing, a time when I suspect that events, services, conversations, and people came to mind, perhaps from long ago. You may have laughed, you may have cried, you may have felt angry or grateful or pensive. All feelings, all memories are worthy and honored.

As we close, I'd ask that we go around the room and each person who wants to can say one or two words that capture a feeling you have, a meaningful memory, a person, an event. Let the chorus of our words be our final prayer.

(Allow participants to share one or two words. In a larger group, this sharing could be done popcorn style instead of around the circle.)

Song

"Part in Peace" (Sarah Flower Adams)

(Lead participants in singing.)

Chalice Extinguishing

(The last two lines of this passage are attributed to Dag Hammarsköld.)

What is new emerges from what has been.
What once was never fully leaves us.
Still, it is the old that gives way for the new.
For all that has been, Thank You.
For all that is to come, Yes!

(Extinguish the chalice.)

For Breaking Ground on a Building Project

Rev. Tricia Brennan

Breaking ground for a new congregational building can be a time of excitement, fatigue, and hope. This is a multigenerational ritual consisting of two parts, each of which can be used on its own. The first part seeks to place the project in the context of previous building losses, changes, and rebuilds and can be done as part of a congregational worship service, during the time usually reserved for a Time for All Ages or other child-friendly element. The second part seeks to nourish the hopes of the congregation as the new build is about to start and can be done immediately after the end of a congregational worship service, as the congregation processes out to where the new build will happen. Both emphasize what congregations can accomplish by dreaming and working together. The ritual should be led by a minister, religious educator, or lay leader, ideally someone involved in the building project.

The ritual assumes that the new building will be close to the current one. If people will need time, and possibly transportation provided, to get from the old location to the new one, adapt it accordingly.

The author is grateful to Louise Marcoux, former director of religious education at the Unitarian Church of Sharon, Mass., with whom she created a number of rituals, including a version of this one.

Materials
- ☐ Children's building blocks, approximately 30–40 of various sizes, divided among four baskets that children can carry
- ☐ Table for the building blocks
- ☐ Photos of the congregation's previous buildings, if possible

☐ Two medium to large bowls of water (If this ritual is being done in a Unitarian Universalist congregation, Water Communion water would be appropriate to use)

☐ Small paper cups, at least one for each participant

☐ Two ladles to fill the cups with

☐ Two sturdy tables for the bowls of water

Setup

Congregations with long histories have typically bought, sold, renovated, and lost buildings along the way. They might have experienced a fire or other trauma, chosen or been forced to move, or have flourished to the point that they needed to buy or remodel a building to accommodate their growth. Knowing as much as you can about this history will enable you to make this ritual deeper and richer. The script is written with some specific historical events; adapt and personalize it to speak to the circumstances and history of your congregation.

This ritual requires fourteen or more helpers, depending on the congregation's history. You may want to recruit and brief some or all of them ahead of time, or call for some or all of them to volunteer in the moment, depending on the culture and flexibility of your congregation. You will need:

- Four children, to bring the baskets of blocks forward in the service
- People of a range of ages to build models with the blocks, in one or more groups of four
- Two adult helpers, ideally leaders of the building project, to hold the bowls of water for the blessing and carry them outside during the recessional
- Four other adult or older teen helpers, to carry the cups outside and assist with the outdoor water ritual

Before the worship service starts, mark off the perimeter of the new build, perhaps by digging a narrow trough or laying out colorful cord or ribbon, and set up the two tables for the bowls of water outside. Ideally, place them at opposite ends of the new build's perimeter, making sure to allow for an easy flow of people coming to get cups of water and pouring them around the perimeter.

A building project is often sparked by the old building's lack of accessibility. Though outside events may be more accessible, be sure that appropriate seating is available for those who need a seat, and an accessible path is evident.

Put the table for the building blocks at the front of the worship space, allowing space for four people to stand around it. You may want to provide stools to stand or sit on. Put the two bowls of water somewhere out of the way but accessible in the worship space. If you have photos of previous buildings, display them or place them where you can easily hold them up to be seen.

Script

Building Our Past and Future

Would [names of child helpers] please bring up their baskets of blocks which we will use today? You can place them by the table on the altar. Thank you.

(The children bring up the baskets and then join the rest of the congregation.)

As we all know, we are soon going to start building our new [name of new space]. This is a very exciting time for us! Can anyone say why we are doing this?

(Invite responses from participants.)

This may be the only time many of us here can remember this sort of big change happening in our community, but in fact it is not the first time.

Before we talk about that, though, I want us to remember that before there was a church on this land, and before anyone who was a part of this [name of congregation] was alive, there were people living here. Can someone tell me the name of the Indigenous people living here? That's right. Long before we or even our great-great-grandparents were here, the [name of Indigenous people] lived, worked, played, celebrated, built homes, worshipped, and died in this region. We and this faith community, [name], came later. [If your community has a standard land acknowledgment, you could use it here instead.]

Here is a picture of the very first church building of the [name of congregation]. I bet someone here knows the year this congregation was founded and the church you see was built.

(Listen for or supply the year.)

Can our first four volunteers come forward and work together, using the blocks, to make something that looks like this church? You have three minutes! While they work, let's remember what we know about our church back then.

(As the volunteers come forward and start working, guide other participants in discussing things like the name of the first minister, the number of people in the first congregation, where its first building stood, and so on. After three minutes, or whenever the volunteers finish their work, wrap up the conversation.)

Good work, builders! You can return to your seats, thank you.

Now, churches can be built using all kinds of materials, like brick, stone, wood, steel, clay; it all depends on what is available in the area. Here where we live, there were lots of trees, so churches were generally built of wood. And that means that churches in this area were often destroyed by—what? Yes, that's right, fires. The original church, built in [year], sadly was lost in a fire in [year]. Can I have four more volunteers come up to take down this building and build the next church building as we tell that part of our story? You have three minutes! Here is a picture of the next church building, constructed after the fire, that you can use as a guide.

(As the volunteers come forward and start working, use questions like the following to prompt more discussion among the other participants.)

How do you think the members of [name of congregation] felt when their church burnt down? Do you think they ever thought of just giving up and not having a church anymore? What do you think kept them going?

We do know that they worked together to create something new after they lost their first church. When people work together, each taking a piece of the work—just like these four volunteers are working together, and like all the many, many volunteers today are working together on our new building project—it is amazing what can happen!

(After three minutes, or whenever the volunteers finish their work, wrap up the conversation.)

Hey, good work, builders! Thank you. You can return to your seats.

(If the congregation has had many homes, then you may want to discuss more of them, as time allows, before moving on to the current build. Show a picture of the project.)

Now here's a picture that probably looks familiar to you—what is it?

(Allow a moment for responses.)

That's right. It is the design of the new [name of build] that we are just about to start building. Can we have four more volunteers to come up and do their best to alter what is here to make it look like what we will soon have? You will have three minutes!

(Continue speaking as the volunteers come forward and start working.)

You know, you have to really want to have a new building to go through all the work to make it happen. You have to have a powerful vision of what you believe your community can become with that new space. Can I hear from three people, in just one or two sentences, why they really want this new building to be built?

(Invite answers from the congregation and name again the originating vision. After three minutes, or whenever the volunteers finish their work, wrap up the conversation.)

All right, take a look at what this group of builders created in just three minutes! Give them a hand! Thank you! As our builders sit down, please join in singing "We Are Building a New Way."

Song

"We Are Building a New Way" (Martha Sandefer)

(Lead participants in singing. Once the song is over, the worship service continues as usual.)

Blessing Our Future

(At the close of the worship service, two of the leaders of the building project bring the two bowls of water forward. They are joined by the last four adult or teen volunteers. All six should stand in front of or beside you, facing the congregation.)

In a moment, I will offer a prayer over this water, which we will use to bless the perimeter of the new building.

But first we will sing our final hymn, "Sing Out Praises for the Journey." We will sing the first verse here in this space together.

Then [names of the two people holding the bowls of water], the other helpers, and I will exit as we sing the second verse. [Name 1] will go to one end of the perimeter and [Name 2] will go to the other end, each joined by two helpers.

Everyone else, please recess out while you are singing the third verse.

Once outside, please go to one of the two teams of water carriers, who will give you a cup of water. Bring your water to a spot on the perimeter, and take a moment to think of your hopes for this new building, and your vision for our congregation's future. Then thoughtfully pour the water in your cup on the perimeter, blessing what is to come.

(Add instructions about what they should do after they are done, such as come back inside for fellowship hour.)

And now I bless this water that we will use to bless our hopes and plans.

Spirit of Life, found in this water here and water everywhere,
found in this congregation's desire for [name the originating vision],
found in the dreams and hopes of people everywhere who yearn
for justice and freedom for all,
for care of the earth and its creatures,
for love of our children and all children,
bless this water in these bowls, and bless the work we feel called to do,
here, together, in this community.

We are not perfect and we may make mistakes,
but like our forebears we choose to work together,
we choose love,
we choose to move forward in faith, adding what is ours to give
to make our world better for all.

And let the people say amen.

Song

"Sing Out Praises for the Journey" (Mark M. DeWolfe)

(Go outside with the helpers, followed by the congregation, as described above.)

For Blessing a New or Renovated Church Building

Rev. Tricia Brennan

The completion of a building project marks both the end of a long journey for a congregation and the beginning of a new phase in the congregation's life as it lives into the new space and the hopes it holds. This ritual is intended for the congregation itself and differs from a more public building dedication. It can be done as part of or after a congregational worship service, or at any other time.

This ritual was created for a substantial renovation of a building. It occurs in three locations: a threshold and two spaces within large enough to hold all participants. Adaptions can be made based on the layout of a congregation's buildings and the new space being blessed.

The author is grateful to Louise Marcoux, former director of religious education at the Unitarian Church of Sharon, Mass., with whom she created a number of rituals, including a version of this one.

Materials

- ☐ Chalice (one that can be carried around)
- ☐ Long-stemmed flowers, one for each participant
- ☐ Vases, twice as many as needed to hold all the flowers
- ☐ Three tables: two large enough to hold the chalice and half of the vases, one large enough for the chalice only
- ☐ Copies of the responsive reading and final hymn

Setup

Outside the threshold to the new space, place a table with the chalice and half of the vases. Put enough long-stemmed flowers for all participants in the vases.

Place a table for the chalice in the location of the first stop in the building.

Set the third table up in the space where the ritual will end, with the other half of the vases and room for the chalice. If possible, arrange chairs in a circle and put the table in its center. Put copies of the responsive reading and final hymn somewhere easily accessible, such as on the chairs or on another table that participants will pass as they enter.

Choose four readers to give different perspectives on the building project. Look for a variety of voices: a youth, an elder, a parent, a choir member, a member of the project committee, a staff person whose work relates to the project's purpose, a benefactor, someone who can articulate the justice aspect of the build, etc. Adapt the readings to suit their particular standpoints and views.

Recruit a helper to carry the chalice. Recruit song leaders to lead the participants in singing "Come and Go with Me" as they walk through the building. You may want to carry a portable sound system or set up amplification at each of the three locations of the ritual.

Script

(Begin the ritual outside the new or renovated space, at the threshold.)

Chalice Lighting

(William Schulz)

Come into this place of peace
And let its silence heal your spirit;
Come into this place of memory
And let its history warm your soul;
Come into this place of prophecy and power
And let its vision change its heart.

(Light the chalice.)

Opening Words

Today is a glorious day.

An incalculable amount of work went into creating this new space;

It truly has been the work of many hands.

Take a breath, look at [name of new build] in all its loveliness

and with all its hopes for the future, and let yourself feel proud.

(Pause to allow participants to look around.)

Today our congregation will bless our [name of new build].

We will bless it with our prayers, intentions, and silence.

We will bless it with the beauty of flowers and song, and with our presence.

It is right that we first acknowledge that before there was a church here on this land, and before we were here, the [name of Indigenous people] lived, worked, played, celebrated, worshipped, and died in this region. We and this faith community, [name], came later. [If your community has a standard land acknowledgment, you could use it here instead.]

We stand here at the entrance, the threshold of this new space.

Thresholds are places of power and intention,

and as part of our blessing today

we will bring our highest and deepest intentions to this moment.

We will sing "Enter, Rejoice, and Come In," a perfect hymn for this moment! After each of the first four verses, a member of the congregation will come forward, take a flower from the vase here, and briefly share an intention for this new building. Then they will mindfully cross the threshold.

After we all sing the fifth verse, everyone please take a flower and likewise cross the threshold into the [new space], bringing to mind and heart your intention, your hope, your prayer for what we have collectively created. Led by [Name] with our chalice, we will process through the building and gather in [location].

Words and Song

(Lead participants in singing verse 1 of "Enter, Rejoice, and Come In." Then the first speaker comes forward and takes a flower.)

SPEAKER 1: Many, many people shared in the adventure of creating this new building, including some who have died. As a young person I am especially grateful, because they worked to create something that they would not live to see, a place that those of my generation will enjoy for many long years. Truly that is a testament of love. Let us remember [names of those who have died].

(The first speaker crosses the threshold into the new space.)

(Lead participants in singing verse 2 of "Enter, Rejoice, and Come In." Then the second speaker comes forward and takes a flower.)

SPEAKER 2: We do indeed, all of us, build for the future. We who are older hold such hope for the future of this congregation which has been a meaningful part of our lives, sometimes for decades. I cross this threshold holding this freshly flowering bud, with hope that within these walls a diverse array of humanity will grow closer to one another and to the Spirit that holds us all.

(The second speaker crosses the threshold.)

(Lead participants in singing verse 3 of "Enter, Rejoice, and Come In." Then the third speaker comes forward and takes a flower.)

SPEAKER 3: I remember well the meeting where we decided to undertake this project. [Name the moment and vision that sparked it.] The power of that collective decision fueled our work through all the time since. May we continue to be a community where all are welcome; may we continue to work for a world where no one is left out.

(The third speaker crosses the threshold.)

(Lead participants in singing verse 4 of "Enter, Rejoice, and Come In." Then the fourth speaker comes forward and takes a flower)

SPEAKER 4: As beautiful as this new [space] is, more beautiful still is the community of faith that sustains us. I cross this threshold grateful for the commitment to right relations that guided our work, mindful that though we did slip up occasionally we chose to stay in relationship to work things out. May we continue this spiritual practice always.

(The fourth speaker crosses the threshold.)

(Lead participants in singing verse 5 of "Enter, Rejoice, and Come In." Then a helper picks up the chalice and leads the participants across the threshold and to the first location. The leader guides each person to take a flower as they pass the table. The leader brings up the rear, taking a flower as well. Once everyone arrives at the first stop, the leader makes their way to the table where the helper has placed the chalice and offers a prayer.)

Prayer

O Spirit of Love and Life,
You who teach us about justice and love,
It was many years ago when this congregation
awoke to its desire for [name the originating vision].
Today we mark the occasion
when that desire has been realized.
In joy do we gather and process and sing and pray.
For it has been a long and sometimes uncertain road
and we are happy to have seen our work through to completion.

We pray today that the originating spark that gave rise to our project
continues to animate this congregation.
For our work is done and our work is not done.
Now the [new space]
is here and it is beautiful.
Now, too, we seek to deepen our commitment to love and justice.

We know there are countless ways to do this,
some tangible and others less apparent yet still real:
the growth of our hearts, our spirits, our consciousness.
As we live into our future, help us to wisely use our time, energy, and resources,
listening closely to your voice,
listening closely to the voices of our children, our neighbors, and the earth,
observing the signs of our times.

Today is a day for celebration, for appreciation, for joy!
And tomorrow calls us forth to new challenges, new visions,
new partnerships, new risks, and new learnings.
May the joy of today give us the courage to meet what tomorrow shall ask of us.

Blessed be what is and what shall be. Amen.

As we process to [the final location], let us sing together "Come and Go with Me." Once there, please place your flower in the vase on the table and find a seat. (If copies of the responsive reading are not already placed on the chairs, add instructions about where to pick them up.)

Song

"Come and Go with Me" (African American spiritual)

The group sings and walks toward the location of the ritual's conclusion. The song leaders can spread themselves out through the group to assist in singing the hymn. Wait until everyone has gathered there before continuing.)

Responsive Reading

Please join me in a responsive reading.

"A Place of Meeting" (Eileen Karpeles)

Out of wood and stone, out of dream and sacrifice,
the people build a home.

PARTICIPANTS: Out of the work of their hands and hearts and minds,
the people fashion a symbol and a reality.

LEADER: May this house be truly a place of meeting:
meeting in warmth and joy and openness;
meeting in courage and love and trust.

PARTICIPANTS: May all who enter here trust one another so surely
that they may share the deep fires
that burst into anger
as much as the sweet spring waters
that swell into laughter;
the slow erosion of wounded tears
as much as the soaring song.

LEADER: May these walls know silence
as a hundred hearts search inward,
each for its own small spark of hope
that might otherwise be snuffed out in the noise.

PARTICIPANTS: May these rafters hear the voice of the child
as surely as that of the orator
and the sound of the lute
and the clack of the typewriter
and the swish of the broom
and know that all are as holy
as the shout of a million stars.

LEADER: May the rain fall lightly on this house
and the sun shine warmly
and the winds blow softly
and bless it
as a place of joy and peace.

Song

"We Are Building a New Way" (Martha Sandefer)

(Lead participants in singing.)

Chalice Extinguishing

Knowing we are here but for a moment in time,
And without each other we accomplish very little,
And without love our achievements are hollow,
Let us use our days well for the earth and our children,
Attuned to life's beauty and responsive to need,
Till the rafters on high cannot hold our joy,
and the beloved community belongs to all.

(Extinguish the chalice.)

Our chalice is extinguished and we have blessed this new space.
Let us go in peace.

For the Days following a Natural Disaster

Rev. Nathan Ryan and Rev. Steve J. Crump

This ritual is for a congregational worship service immediately following a natural disaster. It was created for the Sunday after an unprecedented and catastrophic rainfall in Baton Rouge, La., in 2016 that flooded seventy church families.

Materials

☐ Chalice

Setup

Just be in the space. It can be tempting to try and make something perfect after a major disaster. This is natural. When you can't control the thing that has caused you and your community so much pain, it's natural to try to control something else. Just remember that you can't make things perfect or fix what has happened. All they need from you is to be with them; all they need from one another is to be together. Try to keep this service as simple as possible. Even though you may be looking for a ritual, remember that just being together is the ritual.

Bear in mind that not everyone will be able to be with you. If you have a working phone signal or Internet connection, try to stream the service. If not, keep notes of what was said to send to members of the congregation who couldn't get there.

People usually want to fill this service with content—theorizing, sermonizing, educating, and other kinds of intellectual engagement. Don't. People may not be ready for this type of engagement so soon. Be together. Sing. Share silence. Sing some more. Create just enough structure for people to have a space for their heartache. Also, try to have this service match the regular Sunday liturgy as closely as possible. People will want something that feels normal.

Script

Opening Words

Come into this place.

Come into this place that is safe.

Come into this place as broken as you are right now.

Bring in the truth that you are enough.

Bring in the truth that you are safe here.

Don't leave your fears and worries at the door. Tell them they can sit next to you, but they should be quiet for this hour.

Come into this space that is here for you—all of you.

Come let us be together, a broken together people.

Song

(When this service was held after a rain event, the authors used "I Can See Clearly Now" by Johnny Nash for the first song. For a different type of natural disaster, consider a more relevant song that is hopeful and upbeat.)

Chalice Lighting

Take the long view.

Know, not exactly how, but that we will get through.

Take the long view.

Know what you feel now.

Know, also, that outlooks and feelings change anew. They do.

Take the long view. Look around and know that we are not alone.

Give and receive.

Help and be helped.

Breathe in and out.

Take the long view. Know, not exactly how, but that we will get through.

In that spirit we light this chalice.

(Light the chalice.)

Song

"Winds Be Still" (Richard S. Kimball)

(Lead participants in singing.)

Reading

That Voice (Steve J. Crump)

When things go down or seem to fail or really fail,
Or collapse, or seem to fall to pieces, or really do,
Some things stay in the ditch and it's best to leave them there.
Pronounce them ditched.

But maybe not all things. Not everything.
A voice might tell you the difference.
Some things we ought not try to fix, retrieve, or mend.
A voice could tell us how to choose.

Oh, there will be a clamoring for your attention.
Some will say, "Hey, another door opens."
Many will say, "It all works out in the end."
And there are those pop song lyrics, "Time will heal,"
and "This pain will make you stronger."

Job had his so-called comforters also.
You wonder what Ozymandias would say, but he doesn't call.
When the comforters exit stage right, there remains a voice of a friend
or your own solitary voice. Yes, that voice.

If only folk would speak the truth of the matter: "This is the way life goes.
Life is just as likely to be served up on a plate of absurdity as not."
There is a voice that speaks the truth, and that voice gets us home.
Yes, that voice.

Music

(Play some reflective music designed to give people time to process.)

Prayer

God that we know when we see love and compassion,

Be with us on this day.

Hold all those aching hearts, all those afraid.

Hold all those who lost their things.

Hold all those who lost their safety.

Hold all those who lost loved ones.

Help us to know that no matter how hard things are, we are not alone.

Help us to know that this is not your plan.

Help us to look for you in the help, in the hope.

Help us to transform this heartbreak.

Help make us into beacons of hope.

Help us use this tragedy to make this world more loving and more compassionate.

Amen.

Song

"Filled with Loving Kindness" (traditional Buddhist meditation, words adapted by Mark W. Hayes, music by Ian W. Riddell)

(Lead participants in singing.)

Litany of Connection

Please join in a litany of connection. After each line, respond by saying, "We are not alone."

No matter how afraid you are—

PARTICIPANTS: We are not alone.

LEADER: No matter how damaged you are—

PARTICIPANTS: We are not alone.

LEADER: Even with your fears and worries—

PARTICIPANTS: We are not alone.

LEADER: As you go into this uncertain world, back to your uncertain homes—

PARTICIPANTS: We are not alone.

LEADER: As you try to pick your life up again—

PARTICIPANTS: We are not alone.

LEADER: Go back into this world that isn't fixed, isn't ready, isn't what we were promised. Go back into this world knowing that you carry with you a deep and holy truth—

PARTICIPANTS: We are not alone.

Song

"There Is More Love Somewhere" (African American spiritual)

(Lead participants in singing.)

Chalice Extinguishing

It is time to go back.
It is time for us to leave this sanctuary.
It is time for you to pick back up your fears and worries. They are not your enemy.
They are reminders of what you might have lost, or what a world you might build could look like.
It is time for you to bring some of this sanctuary back to your world.
Go share your love.
Go share your hope.
Go out knowing that no matter what happens,
You are not alone.

(Extinguish the chalice.)

For the End of a Natural Disaster Season

Rev. Nathan Ryan

This ritual is for a congregational worship service once the seasonal threat of natural disasters is over: for example, at the end of hurricane season, fire season, or a terrible winter. The author held a version of it after a terrible hurricane season in Baton Rouge came to an end.

Materials

- ☐ Altar table
- ☐ Chalice
- ☐ Small pieces of flash paper or dissolving paper
- ☐ Way to destroy the paper (bowl of water or a safely contained fire)
- ☐ Pens
- ☐ Items representing the recent threat
- ☐ Basket
- ☐ Music suiting the recent threat

Setup

Set up the worship space as usual. Put the basket and ritual items on the altar table. If it's the end of hurricane season, for example, you might use a storm lantern, an umbrella, and a crumpled hurricane tracker map.

Set up the mechanics of destroying the paper ahead of time. Distribute the small sheets of paper and pens as people enter the space.

If people with limited mobility can't access the altar, recruit a helper to collect their papers.

This service was designed to be imbued with a small amount of indignant irreverence, to give people permission to be exasperated by what they experienced. The author has found that if it's done with a respectfully contemplative overtone, the humor empowers the congregation in surprising ways.

Script

Opening Words

Today is holy.
It is made holy by your presence.
It is made holy by our presence.
If you are willing to join together in this holy space, please say, "We are."

PARTICIPANTS: We are.

LEADER: Are you willing to create a space for collective healing from whatever harm you have borne?

PARTICIPANTS: We are.

LEADER: Are you hoping to mark an end to what was and be open to what is yet to come?

PARTICIPANTS: We are.

LEADER: Then let us join together and be open to the innate divine that is already surrounding us.
Let it find open hearts and healing souls.
Come, let us worship.

Song

"Come, Come, Whoever You Are" (words by Rumi, music by Lynn Adair Ungar)

Chalice Lighting

Today we light this flame

As a marker of the end of a terrible season,

As a reminder that no matter how cold or wet or terrible it is,

There is still light.

You are still light.

We are still light.

We are stronger kindled together.

(Light the chalice.)

Invitation to Naming

Naming is spiritually important. It takes something ambiguous and abstract, like a storm, and makes it concrete. It gives us something to wrestle with.

More often than not, a weather event goes unnamed. Without a name we may struggle to properly grieve or move forward. We need a way to acknowledge what we just experienced.

You've probably already named this weather event a thousand different names—not all church appropriate. I invite you to take the small sheets of paper you were given when you entered and write down one name for what we just experienced. Later in this service they will be read aloud.

During this next musical interlude, please come forward and place your papers in the basket on the altar. If you need a pen, please raise your hand. If you are unable to bring your papers forward, please hand them to a neighbor or motion toward a worship leader, and we will collect them.

Music and Placement

(Play a song that matches your particular miserable weather season as participants come forward and place their sheets of paper in the basket.)

Prayer

The God that we know when we see hope,

The God that we know when we feel held in love,

Be with us on this day

And help all of us who are struggling this season.

Hold all of us who have lost someone or something this season.

Hold all of us who desperately long for safety,

For a clear path forward,

For something that feels normal.

Please help us to put this terrible season behind us.

Please help us to find healing.

Please hold us as we try to move past what was and into what is.

Please steady our hearts

So that we may be agents of healing and reconciliation.

Amen.

Song

"All Will Be Well" (Meg Barnhouse)

(Lead participants in singing.)

Naming

There is power in naming. There is power in knowing. We now invite you to settle and ground yourself in your space. Please join together in this prayerful reflection as we share our names for what we experienced. After each name is read, we will destroy the paper to symbolically let go of this season.

(Read the names slowly, one at a time, preferably with quiet, instrumental music playing underneath your voice. Try to intersperse funny and serious ones. After reading each one, burn or dissolve the paper. Allow space for each name to carry the pain or anger it needs to carry.)

This season has ended.

We know that suffering does not end.

We know you may be processing this for years.

But today marks a change.

Today marks a day we can start processing what we experienced.

May today start the next chapter in our story.

Song

"Life Calls Us On" (Jason Shelton)

(Lead participants in singing.)

Chalice Extinguishing

"Take Courage, Friends" (Wayne Arnason)

Take courage, friends.

The way is often hard, the path is never clear, and the stakes are very high.

Take courage.

For deep down, there is another truth: you are not alone.

(Extinguish the chalice.)

For the First Anniversary of a Natural Disaster

Rev. Nathan Ryan

This ritual is for marking the one-year anniversary of a major weather event or other natural disaster. It is designed as a congregational worship service, but could be adapted for other contexts; in all cases it must be tailored to your specific community and the culture it is immersed in. The outline version given here is based on a service done in Louisiana.

Materials

- ☐ Chalice
- ☐ Art to help set the mood
- ☐ Music

Setup

Arrange seats in rows or a circle, with the chalice visible at the front or center. Use art to set the mood as people enter and find places. For instance, when the author of this ritual did it as an evening service, he projected a ninety-minute video of the sun setting over the Mississippi River, synced with the actual sunset.

The service is meant to retell the story of the disaster and what people experienced in it. Be careful not to push too hard on the bruise. People are very vulnerable on an anniversary. Lightly guide them through the retelling. People cope with tragedy by crafting a narrative, and the goal of this service is to do this.

Identify three leaders in the church to speak at this service: one who had direct experience of the disaster, one who was a part of the recovery, and one who can speak to what the church did. You may want to choose readers as well, or do the readings yourself.

Look for music that speaks to the people who will be participating, and try to choose readings that do not directly discuss the event. You want words, music, and images that will reflect the shadow it cast, rather than relishing its details. If you are doing the ritual in a church context, look at orders of service from the weeks immediately after the disaster and consider reusing those readings and songs.

Script

Opening Words

Come into this place.

Come into this place that is still safe.

Come into this place as broken as you are right now.

Bring in the truth that you are still enough.

Bring in the truth that you are still safe here.

Don't leave your fears and worries at the door. Tell them they can sit next to you, but they should be quiet for this hour.

Come into this space that is still here for you—all of you.

Come, let us be together, a still broken together people.

Song

"Come and Go with Me" (African American spiritual)

(Lead participants in singing.)

Chalice Lighting

As we light our flame,

Let us remember the world that was

And envision the world that we hope will be.

Let this flame illuminate both past and future

Right here in the present.

(Light the chalice.)

Introduction to the Anniversary

(Tell participants what they will experience today. Give them permission to quietly leave the room at any point if they need to. Tell them a little about how the disaster is still affecting you, but be careful not to center your own pain or struggles. This service isn't about content or exposition. It is a time for people to gather together and make space for God's work, to create an emptiness the people will fill.)

Song

(Choose a song that sets the tone for the storytelling; lead participants in singing it.)

Reading

(Choose a text that sets the tone for the first part of the story.)

Speaker 1

(The first speaker describes their firsthand experience of the event.)

Song

"There Is More Love Somewhere" (African American spiritual)

(Lead participants in singing.)

Reading

(Choose a text recounting some aspect of the recovery.)

Speaker 2

(The second speaker describes their experience helping with the recovery.)

Song

(Choose a song that speaks to the recovery and lead participants in singing.)

Prayer

The God that we know when we remember,
The God that we know when we are held in community,
The God that we know when we see the world made better amidst tragedy,
Be with us on this day.
Bless all of those wounded, healing hearts.
Bless all of us who are not yet at peace with what happened.
Bless all those who will never be at peace with it.

Bless all of us who are ready to move on,

And bless those of us who are ready to move on, but feel stuck or are still coping.

Help us heal.

Help all of us heal.

Please know we will never forget.

Please turn us into a people bound by love, committed to justice, and yearning for a more compassionate world.

Amen.

Reading

(Choose a text that describes how the larger community responded to the disaster.)

Speaker 3

(The third speaker discusses the role of the church in the recovery.)

Song

"I Know I Can" (Dennis Hamilton)

(Lead participants in singing.)

Chalice Extinguishing

The year has passed.

Most of us are still here together.

We are forever changed.

Let us try to love this new world as we mourn for what we've lost.

Tell your story.

Watch out for the echoes.

Go love the world.

Go love yourselves.

Make peace.

Be kind.

Amen.

(Extinguish the chalice.)

Seasons and Cycles

For Blessing Backpacks

Rev. Erika Hewitt

This ritual, designed to be used in a congregational worship service or other congregational gathering, invites the congregation—all ages—to bless backpacks, book bags, computer bags, knitting totes, etc., at the beginning of the school and congregational year. Many congregations offer such blessings.

Materials

☐ Optional: Tags, keychains, or other emblems to be attached to bags

Setup

Several weeks in advance, invite people to bring their bag to worship on the chosen day. If you want to distribute tags, obtain and prepare them.

Script

We carry bags with us throughout the week for many reasons. If you have a bag with you and you want to have it blessed, come up front, lift up your bag, or have someone lift it up for you when you hear me describe you.

(Pause after each statement to allow time for participants to come forward or lift up their bags.)

Some of us take books and homework to school.

Some of us bring our lunches to school or to work.

Some of us take computers and other supplies to the places where we work.

Some kids carry overnight bags from one parent's house to another parent's house, and back again.

Some people bring things like books or yarn and knitting needles to places where they might need to wait patiently.

Some of us bring diapers and snacks to daycare or the park.

And some people even have special bags for their dogs or other animals to carry—or be carried in!

(By now, there should be a crowd up front and a number of people lifting their bags from their seats.)

Are your bags already full of things? (You'll likely hear some "no" replies.) Do you imagine that they *might* get full one day? Maybe. For this blessing, it doesn't matter if your bag is full or empty. We're going to add something to your bag—but don't worry, because it won't add any weight and it won't take up any room.

Would any of you like to have some of our congregation's love to take with you to school, or to work, or on your travels? If you feel love here on Sundays, wouldn't you like to know that our love is with you on the other days?

Let's do that. Please bundle some love up from wherever you're storing it (you might rummage through your pockets or look up your sleeves) and make a nice little pillow of love (use your hands, as if making an invisible snowball) and . . . are you ready? Those of you with your bags, make sure they're open and hold them up to catch the love!

(Gently toss an imaginary bundle of love toward the bags being held open, and encourage the congregation to do the same. Make sure that people toss love toward the bags held up by those seated, as well as toward the front.)

That was fun, so let's add some more qualities to your bags. Sometimes we get nervous when we go to school or work. Sometimes we wish we felt braver. I think it would be nice to know that our courage is with you on days when you need to feel brave.

(Again, invite the congregation to "pull out" some courage, to pat it into a "bundle," and then to gently toss it toward someone's open bag.)

What do you wish we could put in your bag, to take with you? Name it, and we'll take it from our heart-supply, and we'll toss it into your bag!

(Once or twice more, ask those with bags what they'd like to carry with them. Feel free to combine requests, like "peace and joy.")

Your bag might not look any different or feel any different, but the next time you use your bag I hope you'll remember that we've added our blessings to come with you when you need them. Remember that the Spirit of Life is with you always: at school, at work, on trips, and everywhere, and that this congregation cares about what happens to you no matter where you are. And if you need more love, or courage, or [list one or two of the other things you offered], you can always ask us for more.

(If you are distributing tags, keychains, or other emblems to attach to bags symbolizing the congregation's blessing, distribute them.)

For Beginning and Ending
a Congregational Year
Rev. Craig M. Nowak and Rev. Sara Ascher

This multigenerational stone communion ritual uses gathered stones to mark the path along which a faith community travels together. It expresses that every person entering the community changes and is changed by it. This exchange of influence is enduring. This is one of the reasons the ritual uses stones rather than some other kind of token: they too endure, and we can hold on to them as a reminder that we are part of something more than ourselves.

The ritual is held twice annually, at the beginning and end of the congregational year, at the Brookfield Unitarian Universalist Church in Brookfield, Mass., where Revs. Craig and Sara served as ministers.

Materials
- ☐ Altar table
- ☐ Small table
- ☐ Stones
- ☐ Bowl for stones (preferably one through which the stones can be seen: glass, wire mesh, etc.)
- ☐ Music

Setup
For the fall ritual, tell people in advance when it will be held, and remind them to bring a stone with them to church that day. If you did a stone communion the previous spring, they can bring the stone they took then, but it can also be a new one. Provide additional stones for those who might have forgotten to bring one or who are new or visiting and wish to participate, and offer them to people as they enter the space.

For the spring ritual, ensure that some stones will be left over after everyone who wants to has taken one. If your attendance has significantly increased since the fall, for instance, you may need to add more.

Put the bowl on the altar table or in some other prominent place in the worship space. (If you have done this ritual before, it should already be there and have some stones in it from the previous spring or fall.) Place the small table somewhere that will be accessible to participants.

Choose quiet, reflective music that will create a contemplative mood. In the fall, recruit a helper to bring a stone to anyone who needs one at the last minute.

Script

FALL STONE COMMUNION

(This version should be held as part of the first gathering of the congregational year.)

Opening Words

As the long days of summer recede and make way for the coming season, we again gather together. And we ritualize, by the gathering of stones, our intention to build together a reminder, a touchstone, of our greatest aspirations and hopes for our ministry together and for the community during the coming months and year.

Our coming together is more than merely returning to a familiar place. It is strengthening and renewing our promise to embody a welcoming faith community of caring, support, and service. A commitment made by each of us to one another. A commitment made by those who were here before us and by those of you who have ventured here today for the first time, a commitment to be taken up by the seekers who will cross our threshold in the weeks, months, and years to come.

Stone Communion

Each of you should have a stone that you have either brought with you this morning or were given when you entered. If you don't have a stone, raise your hand and someone will bring you one. The collecting of these stones represents that each of us in this community adds something beautiful and unique, changing the congregation, and that we each receive something in return, changing us. This exchange is enduring. Those who are no longer with us leave behind something of themselves, as signified by the stones that remain year after year, and today we freely add something of ourselves to this community. The stones will then be placed here [name a prominent place in the worship space] until our last service before summer.

I invite everyone who wishes to participate to come forward now, row by row, in silent reflection to place your stone in this bowl in appreciation of this place and its people, as we once again gather to build this faith community anew.

(Move the bowl from the altar table to the small table. Have music played as people come forward and place their stones in it. Have a helper bring a smaller bowl to anyone who can't come forward, then empty it into the bigger bowl. Once everyone who wishes has participated, put your own stone in and put the bowl on the altar table or in another prominent position in the space. It should remain there throughout the church year.)

Blessing

The stones are now placed, and the congregation gathered anew. In the placing of our stones, each of us contributes to and commits to the growth and vitality of this beloved community. Each of us is called to be, and to become part of, something more. Today we give thanks for this community: a place and a people whom we pledge to journey with, build alongside, have faith in, and love. Amen and blessed be.

SPRING STONE COMMUNION

(This version should be held as part of the last gathering of the congregational year.)

Opening Words

We began this church year by bringing stones, marking the regathering of this congregation and reminding us that each of us brings something beautiful and enduring to this faith community.

Now, at the church year's end, we prepare to take a stone away with us. Not to mark an ending, but to expand our reach and connection. We each take a stone, remembering that we carry something of this faith and each other out into the world beyond these walls: something to hold on to while we may be apart, something to share with those we meet, something to bring back when we gather again.

Stone Communion

I invite everyone who wishes to come forward quietly, reverently, with a reflective heart and mind, to choose a stone from the collection that we created, representing the fullness and richness of this beloved congregation. Take a stone that speaks to you, that reminds you that you are not alone and the heart of this community travels with you even while we are apart.

(Take the bowl from where it has been displayed since the previous fall and set it on the small table. Have music played as people come forward and take a stone from it. Once everyone who wishes has participated, take a stone yourself and then return the bowl to its place.)

Blessing

The stones we now carry are unique and precious. Each is a tangible symbol of our belonging together. May they be reminders of the beauty and strength of this community and our shared faith, until we meet again. Amen and blessed be.

For Celebrating the Harvest

Rev. Ariel Aaronson-Eves

For Mark Cain and Michael Crane, with gratitude

This ritual celebrates all the forces (divine, natural, human) that go into the creation of food. Inspired by the author's experience as a farmer, it serves to strengthen participants' connection to their local foodshed. Recognizing how often both people and planet are exploited in the production of food and that not everyone has easy access to fresh produce, it is intended as a harvest celebration to honor whatever local produce, grown with love, is available. It can be easily incorporated into a congregational worship service or used on its own, with any size group.

Materials

- ☐ Fresh locally grown fruits and/or vegetables, in bite-sized pieces (e.g., pea pod, slice of apple), at least one for each participant
- ☐ Serving bowls or trays
- ☐ Hand sanitizer or serving utensils
- ☐ Responsive reading text
- ☐ Optional: Music

Setup

Be as aware as possible of any potential allergies or sensitivities, and have a variety of fruits and/or vegetables available. They should be washed, cut into bite-sized pieces if necessary, arranged in serving bowls or trays, and set at the front of the space or beside you. Provide serving spoons, tongs, or toothpicks for hygienic serving; hand sanitizer can also be conveniently located nearby.

Depending on how the space is set up and on the needs of the group, the bowls or trays can be passed hand to hand by the congregation, carried from person to person by helpers, or kept at an altar with participants coming forward to them. In the latter case, recruit at least one helper to bring some to those who are unable to come to the altar.

Distribute or project the text of the responsive reading.

Script

Opening Words

Much of religious practice around the world is built on the sharing of food. The necessity of eating reminds us of our dependencies on each other and on forces beyond us. Practices such as participating in the Eucharist, observing kashrut, making offerings to ancestors, and others help us remember our place in the web of existence.

It is a tangled web. Within our food systems, exploitation and oppression are entwined with love and care. There are trade-offs and delicate balances, questions of labor and land management, of intent and impact. Every bite we eat carries with it stories of suffering and stories of joy. Let us be mindful of the pain, even as we choose, in this moment, to lean into pleasure, to delight in the food that soon will touch our lips.

This ritual of sharing food, of communion, brings us into connection with and awareness of the sacred web, acknowledging that Spirit of Life that runs through the food system and through our embodied experience of eating.

Responsive Reading

LEADER: All food begins with a seed,
in its heart the stories of past generations and future promise,
waiting to spring forth.
Environmental pressures push and pull, shaping its response.
But all that is needed is a seed, and air, and water.

PARTICIPANTS: All life stems from this.

LEADER: We have evolved, with other species and the land, to arrive at this moment.

Through careful observation and cultivation,

Following our desires for beauty, for sustenance, for communion,

Joining with the love of the universe to bring love to each other.

PARTICIPANTS: May this love heal us, heal our relations, heal our world.

LEADER: We know not at what cost the farmer planted the seed,

irrigated the field, cultivated the crop.

What we know is that they did,

and thanks to forces beyond them and beyond us, we have food today.

PARTICIPANTS: Because of someone's desire to feed us, we eat.

Sharing of the Fruits of This Land

The produce of this land will now be passed among you [or "Please come forward to take a piece, or raise your hand and someone will bring a tray to you"]. Select one, and hold on to it until everyone has one, so that we may share the moment of tasting.

(As people choose their fruit or vegetable, you may wish to play music, especially for a larger group that will take longer.)

Blessing

I now invite you to savor your fruit or vegetable, chewing it slowly and thoroughly, as I offer these words of blessing:

Let us be conscious of flavors, textures, energy

    Of the simple pleasures of eating

    Of the miracle of photosynthesis, by which air and water are converted into food

Let us be aware of the work of the farmer, who planted the seeds, tended the crop, harvested the greens

    Of the blood, sweat, and tears of making a farm

Let us be aware of and thankful for the rain, and the whole water cycle

Let us give thanks for the livestock whose manure fertilized these crops

> For the plants of seasons past, broken down into compost and resurrected

> For the earthworms and bugs of the soil, for bacteria, for fungi

>> Whose work we cannot see and yet depend on

Let us be grateful for our desires, which pull us outside of ourselves and into communion with other people, with other species, with other places

> Exposing us to new ideas, offering opportunities for growth and change

> May they lead us toward the pleasures of existence

Let us eat together, recognizing that we never eat alone

May we work for a world where everyone will always be able to enjoy such simple pleasures.

For Coming Out Day

Rev. Rose Maldonado Schwab

Dedicated to the author's spouse, Ana Marcela Maldonado Morales

This ritual blesses the LGBTQ+ community in three ways: it creates a sacred space for coming out, blesses those who are out, and provides allies space to offer support to the LGBTQ+ community. It is designed to be included in a congregational worship service immediately prior to National Coming Out Day (October 11).

Materials

None

Setup

Earlier in the service, sing Libby Roderick's song "How Could Anyone." It has been used around the world in spaces where people need to honor and be reminded of their wholeness. Play the tune of the song throughout the service whenever possible, giving it space to swell.

The script given here assumes that the leader is a part of the LGBTQ+ community. If you are not, some of its language may need to be adapted.

Script

Meditation

(If possible, alternate a few lines at a time of the meditation with a few lines of the melody of "How Could Anyone.")

This is the time in our service when we honor National Coming Out Day. During this ritual, I will be inviting members of the LGBTQ+ community forward, and then inviting our allies forward to sing to them.

I invite you to move into a comfortable position in your chairs, whatever that looks like for you. Let your body relax as it wishes to. Take a soothing breath, drawing your awareness to your heart space.

Imagine a little glowing diamond, deep inside your chest. When you breathe in, it glows, and when you breathe out, it dims. Draw to mind someone you love; imagine their face, and breathe. And now take your hands and place them face up in your lap. And feel, right in the very middle of your palm, a golden orb. When you breathe in, it glows; when you breathe out, it dims. It has pressure and a pulse. And now, draw your hands up and place them over your heart and repeat after me.

(Read the following text line by line, pausing after each to let participants repeat what you have said.)

May I be free from suffering.
May I find sanctuary.
May I be healed.

Invitation to the LGBTQ+ Community

And now I am going to list some categories. If the words I use apply to you, I invite you to be brave, rise, and join me here as you are willing and able. You may also stay in your seat and raise your hand if that is more comfortable.

(Pause after each line to give people time to come forward or raise their hand, and to bear witness to those who do so.)

I invite you to join me if you are a lesbian.
If you are gay.
If you are transgender.
If you are nonbinary or gender nonconforming.

If you are bi.

If you are queer.

If you are queer but pass as straight, whether through your presentation or through the relationship you are in.

If you are questioning, if you have ever questioned, if you are closeted.

If you hold an identity that wasn't named but that is part of the beautiful, expansive universe of nonmainstream sexual orientations and gender identities.

Sending Out Compassion

And now, let us send out compassion to anyone here with us, and everyone out there in the world, who has chosen not to come out today. There are many reasons people may feel unsafe or uncomfortable with publicly sharing this part of themselves.

Imagine the glowing orb in your palm growing warmer and brighter. Now send that warmth out to anyone who feels pressure not to come out. It may be someone you know; it may be a stranger; it may be yourself. Send them love; send them prayers for their physical and financial and emotional safety; send them hope.

Laying on of Hands

And now, everyone who has not come to the front or raised your hand, you have a very special job: to make this sanctuary one of the very few places in the world, even today, where LGBTQ+ people are considered full spiritual beings, with the right to worship and the right to the fullness of human relationship.

Go ahead and take another soothing breath, and help us hold all the years of shame and anxiety that so many among us have gone through. Help take away the curse of ostracism, the pain of broken families. Here in this community, we believe that the human heart is a good and powerful agent in this world. In that spirit, I invite us into a laying on of hands for our LGBTQ+ community gathered here today.

All you beautiful people who have come forward, and you beautiful LGBTQ+ people who have stayed in your seats: If you prefer not to be touched in this way, please cross your arms over your chest like this [demonstrate].

As we imagine a world without stigma or hatred for queer people, I invite the children and youth who have identified yourselves as LGBTQ+ to move toward an adult you know and like, especially one who is also LGBTQ+. And you trusted adults, unless they've crossed their arms, please put a hand on their shoulder. If they have crossed their arms, hold your open palms out to them, like this [demonstrate]. Other adults who have come forward, please gather around the young people.

(Pause to let people move around.)

And now, if you are an ally in the front row, I invite you to come forward as you are able and lay a hand on the shoulder, or back, or arm of one of the adults up here. If someone has crossed their arms, hold your open palms out to them. You can also stay in your seat and lay your hand on someone who has identified themselves as LGBTQ+, or open your loving palms to them if they're too far away, or if either you or they prefer not to touch. And if you are LGBTQ+ but have chosen not to identify yourself today, know that the blessings are for you as well, even though we don't know who you are. May you bless yourself as we bless you.

(Pause to let people move around.)

Allies in the next rows, please do the same, laying your hand on any willing adult or holding out your palms, joining in the interconnected web of blessing. You can come forward and join the gathering here, or stay in your seat, extending the web through the whole of this space.

(Pause until everyone has joined the blessing as they wish to.)

And now, take another breath and touch base with that diamond in your heart. Think of someone up here who you love; maybe it's someone you've watched come out, or someone you just saw for the first time today. Bring them into your heart and send them loving kindness.

Prayer

May we be free from suffering.

May we be free from shame.

May we be free from the storms of guilt and rage.

May we find here acceptance and love.

May we know that we are whole and good in all our complicated beauty,

that we are powerful beyond measure,

that the fire of our creativity is needed to light this world.

That one lightning flash of our beauty illuminates a whole new world.

May the hands in this room be used for good.

May we find a compassion bigger than our ego,

a bravery wiser than our insecurities, a love stronger than our fear.

Song

"How Could Anyone" (Libby Roderick)

(Lead participants in singing the song at least three times through, with swelling music.)

For Veterans Day

Rev. Barbara McKusick Liscord

This ritual honors the service and experience of military veterans, active service members, and their families on or near Veterans Day (November 11). The script here assumes that the ritual is being done in the context of a congregational worship service. A few weeks prior to the service, you might gather a group of people to share their military experiences; knowing more about them will help you shape the ritual.

Materials

- ☐ Altar table
- ☐ Table for photos
- ☐ Five pillar candles

Setup

Recruit five helpers, one each from the Air Force, Army, Coast Guard, National Guard, and Navy or Marines. They may be past or current service members. If necessary, you could recruit a family member of a current service member instead.

Ahead of time, ask congregants who are serving or have served, or who have relatives who have, to bring photos of themselves or their relatives, in uniform if possible. Set up the altar table at the front of the space, and put pillar candles on it; put the table with the photos in another prominent and accessible location.

Recruit a trumpeter to play "Taps."

Script

Opening Words

How many people here had a day off this week for Veterans Day? This morning we are having our own Veterans Day observance. We are remembering, honoring, and praying for all those who have served and still serve in the armed forces of our country.

Veterans Day used to be called Armistice Day. It was the celebration of the end of World War I, which was such a terrible war that it was called the War to End all Wars. Armistice Day became a national holiday in 1938, a day to honor veterans of World War I and the cause of world peace. Sadly, we have had many wars since then. In 1954, the United States Congress renamed the holiday Veterans Day, saying that it should be a time when we honor all our country's veterans for their patriotism and their willingness to serve and sacrifice for the common good, as well as rededicating ourselves to the cause of world peace.

In our liberal religious tradition, we know that there are many ways to serve our country. We also know that there are many paths to military service; people may serve by choice, by draft, or because of difficult circumstances. Today, no matter your path or circumstances, we honor you who currently serve and those of you who have served in the US military. We acknowledge that military service often affects those who have served and their families every day, not just one day of the year.

As we honor those who have served, we also acknowledge the range of feelings people may have about their service. As part of our ritual today, I'll invite all of you who have served or are currently serving, and family members of those who are currently serving, to be recognized, so that you and your loved ones may be honored. You were invited to bring pictures of yourselves in uniform, or pictures of your loved ones who have served in the military. They are on the table here, for you to look at after the service.

Candle Lighting

Now we will light a candle for each branch of the armed services and ask those here who have served in those branches to stand up and say your name. As we go through this part of the ceremony, we may feel moved to clap to show our appreciation for our veterans. But I ask you to hold your applause until the end, so that we may honor each person in silence.

I'd like to invite those who will be lighting candles for those who have served in the various branches to come forward: [Name 1], [Name 2], [Name 3], [Name 4], and [Name 5].

(The five helpers come up to the altar table.)

HELPER 1: I am [Name]. I served in the Air Force.
I light this candle for all those who have served in the Air Force
and for those who are serving in the Air Force today.

(They light the candle.)

Will those who serve or have served in the Air Force please stand or raise your hand and give your name, so that we may honor you?

(Pause to allow participants to stand or raise hands and call out names.)

Will those of you who have loved ones who serve or have served in the Air Force please stand or raise your hand and say their names?

(Pause to allow participants to stand or raise hands and call out names.)

Thank you. Please be seated.

HELPER 2: I am [Name]. I served in the Army.
I light this candle for all those who have served in the Army
and those who are serving in the Army today.

(They light the candle.)

Will those who serve or have served in the Army please stand or raise your hand and give your name, so that we may honor you?

(Pause to allow participants to stand or raise hands and call out names.)

Will those of you who have loved ones who serve or have served in the Army please stand or raise your hand and say their names?

(Pause to allow participants to stand or raise hands and call out names.)

Thank you. Please be seated.

HELPER 3: I am [Name]. I served in the Navy.
I light this candle for all those who have served in the Navy and Marines and who are serving in the Navy and Marines today.

(They light the candle.)

Will those who serve or have served in the Navy or Marines please stand or raise your hand and give your name, so that we may honor you?

(Pause to allow participants to stand or raise hands and call out names.)

Will those of you who have loved ones who serve or have served in the Navy and Marines please stand or raise your hand and say their names?

(Pause to allow participants to stand or raise hands and call out names.)

Thank you. Please be seated.

HELPER 4: I am [Name]. I served in the Coast Guard.
I light this candle for all those who have served in the Coast Guard and who are serving in the Coast Guard today.

(They light the candle.)

Will those who serve or have served in the Coast Guard please stand or raise your hand and give your name, so that we may honor you?

(Pause to allow participants to stand or raise hands and call out names.)

Will those of you who have loved ones who serve or have served in the Coast Guard please stand or raise your hand and say their names?

(Pause to allow participants to stand or raise hands and call out names.)

Thank you. Please be seated.

HELPER 5: I am [Name]. I served in the National Guard.
I light this candle for all those who have served in the National Guard and who are serving in the National Guard today.

(They light the candle.)

Will those who serve or have served in the National Guard please stand or raise your hand and give your name, so that we may honor you?

(Pause to allow participants to stand or raise hands and call out names.)

Will those of you who have loved ones who serve or have served in the National Guard please stand or raise your hand and say their names?

(Pause to allow participants to stand or raise hands and call out names.)

Thank you. Please be seated.

I ask all veterans and active service members to stand or raise your hands, so that we may show our appreciation.

(Pause for applause.)

Thank you. Please be seated.

Let us join our hearts and minds in a spirit of prayer.

Prayer

"A Prayer for Memorial Day" by David Pyle

Spirit of Life, to you we consecrate our silent tears,
For the memory of all of those who have fallen in war,
For the lives of families broken by loss,
For the spirits of those who live with the memories every day,
For the loss of our innocence.

Spirit of Life, to you we consecrate our silent tears,
For the innocent victims of the evil of war,
For the destruction we visit upon the miracle of life,
For the fear that is spread by the sounds of battle,
For the creation of children with haunted eyes.

Spirit of Life, to you we consecrate our silent tears,
For the young men and women who have come back wounded,
For all those who never came back at all.
For viewing others as our enemies,
For making enemies of ourselves.

Spirit of Life,
For the memory of all, for our responsibility to all, and for our hope in a better
future for all… We consecrate to you our silent tears.

Music

(The trumpeter plays "Taps.")

For Transgender Day
of Remembrance

Rev. Otto Concannon

A ritual for Transgender Day of Remembrance, an annual day of mourning on or around November 20 which gives names to lives lost to anti-transgender violence around the world.

Materials

- ☐ Altar
- ☐ Chalice
- ☐ List of names of those known to have been lost to anti-transgender violence in the past year
- ☐ Tea lights, one for each person named (you will need more than three hundred)
- ☐ Music
- ☐ Taper candles with drip guard, one for each participant
- ☐ Receptacle to collect taper candles
- ☐ Optional: Transgender pride flag

Setup

Expect an event like this to be attended by folks from outside of your community, many of whom may not be comfortable in a church setting. Be sure to have welcoming signage and helpers who can help people get oriented. They should give each person an unlit taper candle as they come in, and make sure guests know where there is a gender-neutral and accessible bathroom.

Find a list of people known to have been killed in anti-transgender violence in the past year (October through September); one reliable source is Transrespect versus Transphobia Worldwide (transrespect.org), a research project initiated by Transgender Europe (TGEU). (On TvT's list, "N.N." means that the person's name is not known.)

Print out the list of names in large print and recruit seven to ten helpers to read them. Most of the people named will come from Latin American countries, so it's helpful to have readers who can fluently pronounce Spanish and Portuguese names. If there are anonymous people on the list, instruct the readers to say "Name unknown" for each.

Set up an altar, and place on it a lit tea light for every life lost to anti-transgender violence. Note that you will need a large altar, as you will have more than three hundred candles. You may wish to use a transgender pride flag as an altar cloth.

The script given here assumes that the leader is not trans; if you are, change "they" to "we" as appropriate.

Consider having a reception after the ritual. Especially for smaller gatherings, such an event can be a place for people to bring their tears and grief, a much-needed space for healing and connection.

Script

Music

(Play soft gathering music as people enter the space.)

Chalice Lighting

Welcome to [name of space or community] for this service honoring Transgender Day of Remembrance.

We will now light our chalice, marking the sacred space we will share.

By the glow of the lights of those lost
We light the flame of life that burned within each life we mourn today.
May we find healing and connection here.
May we be reminded that we are part of a larger movement
Of souls and bodies
Beautifully and wonderfully made
Just like the lives we now mourn.
May we find ourselves inextricably connected
To the hope of a better world for all transgender people.

(Light the chalice.)

Song

"There Is More Love Somewhere" (African American spiritual)

(Lead participants in singing.)

Reading or Reflection

(You or someone else could offer a reading or short reflection here.)

Introducing the Candles

I'm [Name], the [role] here at [congregation's name], and my pronouns are [pronouns]. I want to acknowledge how important this service is for our community. It is a time for us to pay our respects to those who have been killed by anti-transgender violence worldwide. Many who are killed by anti-transgender violence are not honored or remembered in a way that recognizes their full humanity, and so we come together every year to say these names, to give them the respect they deserve. Let the names we read remind us, as Mother Jones did, to "pray for the dead, and fight like hell for the living."

Behind me, there are [number] candles lit, one for each life lost to transgender violence this past year. In a moment, we will read the names, but first I would like to invite you to join in singing two verses of the song "Comfort Me." You can sing, or hum, or just listen; whatever you like. Once we've sung twice through, we will begin reading the names of our beloved dead.

Song

"Comfort Me" (Mimi Bornstein-Doble)

(Lead participants in singing.)

Reading the Names

(As the musician quietly plays the melody of "Comfort Me," the helpers should begin reading the names, slowly and reverently. This section can take up to twenty minutes.)

Prayer

Spirit of Life,

We are a people hurting and mourning our beloved siblings,

Killed by anti-transgender violence.

We know not what to do, holy one,

Nor what is asked of us when we must bear witness to such horrible deaths.

Spirit of Life, you know that it is hard to find hope in times like this.

May love embrace us and all our transgender siblings the world over.

Help us to remember that transgender people are whole and wonderful beings worthy of love and safety, joy and contentment.

Spirit of Life,

Hold in love all those who struggle with their gender identity,

All those who struggle to know that they are loved,

That they are worthy,

And that we need their light burning brightly to guide us in this beautiful, terrible world.

We say a prayer of compassion for all those who love the hundreds of names listed today.

May they be comforted in their grief.

And we say a prayer of justice

Of hope

That the killing of transgender people ends today.

We recognize that each of these names represents a whole person,

A person who loved, and lived, and struggled, and laughed, just like all of us.

We know that this violence impacts each of us differently,

And tonight we lift up especially transgender women of color, who are so much more often the targets of such violence.

May we be reminded of the resilience that transgender people have shown throughout history,

And may we be reminded in these difficult times of that resilience:

Of those who will not be erased,

Who will not be silent,

Who exist and will continue to exist until the end of time,

Wholly and beautifully made.

And, finally, may these lives be remembered for what they brought to our world. Blessed be, and amen.

Lighting Candles for Those Present

The solemn and sacred task of Transgender Day of Remembrance is to mourn and remember those who have died in the holy act of simply being who they are, beautiful and beloved creations of God. It is right that we take time today for sadness and grief, that we recognize the fear that resides in all transgender people and those who love them, and that we honor the lives that were cut short by the scourge of transphobia in our world.

But even amidst this mourning, we are reminded by our presence here today of the resilience of transgender people. We are reminded by those who live their lives as they are, whether out loud or in the quiet space in their hearts; we are reminded by all the beloved transgender people in this room and the power they hold; we are reminded by those who love transgender people, and those who loved those who have gone from this world.

We know that transgender people aren't going away; they will not be silenced or erased. They are part of the masterpiece that is the human experience. The resilience of transgender people must be honored and celebrated as well.

And so, as a reminder of that resilience, and the power in this room of transgender people and those who love and have loved them, let us light our candles as we sing again together. If you didn't get a candle as you came in, please raise your hand now and a helper will bring you one. Then accept the flame from your neighbor and pass it on to the next person.

(Allow a few moments, if needed, for taper candles to be delivered. Then light a taper of your own from one of the tea lights and use it to light the tapers of a few participants. Offer guidance as needed as they light others' in turn. When all candles are lit, invite participants to sing.)

Song

"Go Lifted Up" (Mortimer Barron)

(Lead participants in singing.)

Chalice Extinguishing

We will extinguish our chalice and the candles we are holding. But as we go forth into the world we still carry our light, our resilience, in the face of such sadness. Lift it high, and go in peace.

(Extinguish the chalice and your taper candle.)

You are welcome to leave as the music plays, or to stay as long as you like in the silence afterward.

(Add an invitation to the reception, if you are having one.)

Music

(Reprise the tune of "Go Lifted Up.")

For the Season of Creative Dormancy

Rev. Ron Phares

This ritual is designed to be used as part of a congregational worship service in the late fall or early winter. It welcomes the oncoming darkness of winter as a time of deep internal breakdown, decomposition, re-creation, and creative dormancy.

Materials

- ☐ Altar table
- ☐ Bowl for soil (preferably transparent)
- ☐ Smaller bowl that can be carried to participants
- ☐ Small cups of soil for participants who did not bring any
- ☐ Bowl of water

Setup

Announce well in advance that each participant should bring a small handful of soil from their home to this ritual.

Place the altar table somewhere accessible to participants, and set the empty bowl and the bowl of water on it.

Recruit a helper to carry a second soil bowl to participants who cannot come forward, and one to bring small cups of soil to participants who did not bring any.

The Soil Communion element of this ritual is intentionally silent, to acknowledge that meaning need not be expressed in words, or in sound at all. The quiet is a reminder of the soil.

Script

Opening Words

The planet that sustains us is the only known planet with living, breathing skin. That skin is called dirt. From a far enough distance away, we are indistinguishable from that planetary skin. From right up close, closer than our eyes can see unaided, it is the same. We are land with legs. Many of the ancients believed this too. Jewish, Christian, and Islamic traditions hold that the first human, Adam, was made of clay and breath; the name "Adam" means "earth being."

And now, all around us in this hemisphere, the earth is breaking itself down. But fields and gardens that appear fallow are actually quite lively as the internal processes of decomposition create rich, healthy soil.

Let us, like earth, find life in the quiet internal churning of the breakdown. What in your life is dying? What do you need to let go of in order to allow more life into your world? A grudge? A regret? An attitude? A habit? A relationship? A status? A sadness?

What is it that you will let decompose, so that its death can bring new life into your world? Put a name to it if you can. Remember what you have named it.

And what will you plant in the compost it becomes? What seed will you push under that earth, that will use the soil as food, to grow into something new? Put a name to that seed. Remember it.

Now you have two words: something that you are letting go to decompose, and something that you are planting to grow. Hold on to them. We will use them in the ritual to come.

(Pause.)

You were asked to bring a handful of soil from your home to this ritual today. If you forgot, or if you're visiting, or if you need more soil for any reason, please raise your hand and a helper will bring you some now.

(A helper distributes cups of soil as you continue speaking.)

Without decay, there would be no soil. Without soil, no seed could flourish, no seed would be fed. Just so, parts of us must decay so that new parts can flourish. Chapters, themes, and characteristics of our identities must be allowed to compost so that fresh characteristics, themes, and chapters may flourish.

Embracing our dissolutions is scary. They are a window into dying. But refusing to do so leads to suffering and prohibits new life. Why are we so afraid? Why is it so hard to trust our own becoming? The seeds of you need the decay of you. This ritual gives us some practice. Here we can ease into decay. Embrace it and trust the seeds. Trust the soil. Our home. Our place of rejuvenation and return.

In this ritual we may return to our most fundamental home, the earth. Return to who you fundamentally are. Return to what you are in essence. Return to where you are born and reborn again. The home of your soul. The soil.

Let us prepare for this return with song.

Song

"Return Again" (Shlomo Carlebach)

(Lead participants in singing.)

Soil Communion

I will ask each section to come forward in turn and form a line over here, in front of this bowl. If you prefer not to come forward, raise a hand and a helper will bring our other bowl to you.

(Indicate how participants should move through the space.)

When you're ready, with the bowl in front of you, pour your dirt into your hand. Feel its texture, its richness. Remember what you named in your meditation earlier that you will let go of this season. Press it into your soil . . . and then silently let it go, into the bowl.

After that, recall the seed deep within, the seed that you trust. Find it in your heart and plant it in the soil with the tips of your fingers. Again, do this in silence. Seeds work unseen.

We are of the earth. This is our body. Let us, like earth, find life in the quiet internal churning of the breakdown. Decomposition feeds the seed. What will you let go of in order to discover a new flourishing? What part of you will you let decompose, in order that its death may bring new life into your world?

(Indicate that the first section should approach the altar. The ritual is performed in silence, without musical underscoring. Continue in silence until everyone has participated. Put the smaller bowl of soil on the altar table next to the main one, or empty it into the main one.)

Blessing

Here is the ground of our living and dying. Here is the stuff of us, our body, death and life, the nexus of creation and destruction, our creative dormancy.

(Sprinkle water on the soil.)

May this water be a blessing from our community upon our creative dormancy. May this water encourage growth. May we anticipate the new shoot and the flower, and find confidence in the grace of this world. May we trust the depths and call them into the light.

(Close with a reprise of "Return Again.")

For Grief during the Winter Holidays
Rev. Emily Bruce

This Longest Night ritual is a meditative ritual designed to create sacred space for the grief and loss that so often accompany the winter holidays, and yet can be obscured in the blur of celebrations.

It is usually held as part of a worship service on an evening near the winter solstice, a date often concurrent with the Christian feast day of St. Thomas the Apostle. In Christian belief, St. Thomas struggled to accept the truth of Jesus' resurrection as the other apostles did, and is therefore called "doubting Thomas"; this ritual can make space for one's struggles with faith in the midst of grief and sorrow.

The celebration of the winter solstice centers on the idea of waiting, in winter darkness, for the coming of the light. (The Christian observance of Advent at this season similarly anticipates the birth of Jesus.) This ritual provides a space of quiet and reflection so that participants may contemplate the struggles that lie on their hearts and how the coming light may provide illumination for them in their spiritual journey.

Materials

- ☐ Altar table
- ☐ Chalice
- ☐ Taper or tea light candles, at least two for each participant
- ☐ Taper candles with drip guards, at least one for each participant
- ☐ Twinkle lights, candles, etc., for decoration
- ☐ Singing bowl or bell

Setup

To create a quiet and reflective meditative space, hold the ritual at dusk or in the evening. Turn off all overhead lights and bright lights of any kind; use warm, soft, and low lights, especially candles and twinkle lights (shining steadily, not flashing). Put the chalice on the altar table, and put at least two candles for each participant either on the altar table as well or on another table in an accessible location; have some extra candles nearby in case they're needed.

Recruit helpers to give each participant a taper candle (with drip guard) as they enter, and to help with candle lighting during the ritual.

The songs suggested here are from the Taizé Christian monastic community. Taizé songs have simple and repetitive lyrics, meaning that people can learn them quickly. Any alternative song choices should be similarly simple.

Script

Opening Words

Good evening and welcome to [congregation's name]. Whoever you are and wherever you are on your spiritual journey, you are welcome here.

On your way into our space, you should have been given a small taper candle. If you did not receive one, please raise your hand and the helpers will bring one to you. Please just hold on to it for now; we will light some other candles first, and come to these ones toward the end.

We invite you now to relax into your seat and take a cleansing breath in . . . and out. This time is for you. This is a time for rest, for prayer, for meditation, and for healing. This ritual is an opportunity to hold space for all that lies on our hearts during this holiday season. To give ourselves the grace to just be here, now.

So we invite you to mentally put down your to-do list—it will be there when this ritual ends. Please silence your cell phones—they will also be there when this ritual ends. Give yourself the gift of being present to this sacred space, to these people, to this moment.

Chalice Lighting

We begin by lighting our chalice, a symbol of light and faith, with these words:

For those who are grieving, for those who are longing, for those who are lonely, For those who are tired, for those who are stressed, for those who simply crave a moment's peace.

For each of you who are in this sanctuary tonight, you are the reason we are here. This chalice is lit for you.

Song

"Stay with Me" (Jacques Berthier)

Please join us in singing our first meditative song, "Stay With Me." We will sing this song several times through, so as you come to feel comfortable with it you are encouraged to put down the music and close your eyes as you sing. While you sing, contemplate why you're here, what burdens rest on your heart, and what you might want to release in this space.

(Lead participants in singing the song through up to ten times.)

Reading

"Blessing for the Longest Night" (Jan Richardson)

All throughout these months
as the shadows
have lengthened,
this blessing has been
gathering itself,
making ready,
preparing for
this night.

It has practiced
walking in the dark,
traveling with
its eyes closed,
feeling its way

by memory
by touch
by the pull of the moon
even as it wanes.

So believe me
when I tell you
this blessing will
reach you
even if you
have not light enough
to read it;
it will find you
even though you cannot
see it coming.

You will know
the moment of its
arriving
by your release
of the breath
you have held
so long;
a loosening
of the clenching
in your hands,
of the clutch
around your heart;
a thinning
of the darkness
that had drawn itself
around you.

This blessing
does not mean

to take the night away
but it knows
its hidden roads,
knows the resting spots
along the path,
knows what it means
to travel
in the company
of a friend.

So when
this blessing comes,
take its hand.
Get up.
Set out on the road
you cannot see.

This is the night
when you can trust
that any direction
you go,
you will be walking
toward the dawn.

Silent Meditation

As we move into a time of meditation and prayer, we invite you to reflect on what lies on your heart in this moment. What did you bring with you into this space? What are you sitting with right now? Whether it is something that brings you grief, anxiety, or joy, we encourage you to allow its presence as you rest in this space.

We will now take meaningful time to sit in silence—for prayer, for meditation, or if you prefer, simply to breathe slowly and intentionally. The bell ring will signify the beginning and end of this time of silence.

(Ring the bell once. Hold space for meditation for approximately five minutes. Ring the bell again at the end.)

Candles of Loss

This season is a time of remembrance and reflection—remembering the loved ones we have lost and reflecting on the year that is coming to an end. Holding grief for those whose absence we feel and reckoning with the events of the past year.

We now invite you to light a candle for those beloveds whose absence you are feeling most strongly at this time of year: the family, friends, and loved ones whose spirits remain with you in memory. You can also light a candle for other losses you may be grieving this year, such as loss of employment, loss of a relationship, or loss of health.

If you like, you can come forward and light a candle here, whenever you feel called to do so. You can also raise your hand, and a helper will bring a candle to you for you to light or offer any other help you may want. As we are lighting candles, we will sing our second meditative song, "Within Our Darkest Night." You are invited to join in singing whenever you are ready.

(Allow ample time for everyone to light their candles, repeating the song as many times as needed. Helpers bring candles to participants as needed, and put their lit candles on the table with the others.)

Song

"Within Our Darkest Night" (Jacques Berthier)

(Music begins as the candle lighting ritual starts. Lead participants in singing it as many times as needed, until all who wish to light candles have done so.)

Candles of Blessing

Life is both loss and blessing, sorrow and joy. So often, both are intricately intertwined. For that reason, we now invite you to light a candle for what you have not lost—for the blessings of this life for which you are grateful, for the loved ones who surround you in body or in spirit, and for the richness of community that encourages you to keep faith in yourselves and each other. For all of these blessings and many more that may remain unspoken, we invite you now to light another candle.

Please raise a hand or come forward as you feel called. As we are lighting candles, we will sing our next meditative hymn, "Ubi Caritas." You are invited to join in singing whenever you are ready.

(Again, allow ample time. Helpers assist as before.)

Song

"Ubi Caritas" (traditional Christian hymn)

(Music begins as the candle lighting ritual starts. Lead participants in singing it as many times as needed, until all who wish to light candles have done so.)

Candles of Hope

Finally, we now invite you to light a candle for yourself—for that divine spark that resides inside of you. You may light a candle to set your intentions for the year to come, to make space for the journey that lies ahead, or as a silent prayer for the hopes and dreams that are in your heart.

For this, you may use the small taper candle that was given you when you entered. Please remain seated; we will pass the flame one to another, around the room. And we will sing again, this time "Nada Te Turbe."

Song

"Nada Te Turbe" (words by Santa Teresa de Jesus, music by Jacques Berthier)

(Light a taper candle of your own from the chalice, and use it to light one or a few participants' tapers; guide them in passing the flame on. Helpers might assist here. Lead participants in singing the song as many times as needed, until all participants' tapers are lit.)

Prayer

Friends, will you please join me in the spirit of prayer?

Holy Light, Holy Presence, Holy Love,

We honor all of the souls whose light is represented by these candles. May this light be a blessing to those who miss them and a symbol of the love that remains ever present between them.

We witness the pain and the grief that is present in this space. May this light assure you that you are seen, that you are held, and that you are not alone. May you feel the presence of the ancestors, saints, and loved ones that journey with you today and every day.

We raise up all of the tender hearts present in this space. For the weariness, for the anxiety, for the overwhelm, may this light be a symbol of peace. You are not forsaken. We all struggle with you and we all pray for you, that you may receive the blessings of nourishment, rest, and well-being.

We turn our faces to the light to witness the holy presence in our lives, the holy love in the world that surrounds us, and to lift up our gratitude for the many blessings of this world. Amidst your daily strife, may you remember that you are enough, you are worthy, and you are loved.

May it be so. Amen.

I invite you to extinguish your candles, but not the divine spark that resides within you.

(Extinguish your own taper.)

Silent Meditation

As we move into a final time of silent meditation and prayer, we invite you to reflect on whatever is rising in your heart right now, after this ritual of contemplation we have shared together. It may be grief, or joy, or both, or something else. Breathe peacefully into the peace of this sanctuary, and allow your heart to rest open. We hope that this time of silence can offer you healing and blessing.

(Ring the bell once. Hold space for meditation for approximately five minutes. Ring the bell again at the end.)

Song

"Spirit of Life" (Carolyn McDade)

Please join us in singing once more, in whatever way you are comfortable. We will sing "Spirit of Life." As we sing, contemplate who or what is present to you in this moment. Whether it is the holy presence of God, the memory of a loved one, or a presence that's in your life today, you are invited to reflect on how they love and support you, on how their role in your life is meaningful.

(Lead participants in singing.)

Chalice Extinguishing

Friends, as we go from this place,
May we remember that light and shadow are the rhythms of the world.
We need not be afraid. We are not alone in our experience of either.

May this time of shared solitude and song be a grace upon you, bringing you comfort and connection, soothing your soul, whether it is weary, worried, or longing.

And as we extinguish this chalice [do so now], may the love that is present in this sanctuary surround you. May you see with soft eyes the interconnected web of existence, of which we all are a part. May the coming of the light fill your spirit and guide you, as we leave this space.

May it be so. Amen.

(Instrumental music plays as people leave the space.)

For the Winter Solstice

Rev. Wendy Bartel and Rev. Lynn Gardner

This ritual honors both the dark and the light on the winter solstice. It can be adapted for a small or larger group of any age range. The authors have participated in and facilitated a variety of Earth-centered traditions, rituals, and ceremonies. This ritual was first co-created to conclude a full evening winter solstice service in Auburn, California, and has since continued to evolve.

Materials

- ☐ Altar table
- ☐ Chalice
- ☐ Chocolate, at least one piece for each participant
- ☐ Mandarins or other citrus, at least one slice for each participant
- ☐ Alternative foods for those who do not eat chocolate or citrus
- ☐ Trays or plates
- ☐ Music

Setup

This ritual should be held at night, when darkness and candlelight help to set a tone for the turning of the seasons. If possible, dim the lights and/or light candles around the outside of the circle, at a safe distance from participants.

Place chairs in a circle, leaving openings for folks to enter and exit the circle and for those using wheelchairs, scooters, etc. If you have a large gathering, you might consider concentric circles. It is ideal to have nothing but the altar table in the middle so you can move about.

On one tray, lay out alternatives for those who do not eat chocolate or citrus. Choose something dark and something light; one simple option is individually wrapped purple and yellow sugar-free hard candies. Lay them out on a tray, arranging the dark ones on one side and the light ones on the other.

Break the chocolate bars into bite-size chunks and lay them out on one side of each remaining tray. Peel the fruit and lay out wedges on the other side, arranging them like sun rays. Provide enough that all attendees can have one of each item, with a few left over so there is a sense of abundance. You may want to set out napkins or paper muffin cups for participants to use as well.

On the altar table, place a chalice and the prepared trays.

Consider draping fabrics, placing some local evergreens or bare branches, lighting candles, and having soft wintery (but not Christmas) music playing as folks are arriving.

Script

Chalice Lighting

Welcome, one and all, to this ritual of nourishment as we honor the winter solstice!

[Offer greetings and orientation to the space as is appropriate to your context.]

I open this gathering with the lighting of a chalice. The cup holds this community, and the flame is a spark of possibility, held in the circles of darkness and light, for we need both to live.

(Light the chalice.)

Opening Words

As we gather on this longest night in the northern hemisphere on this beautiful planet Earth, let us abide in the wonder and mystery. What was it like so many millennia ago when the days grew shorter and the nights grew longer, and often colder, and people did not understand why? Were they afraid? Many stories suggest they were. How would they survive? Would the animals and the plants upon which they depended for their own survival die?

In the early incarnation of our human species, I wonder what else they felt and what history they passed on to their children. What meaning did they make of the growing darkness? Did they gather around the fire and tell the stories of their people? Did they overhunt or overharvest for fear this was the beginning of the end? Did their spiritual leaders suggest they needed to make more offerings to the gods of their understanding, to implore them to bring back the sun?

And then . . . what did they do when they realized the days were finally getting longer? Was there confusion? Relief? Or maybe even jubilation? When did the observers or the wise ones or the elders realize they could predict the cycle and know when to enact whatever rituals they believed would call back the light?

It is, of course, also possible that they welcomed the growing darkness. Maybe they were glad to have a bit more downtime from hunting and gathering, and instead settle into the gifts of the darkness: rest and reflection, connection and devotion. We cannot know for sure.

(Pause.)

At this time of year, we often gather to tell stories both ancient and new. We offer one another gifts. And we participate in rituals, like this one, as we arrive in winter, with hope to find our way toward spring.

We need not rush out of the dark, though. Many messages in our culture devalue the dark and teach us to fear. Our language often conveys that darkness is dangerous—monsters are in the dark, bad things happen in dark alleys—and yet so much relies on the dark: the gestation of new life, including our own; decomposition that nourishes the soil; the practice of hibernation or going within that allows us to heal, reintegrate, and recover so we are ready for what will come. Many of us sleep better when it is dark, whether or not it is nighttime. There is a sweetness, a vulnerability, in gestation, in decomposition, in hibernation, in restoration. Have you ever felt moved watching a loved one sleeping? And many of us say "Sweet dreams" when someone is heading off to sleep. There may be danger in the dark, but there is also sweetness.

And we often associate light with goodness, with the divine. The sun's warmth and light help plants to grow. Light helps many of us to do our daily tasks. And yet, too much light is exhausting and even harmful for many species. Both are true. And there is something joyful as the Earth orbits the sun and birds begin to return, the days grow longer, and we see new life growing. There is joy in the first crocus pushing through snow. Let us not rush toward the light. We need both darkness and light to thrive.

These cycles of life and death and rebirth are apparent in the seasons too. Tonight, we rest in the dark as the winter solstice comes upon us. What will we pass on to our children about the importance of light *and* darkness? How might we celebrate both together? Let us take some quiet time to just slow down, noticing our breath as it moves in and out of us, and consider the ways we can celebrate dark and light.

(Pause for contemplation. After a few moments, begin the melody of "Honor the Dark" to invite folks back to the present moment. You might have a musician playing live, or a recording.)

We invite you to listen to this beautiful song by Lea Morris, "Honor the Dark." You are invited to sing along as the words become familiar.

Song

"Honor the Dark" (Lea Morris)

(Lead participants in singing.)

"Until only love remains." As we near the winter solstice, we journey into the darkness and also celebrate the return of the sun. I invite you to consider quietly what you might need as nourishment for the journey.

(Pause.)

Sharing Nourishment

We are invited into this circle tonight, a circle of worth, a circle where all are held, a circle where we honor the dark and the light at this winter solstice time, for we need both darkness and light to survive. We also know that in many ways the dark, the darkness, the shadow is not valued—is actually denigrated. Tonight we interrupt that false narrative and declare our appreciation of the dark and of the sweet time it allows for reflection, renewal, and nourishment. And as we kindle fires and candles, we celebrate the light with joy, too.

Tonight, we will offer one another a blessing of nourishment—a reminder of the nourishment we get from both the light and the dark. We will pass around trays of chocolate and oranges, or if you prefer, there are also sugarless candies [or whatever you have provided].

When you receive a tray, offer it to your neighbor and say, "May the darkness bring sweetness. May the light bring joy." They choose a dark treat and a light one. If you need a different tray, just give a gentle wave and we'll bring you one. After your neighbor has taken their treats, give them the tray, and they will offer it to the next person. And so it goes around the circle. As you feel ready, you are invited to enjoy the sweetness of the chocolate or dark candy. Then let the brightness of the mandarin or light candy bring you joy.

At the end we'll share our blessing all together, and it is my hope you will join me in saying, "May the darkness bring sweetness. May the light bring joy." Let's practice, shall we?

PARTICIPANTS: May the darkness bring sweetness. May the light bring joy.

LEADER: We will all hold the sacred space of the circle, attend to the passing and receiving, and open our hearts as the blessings of nourishment travel around. Let us begin.

(Begin to pass the trays of chocolate and citrus, one in each direction. Then pick up the tray of alternative options and make your way around the circle, offering it to anyone who may want it. When everyone has participated, bring all the trays back to the table.)

LEADER: We have shared the blessings of nourishment with one another. Together, let us share our affirmation:

PARTICIPANTS: May the darkness bring sweetness! May the light bring joy!

LEADER: May they indeed!

Responsive Blessing

Please join me in a responsive blessing. You'll repeat the last part of each line, the thank-you.

Let us give thanks to the Earth for these blessings of nourishment! Thank you, Earth!

PARTICIPANTS: Thank you, Earth!

LEADER: Let us give thanks to the Sun for these blessings of nourishment! Thank you, Sun!

PARTICIPANTS: Thank you, Sun!

LEADER: Let us give thanks to the seed savers, farmers, harvesters, transporters, and grocers for these blessings of nourishment! Thank you, food providers!

PARTICIPANTS: Thank you, food providers!

LEADER: And we give thanks to the Love that holds us all. Thank you, Love!

PARTICIPANTS: Thank you, Love!

Chalice Extinguishing

As you head off into the night, go gently. Take time to notice the gifts in the darkness.

We are so grateful for your presence and your participation. You are welcome to stay and talk with one another and partake in more blessings.

When you are ready to head out on this longest night, go with peace, go with anticipation, and go with these blessings. A blessed winter solstice to you all!

(Extinguish the chalice.)

For a New Year
Rev. Kendra Ford

This New Year's ritual is appropriate for a congregation or small group. It can be embedded in Sunday morning worship or done as a separate ritual.

Materials

- ☐ Two small tables
- ☐ A freestanding doorway or something to evoke one
- ☐ Small pieces of paper, at least one for each participant
- ☐ A cauldron (bowl or cooking pot)
- ☐ Larger sheets of paper, one for each participant
- ☐ Envelopes, one for each participant
- ☐ Pens or pencils, one for each participant
- ☐ Basket or bowl big enough for all the letters
- ☐ Timer
- ☐ Music

Setup

If you do not have a freestanding doorway, set up something that evokes one, such as a garden arch, or two helpers holding up a horizontal pole with ribbons dangling down from it. A 36-inch opening will allow nearly all wheelchairs, scooters, and other mobility devices to get through; most standard doorways are 32 inches, which may be a problem for some. If there is a step or lintel at the base that people would have to get over, lay a nonslip rug over it. Place the doorway where all participants will be able to approach it, pass through it, and return to their places. On one side of it, set up the cauldron where participants will place their papers to be burned. On the other side, set up the other table with the basket for letters.

As people enter the space, they should receive a small piece of paper, a sheet of regular paper, an envelope, and a pen or pencil.

Be prepared to hold on to the letters until May and then mail them to participants.

Script

Opening Words

Welcome to the future, where you will live from now on! This isn't really the future; we only have this breath right now, so really I welcome you to the present, to this one moment between past and future. This is the only moment we ever live in. In this present, in this suspension between past and future, this cusp, a new year's beginning, I thought we might take as our traveling companion the ancient Roman god Janus, the god who looks forward and looks back, the god of beginnings and endings, the god of doorways.

Hymn

"May Nothing Evil Cross This Door" (Louis Untermeyer)

(Lead participants in singing.)

Reflection

In this ritual we will take some time to look both backward and forward, like Janus. We will open our hands to let go of what we want to leave behind in the old year, and open our hearts to what we want to carry with us in the new one.

Let us begin with a moment of reflection. Take a moment to breathe, the breath going in and out through the door of the body.

How do you want to live this coming year?
What will you have to give up, to do so?
What will you have to let in, to do so?

Writing: Letting Go

There may be things from the past year that you'd like to let go of in the coming one. Maybe they don't serve you well, or aren't good for you; maybe they've been wonderful, but their time is over now. Maybe they're things you don't want to get rid of, but you know you need to. Whatever they are, hold them in your heart for a moment, those things that belong to the old year and not the new one. Then write them on your small piece of paper.

(You may want to play quiet music as people write. After a few minutes, when most people seem to be finished, tell participants that they have about a minute left. When everyone has finished, ask for their attention again.)

Writing: Intentions

The new year will bring new challenges, new joys, and new times with the people and places we know well already. What do you want to have with you? What will you need to gather, or what do you already have that you want to be sure to keep, as you move forward?

Please take ten minutes to write a letter to your future self on your big sheet of paper. We will send your letter to you this spring! Remind your future self what you want to be doing and remembering, what you want to have with you. When you're done, put it in the envelope and address it to yourself, so we can mail it. Please write your letter now; I'll let you know when time is almost up.

(You may want to play quiet music as people write. After nine minutes, tell participants that they have one minute left. When time is up, remind them to put their letters into their envelopes and address them.)

Doorway

Be aware, now, that we are in the presence of the ancient of ancients—the doorway.

(If you have helpers creating a temporary doorway, they should come forward now and set it up.)

People have been building doorways as long as we have been creating shelter, collecting food, leaving for journeys. Doorways mark shelter and safety, doorways mark going out and a fresh start. They are the place where we change from inside to outside, from home to away, from traveler to guest. Doorways mark endings and beginnings all at once.

We stand in the doorway of the year this weekend. One year is ending and another is beginning—but we are not fully in the new year, nor entirely out of the old. We are in between years. Like the Roman God Janus, we look both ahead and behind simultaneously. He is the dweller on the threshold, a divinity presiding over the change point of a building and the change point in many lives. The month of January is named for him; it is the month of moving from one year to another. Janus, god of beginnings and endings, reminds us that we always have a chance to begin again.

In a moment I will invite you not only to think about the animating power of the doorway, the concept of a being who looks both backward and forward; I will also invite you to experience moving through a doorway yourself, here. I invite you to move into something new, move out of something old.

On this side of the door, the past, there is a cauldron. Before you go through the doorway, put what you are leaving behind in the cauldron. It will be burned outside, after the service, to release it.

[Indicate the other side of the doorway.] On the other side, over there in the future, there is a basket for your letter to your future self. Leave your self-addressed letter there, and we will mail it to you this spring. Then you can go back to your seat.

So now I invite you to move through the doorway here. I invite you to take a breath as you pause on the threshold between past and future, here in this shining present moment. When everyone who wishes to has passed through the doorway, we will share a blessing.

(Have music playing as people move through the doorway. Once everyone has finished, offer the following blessing.)

Blessing the Doorways

May you always have a door that is wide enough and high enough to move through.

May you notice your endings and your beginnings.

May you put down what you do not need;

May you carry with you what you do.

For Earth Day

Rev. theresa rohlck

This is a ritual for honoring the fragility and resilience of this Earth, the beauty of the natural world, the impermanence of life, and the interconnectedness of all beings. The ritual invites participants to create an Earth circle from a variety of objects found in nature, while contemplating beauty and interconnectedness; the circle is dismantled at the end. This is a particularly accessible ritual for young people. Even the very young can participate when guided by a caregiver or teacher. This ritual was inspired by the abundance of chestnuts and pine cones, stones and shells, seeds and leaves the author collects on walks and was originally created as a virtual ritual during the Covid-19 pandemic.

Materials

- ☐ Chalice
- ☐ Stones, feathers, pine cones, chestnuts, leaves, twigs, shells, and similar natural items, enough for each participant to create a design a foot across
- ☐ Tables for participants to work on
- ☐ Sheets of paper or placemats, square or round, at least a foot across

Setup

Set up tables and chairs, and lay a place mat for each participant. (If some people want to work in pairs, that's fine.) Spread out the nature items on the tables so that a variety of them are accessible to all participants.

Adapt the language given here to your participants: adults, intergenerational, youth only, etc. In particular, when working with younger participants, you may want to make clear at the beginning that the Earth circles let us practice letting go of things, because they will be wiped away at the end of the ritual.

Script

Introduction

Today we are going to create, together, an Earth circle. What comes to mind when you think about a circle?

(You can encourage participants to answer out loud, or to just think about their answers. If they are answering out loud, acknowledge the responses before moving on.)

We honor the interdependent web of existence, and we celebrate that we are part of it. When I visualize that web I see concentric circles, starting from a small center point, but growing wider and wider. We are called to widen the circle that connects us all, to truly include everyone. Instead of just inviting someone into the small center of our existing circle, we can think about expanding, widening our circle to include more and more. As we see just how interconnected everyone on the planet is, we realize that our actions have an impact far beyond ourselves or our immediate community.

The Earth itself is a three-dimensional circle, a sphere. As we make our Earth circles today, we will also center our thoughts on our relationship with the plants, animals, land, water, air, and all beings on this Earth.

Will you join me on this spiritual journey now?

Chalice Lighting

We light a chalice to mark our beginning, and by doing so recognize that we are in sacred space together.

(Light the chalice.)

May this light represent the creative energy we each have burning within us that helps us imagine a world that is healthier, safer, and more just for all who inhabit the Earth, now and in the future.

Creating Earth Circles

Let's begin creating our Earth circles. Each of us has a space to work in, marked out by the placemat. I am placing a smooth stone in the center of my space. Will you do that with me?

Take a handful of breaths with me, breathing as it feels comfortable for you. You might want to close your eyes for a moment to help center yourself.

(Pause and take a few breaths.)

Now let's begin to create a circular design, moving out from the center. You may use any of the materials you have near you, in any way you wish. There is no right or wrong way to do this meditation.

(Begin creating your own Earth circle. You are modeling the steps for participants; doing it yourself also helps you pace your speaking. The creation should not be rushed.)

As you place each item, take a moment to notice the beauty of the object you are holding. Feel how the stone fits into your palm, feel how smooth an old chestnut is, notice how symmetrical the seashell is. Place each one with intention and gratitude for all that the Earth provides for us.

As you do this, reflect on who or what is within your circle right now. Who or what is excluded? What actions can you take to make the circle wider still?

(Pause for a few moments.)

Let's continue now in silence.

(Continue for as long as the meditation needs; do not rush.)

As you are finishing your Earth circle, take a few more intentional breaths.

(Pause and take a few breaths.)

Do you feel more centered, more connected to the Earth, to each other, to nature?

If you would, join me in singing "Circle 'Round for Freedom." Use this time to finish your Earth circle if you are not quite finished.

Song

"Circle 'Round for Freedom" (Linda Hirschhorn)

(Lead participants in singing.)

Practicing Impermanence

As human beings with agency to act, we are called to care for this planet, the Earth, our home.

The Earth has existed for over 4 billion years, and the amount of time humans have existed is miniscule in comparison. Yet within only the past few hundred years, the actions of many human beings, countries, and governments have jeopardized the future of this planet, the future for our children and our children's children.

We are part of the natural cycles of life in which things are born, grow, and die, and new life begins again. You may have grown up never thinking that the Earth would die—it will, but the time frame is just too big to comprehend. What we do need to comprehend is that we are responsible for the ongoing devastation of this planet; the climate crisis is a very real reminder of this.

Now, I invite you to slowly sweep away the design you created. Gently push all the items off to the side. (Demonstrate doing this. You may also invite participants to push items into a container, if that makes sense for your setup.)

May this action remind us how fragile and impermanent life is, this world is. When there has been damage or loss to the environment, the Earth typically has been able to heal; as humans we can take action to help the healing, or we can choose to do nothing. We have the power to make a difference, no matter how small.

What does the world look like, as you imagine it, when it is both whole and holy?
Hold this image for a moment in your imagination.

(Pause for several moments.)

Extinguishing the Chalice

Dear ones,
May we not be discouraged when things end
may we see that ending creates the potential
for healing, for growth, and for renewal
may we believe in our creative vision
for what this Earth can be
in the not too distant future
and act to make it so.
It is not too late.

Amen. May it be so.

(Extinguish the chalice.)

For Acknowledging Mother's, Father's, and Parents' Days

Rev. Lynn Gardner and Rev. Wendy Bartel

Inspired by our families and our first co-ministry with
the Sierra Foothills Unitarian Universalists

Many people have mixed feelings about Mother's Day, Father's Day, or Parents' Day. This ritual acknowledges a variety of relationships between parents and children: the beautiful, the challenging, and the complicated. Many familial experiences are hidden from those outside the family and not acknowledged. This ritual was designed to be used as part of a congregation's worship service, to name prayerfully and out loud the deeper complexity and pain that many of us carry.

In their family and professional experiences in childcare, music therapy, and co-ministry, the authors have faced and witnessed the amazing, difficult, awful, incredible, and perplexing experiences people have had with their parents and as parents. They want Unitarian Universalism to continue to expand nuance and inclusion.

Materials

- ☐ Altar table
- ☐ Thirteen candles and holders (or twelve, for a Parents' Day ritual), as alike as possible
- ☐ Small taper candle
- ☐ Small plate

Setup

Arrange the candles on the altar table so they are visible to those who will gather, and so that a person lighting them won't block the view of them; set a taper beside them to transfer the flame with. If the candles are not near a lit chalice, place a small lit tea light near them, with the taper.

Recruit a helper to light the candles.

Script

(Say "Mother," "Father," or "Parent" as appropriate throughout, according to the day you are marking.)

We want our congregations to be places where each of us can be more fully welcomed and known. When we look at the array of cards available for [Mother's, Father's, Parents'] Day, we notice that there are many relationships and experiences that aren't named . . . that are invisible. This includes the gender identities of parents who identify beyond the binary. We invite us all to broaden the terms of [mothering, fathering, parenting] to expand past society's gendered definitions of these words and to more intentionally include people of many fabulous genders.

We begin this ritual by acknowledging and honoring the complexity of this day, the complicated relationships and experiences that may be present here in this gathering, and by lighting candles.

(The helper lights the taper from the tea light or an already lit chalice. After you read each line below, the helper lights one of the candles on the altar table. Go at a calm, thoughtful pace, allowing each line and each candle to have its own significance.)

For those who wish their relationship with their [mother, father, parent] was different than it is.

For those whose [mothers, fathers, parents] have died.

For the [mothers, fathers, parents] who foster, for those who have adopted, and for the birth [mothers, fathers, parents].

For all those who want to be [mothers, fathers, parents], and who may not have this experience.

For those [mothers, fathers, parents] whose children are far away.

For the [mothers-in-law, fathers-in-law, parents-in-law], [stepmothers, stepfathers, stepparents], and coparents who are redefining family.

For those who didn't receive the [mothering, fathering, parenting] that they needed.

For those who didn't offer the [mothering, fathering, parenting] they wish they had.

For those [mothers, fathers, parents] who have lost children, whether not born, infants, children, youth, or adults; for the ones who are missed.

(Choose from the next three options as appropriate.)

For those families that don't include a mom, yet are mothering, who are loving and whole just as they are.

For those families that don't include a dad, yet are fathering, who are loving and whole just as they are.

For those families who have parents whose gender identity is expressed beyond "mother" or "father," who are loving and whole just as they are.

For the [mothering, fathering, parenting] of the furry, the finned, the spiny, the scaled, the winged.

For those with wonderful and complicated relationships with their [mother, father, parent], or with their children, all practicing the art of being human.

For those who are grateful for the blessings of their [mothers, fathers, parents].

(All the candles should now be lit.)

Call to mind, now, those who have been a [mother/father/parent] or [mother/father/parent] figure to you. (pause) You are invited to speak those names aloud.

(Pause for speaking of names and then another breath.)

Blessed be these names. Blessed be our memories. Blessed be this moment.

(Pause here, staying focused on the candles and allowing space for feelings to emerge and be expressed, before ending the ritual or moving on to the next element in a worship service. You might transition with a brief musical interlude, if appropriate to your setting.)

For Pride

Rev. Hannah Roberts Villnave, Rev. Kayla Parker, and Rev. Caitlin Cotter Coillberg

This is a ritual for Pride. It could be done as part of a congregational worship service, or by a group of congregation members before going to a Pride event. It could also be used as a stand-alone ritual, to provide a spiritual and religious LGBTQ+-affirming space within the Pride festivities of the larger community. It is a time for prayers of protection and celebration, a time to send others and ourselves off with armor and joy. It is a blessing for, of, and by the LGBTQ+ community. The authors co-created this ritual out of their lived experience as queer clergywomen who love both blessings and parties.

Materials

- ☐ Altar table
- ☐ Glitter gel

Setup

Give special attention to how to center LGBTQ+ community members without putting them on display. Invite them to participate (as they are willing) in planning and leading this ritual, particularly if you are an ally rather than a member of the LGBTQ+ community yourself.

The responsive litany in particular should be led by a member of the LGBTQ+ community.

If this ritual is taking place outside, find space that will not be in the way of pedestrians to set up an altar and have enough space for participants to gather. Make some seating available. Use a sound system, and be aware of competing noise; many Pride events are quite loud! If you have a larger group, you can invite helpers to assist you in offering blessings.

Script

Opening Words

(This section may need to be modified if using this ritual as part of a larger congregational worship service.)

Welcome to our Pride blessing! [If you are doing this ritual as a faith community, name your community here.] Whether you've been here before or not, welcome! Whether you are a member of the LGBTQ+ community or an ally, welcome! Here, we'll share some words and music together, and then we'll have an opportunity for you to receive a glitter blessing. However you name and understand the divine, you are welcome in this community of precious, powerful LGBTQ+ siblings and allies!

Reading

"A Protest and a Party" by Hannah Roberts Villnave

People sometimes ask:
Is Pride a protest
Or a party?
And the answer is
Of course
Yes.

And why not?

Why not
Rejoice as we resist
Dance as we demand change
Celebrate as we create community that delights in
All of who we are?

So bring all of that
With you this morning.

Bring your policy demands
Bring your glitter
Bring your Supreme Court–broken heart
Bring your rainbow socks
Bring the emptiness you feel
For our siblings gone too soon.

Bring your Gloria Estefan remix
Bring your tender hope for change
Bring your most garish eyeshadow
Bring your spirit, tattered and battered
By a world that seems insistent on
Choosing fear and hate.

Gather up all these things
And bring them here
To a place where we don't
Have to shoulder these burdens
Or celebrate these joys
Alone.

Song

"How Could Anyone" (Libby Roderick)

Please join us in singing "How Could Anyone." This song was written by Libby Roderick, an Alaskan singer-songwriter, poet, activist, and teacher. It has been used around the world in spaces where people needed to honor and be reminded of their wholeness. We will sing it three times in the course of this ceremony.

(Lead participants in singing.)

Responsive Litany

Please join us in a litany of blessing. Your response will be "We are precious and we are powerful." Let's try that now!

(Lead participants in reciting "We are precious and we are powerful." Cue them by gesture for each subsequent recitation.)

We come from fierce freedom fighters.
From the survivors and the dead of the HIV crisis,
    who organized and fought for their lives.
From the Black Kings and Queens who ruled the ballroom,
    who insisted we dance even amidst death and devastation.
From these ancestors, we learn:

PARTICIPANTS: We are precious, and we are powerful.

LEADER: With the tenderhearted butches and the powerful femmes
With the strong twinks and the soft bears
With all the complexities that live within each of us
We know that we are whole, just as we are:

PARTICIPANTS: We are precious, and we are powerful.

LEADER: From the Black dykes, the trans Chicana sisters, the Boricua bois,
And every other sibling who is told they can't bring their full self to queer community,
From them, we learn:

PARTICIPANTS: We are precious, and we are powerful.

LEADER: To the elders who've seen it all
To those with one toe out of the closet
To those who are still in it
To those who tore down the closet altogether, we say:

PARTICIPANTS: We are precious, and we are powerful.

LEADER: In the face of hatred,
In the faces of those who deny our wholeness

We root ourselves in the truth we know:

Participants: We are precious, and we are powerful.

Leader: From the dance floor to the Capitol rotunda,
From our kitchen tables to the White House,
From jail cells to classrooms to pulpits,
Whether whispered or shouted,
We will and do proclaim:

Participants: We are precious, and we are powerful.

Song

Let us sing together, again, "How Could Anyone."

(Lead participants in singing.)

Glitter Blessing

Today we offer a glitter blessing, a recognition of the sacred beauty inherent in every person.

Glitter has long been a symbol for the LGBTQ+ movement of gritty, sparkly hope in the face of prejudice and oppression, of joy and pride in the face of hatred and bigotry.

Glitter is resilient and tenacious. The briefest beam of sunlight causes it to shine out even in the dustiest and dreariest of spaces, and its beauty comes from its brokenness.

Glitter sparkles because it is many different broken pieces coming together, changing in every moment as the light changes.

This glitter that we share with each other today is a reminder that each of us is beautiful in our sacred imperfection, our ever-changing selves, our glorious plurality.

As we play some music, you are invited to come forward, show us where on your face, neck, arm, or hand you would like to receive your glitter blessing, and then circle back to your seat. If you cannot come forward today and wish to receive this blessing, please raise your hand and one of us will come to you.

(As each person comes up, give them a small smear of glitter and say something like "May you sparkle inside and out," "You are fabulous, keep shining on," "Remember, you are made of star stuff," or "May the beauty that you are shine as bright as the stars." Be sure to not put glitter too close to anyone's eyes or where someone with physical disabilities might accidentally swipe it into their eyes or mouth. People who have severe disabilities may do better with the glitter on their upper arms or on their neck. Once all who wish it have received the blessing, continue.)

I invite you to pause with me, as we come to the close of this ritual. Look around at all the beautiful shining faces that surround you, at the amazing thing that is our blessed bodies gathered in this sacred space together. Everybody in this space and beyond it is a holy thing, every person a sacred being made of stardust.

Take a moment, now, just to marvel at how extra glittery we are today, how fabulous we are.

(Pause.)

Song

Let us sing once more together "How Could Anyone."

(Lead participants in singing.)

Closing Words

As we go forth, I offer you this final blessing.

May you receive and reflect love, everywhere you go, and know—in your deepest heart and in every day—you matter and you belong.

May you hold on to hope and your inner sparkle even when discouragement and despair beckon.

May the beauty that is you shine out, bright as the stars from which we came and to which we will return.

Together may we make this a place of welcome and healing, of connection and plurality.

Together may we practice compassion and courage, seeing and celebrating and supporting each other.

Together may we be the sparkling force of love that our world needs.

Blessed by this community and by the divine, go forth and celebrate with pride!

Working for Justice

For Blessing the Organizers

Ruth Idakula and Rev. Deanna Vandiver

This is a ritual to bless movement organizers and all those working for social justice and collective liberation. The authors co-created the original version of this ritual in 2016 as a resource for the movement, a way to strengthen people for the journey toward collective liberation, and have been adapting it ever since.

Materials

None

Setup

Anywhere—in a church sanctuary, online, on the street, in the forest; this is a portable ritual.

This ritual may be adapted to serve whoever needs blessing in your community.

Script

Beloveds, thank you for showing up for each other, for the beloved community that we are always in the process of creating. We bear witness to the courage and the power among us.

In this sacred time, we ask everyone present to join in a ritual of blessing for all of us who organize for justice and collective liberation.

Beloveds, you are invited to take a centering breath in and then, with intention, release it.

As you breathe in and breathe out, know that you are not alone
Know that the ancestors that fought before you are with you now
Know that you are forever guided by their wisdom
And sustained by their love and courage

As you are willing and able, reach out and connect with a human being near you, with a hand, an elbow, a wave, a gentle smile . . . some acknowledgment of our connection.

(Pause as participants get connected.)

You are invited to be a part of this blessing, offering your love and energy and support.
You are invited to be a part of this blessing, receiving love and energy and support from those around you.

Breathing in and then slowly releasing your breath, please repeat after me.

(Read the following eight lines, pausing after each to let participants repeat what you have said.)

I am worthy.
We are worthy.
My life matters.
Our lives matter.
I am not alone.
We are not alone.
I am held by a community of power and love.
We are held by a community of power and love.

Now, breathing in and then slowly releasing your breath, please repeat after me, offering this blessing to each other.

(Read the following two lines, pausing after each to let participants repeat what you have said.)

We are grateful for you.
We need you.

Receive this blessing, and go forth with courage and compassion to organize for justice and mercy. Breathing in a breath of love, breathing out a breath of liberation, we say asé and amen.

(Close with a song or chant relevant to the group you are blessing.)

For Direct Action

Rev. Elizabeth Nguyen

This ritual is to bless and support a person or group engaging in direct action or civil disobedience. It developed from the author's own experiences participating in, and supporting others' participation in, acts of noncooperation, protest, disruption, and community defense. It's intended to be flexible and adaptable; it can be used in whole or in parts or expanded, depending on the need of the moment. The methods of direct action and civil disobedience are neutral. Any action can be grounded in love and justice and move our world toward liberation and thriving, or it can be grounded in hegemony, oppression, state violence, genocide, or hate. This ritual is intended to support the intentional disruption of unjust laws, practices, or actions through acts of love that confront systems of oppression.

Materials

None

Setup

This ritual can be done as part of training or preparation to engage in direct action, in the days or weeks beforehand. It can also be used in a quiet moment a few hours or a few moments before an action, or even while actually doing direct action. Consider whether law enforcement are present and whether anything you say (or ask others to say) could incriminate, or have other legal consequences for, the person or people acting or anyone else, including organizers, trainers, supporters—and you yourself.

The ritual is written with spaces for you to fill in details and specifics relevant to the action. This is intended to be a gentle space to ground participants in their bodies and communities, acknowledge their fears and the challenges they face, and connect them to their vision of the world they are fighting for.

Script

Grounding

(Begin with a way for participants to pause and ground themselves. Some ways to do this are:)

- *Making eye contact*
- *Feeling their weight pressing them to the ground*
- *Bringing attention to a specific part or parts of the body*
- *Taking a centering breath, or three, or ten*
- *Humming together*
- *Closing or lowering eyes*
- *Holding silence for thirty seconds or several minutes*
- *Holding hands, touching one another's shoulders, bumping elbows, or making some other physical connection* (with consent)
- *Singing a song*
- *Doing three neck rolls*
- *Stretching or making another movement*

(If you have more time, consider doing several of these. When it feels right, move on to the blessing.)

Blessing

[Name(s)], as you take this action for love and justice, you do not act alone.

[I, We] give thanks for [name the teachers, trainers, activists, leaders, and individual community members whose lineage this action is in or who it is dedicated to].

You are part of a long struggle toward liberation.
Act with humility, knowing you are [one, a few] of many.
Do what is yours to do.
Many fears, doubts, questions, challenges may be part of this moment.
We acknowledge them, and we know that many have had those same fears, doubts, questions, challenges and have acted anyway.
We act anyway.

Know that you are worthy and beloved,
And nothing can take that away from you,
As we fight for a world where we are all free and safe and well and thriving,
Act by act.

(End the blessing with a phrase that is relevant to the action. This could be a line from a chant or a song, a grounding phrase, or the core messaging or goal of the action, such as "Water is life," "Not one more deportation," or "Black lives matter." Then close with another form of shared grounding, either the one you used at the beginning or a different one.)

For Nourishing Justice Makers

Rev. Aisha Ansano and Rev. Emily Conger

This ritual explores the power and possibility of building beloved community, sharing the challenges and blessing one another for this long-haul commitment of generations. We recommend it for anyone striving for justice who needs nourishment for the long haul: youth groups going on a service trip, a social justice committee preparing for or in the midst of a new project, boards doing visioning, or even a whole congregation, as part of a worship service.

Materials

- ☐ Chalice
- ☐ Food or drink, a few bites or small cup for each participant (could also be imaginary)
- ☐ Copies of the litany of challenges

Setup

This ritual could be used to start a meeting, as part of a retreat or worship service, or on its own. It includes both full group and small group parts. Arrange the space so that folks can see one another. Chairs in a circle or around a large table would work well, or if the group is very large, smaller tables or clusters of chairs. If you have eight or fewer people, you can do the entire ritual together. Otherwise, you should create space to split into groups of four or five people who will bless one another.

Set up the food or drink as needed in the space. If you don't know what dietary restrictions folks have, it's better to invite them to imagine food or drinks than to provide something that not everyone can share. You could also just provide water.

If your group is too large to begin in a single circle together, plan to read the litany of challenges yourself or recruit helpers to do so. Ensure that the helpers are scattered around the room, not clumped together.

Script

Opening Words

Welcome to this ritual of renewal and nourishment for the long-haul commit-ment of building beloved community together. This ritual includes sharing from our hearts, eating together, and blessing one another.

When we gather around a table, we can build community, find beauty in our shared experiences, and celebrate our differences. We can feed one another in body and spirit to sustain this important ministry together.

We want to acknowledge that food and eating can be complicated for many of us. We come to the table with experiences and stories that are joyful and painful and everything in between. We welcome you into this space and honor the expe-riences that you are bringing, the feelings you are holding, and all of who you are.

Chalice Lighting

(Invite someone to light the chalice as you read these words.)

Let us join together in a spirit of gratitude.
We light our chalice, marking this time together as sacred.
Let us enter into this space, nourished by the love and warmth of community.

Framing Our Task

To paraphrase the nineteenth-century Unitarian minister Rev. Theodore Parker, although the arc of the moral universe is a long one, and although we cannot experience its full curve, we can still deeply believe that it bends toward justice—and that we can have a part in bending it that way.

Together we are striving to bend the arc, to build beloved community. To build a world rooted in love and justice, with accountability and sustainability at its core. This is an important commitment that will take all of us.

This is a task that will take generations. We build on the legacy of those who have come before us, and we do our part during our lifetimes. And we will pass on what we have done to those who come after, creating foundations upon which they can build. We may experience some of the results of our efforts, but their effects spread in ways we may never fully know. It is hard to stay committed to such a long task with few clear results.

In order to make this powerful, sustaining, generational transformation, we must create a container that is sustainable, that nourishes us even as we do so much, that allows us to continue on even when things are challenging.

Naming the Challenges

Together, let us take time to notice and name the challenges that are present in this powerful commitment we are making together.

[If participants are in a single circle together] For this litany of challenges, we'll go around the circle. You can pass, or if you like you can read a challenge from the list. Each time someone reads, we will all respond by saying, "Together, we journey in love." At the end, there will be time for naming other challenges that come to mind.

[If participants are split into several groups] We will hear a litany of challenges read aloud. After each one, we will all respond by saying, "Together, we journey in love." At the end, there will be time for naming other challenges that come to mind.

(Participants or designated helpers read the challenges below one by one, pausing after each to let the group respond.)

READER: We are confronted with our fears of doing or saying the wrong thing.

PARTICIPANTS: Together, we journey in love.

READER: We wonder if we have the capacity to do this, if we are enough to do this, if we are the right ones to do this.

PARTICIPANTS: Together, we journey in love.

READER: We face the scary possibility that we have not built trusting, accountable relationships.

PARTICIPANTS: Together, we journey in love.

READER: We worry that we are not following the lead of those most affected by what we are addressing.

PARTICIPANTS: Together, we journey in love.

READER: We fear that we won't learn from our mistakes and will continue to make them.

PARTICIPANTS: Together, we journey in love.

READER: We worry that it will be hard to follow through on our vision with time, money, and other resources.

PARTICIPANTS: Together, we journey in love.

READER: We know that institutions move as slowly as glaciers, and fear that ours will move more slowly than the speed of trust.

PARTICIPANTS: Together, we journey in love.

READER: We face systemic problems that are embedded and entangled in everything.

PARTICIPANTS: Together, we journey in love.

READER: We fear that in the face of so much, we might freeze and our institutions might die.

PARTICIPANTS: Together, we journey in love.

READER: We know that we are mired in white supremacy culture.

PARTICIPANTS: Together, we journey in love.

READER: We face internalized oppression, taking in all that our society has told us is true about ourselves and the world around us.

PARTICIPANTS: Together, we journey in love.

READER: We worry that our approach may be unsustainable and cause us to burn out.

PARTICIPANTS: Together, we journey in love.

LEADER: I invite you now to name other challenges, fears, and worries that we face in movement building, leaving space after each one for us all to respond with "Together, we journey in love."

(Allow some quiet space for people to name challenges. When all who wish to have spoken, allow a bit of silence, then continue.)

These challenges can be daunting and overwhelming. May we be comforted by knowing that we are held by a larger community and a greater love.

Song

"Comfort Me" (Mimi Bornstein-Doble)

Let us pause for sacred rest as we sing, hum, or sway along to "Comfort Me," by Mimi Bornstein-Doble.

(Sing or play the first verse of "Comfort Me.")

Blessing

(If you have eight or fewer participants, you can do this activity as a single group; if not, split participants into groups of four or five before proceeding.)

We've talked about the power and possibility of beloved community, and the challenges that we are each facing on the path toward it.

Holding those, I want you to think about what blessing you need to receive to help you move toward beloved community, to keep engaging sustainably.

When we're ready, someone can share the blessing they need to hear with the group. Then one person who feels moved to speak will offer that blessing to them.

For example, I might say, "I need the blessing of joy to continue finding pleasure in movement building."

And you might respond with "May you be blessed with joy" or "Blessed be."

Whoever feels moved to do so can begin by naming the blessing that they need. Anyone else can offer that blessing. And then the next person can speak the blessing they need. You can ask for a specific blessing or a very general one, or you can pass if you prefer. Let us begin.

(Allow five or ten minutes for everyone to name and receive their blessings.)

Nourishment

(If you've split into smaller groups, invite everyone back together.)

This commitment that we are making together, of building beloved community and sustaining one another, is challenging, and it is a long-haul commitment. It can only be done through learning, growing, and supporting one another in community. Some of how we support one another is by literally providing sustenance to each other, feeding the bodies and spirits of our community to allow us all to continue moving forward.

To embody this practice of finding nourishment for the long haul and supporting one another in it, we're going to do a ritual where we nourish one another.

In this moment, I invite you to find a bit of food or a sip of drink, whatever you choose, whether it is real or imagined. We'll each hold up our food or drink and say, "I offer this nourishment for the long haul." Then we eat or drink what we're holding, to receive the blessing.

So first, I'm going to offer a blessing to all of you. For this one, just eat or drink half of what you're holding, because we'll do a shared blessing next. But first—

(Hold a bit of food or a drink up and look at everyone.)

I offer this nourishment for the long haul.

Now take a bite or sip to receive the blessing.

(Participants take a bite or a sip.)

Now I invite you to look around the room and hold up your offering of food or drink, and say the blessing with me: "I offer this nourishment for the long haul."

PARTICIPANTS: I offer this nourishment for the long haul.

LEADER: And eat or drink again, to receive this blessing that we have all offered each other.

(Participants take a bite or sip; eat or drink what you are holding as well.)

Beloveds, as we go forth, may we be the people who know the challenges we face, and who journey through them in love, together. May we use the deep wisdom within us to know that we are connected to each other in love and generosity and nourishment. May we know that our powerful collaborative community is stronger than any of us alone. Together, we can sustainably build toward the beloved community.

Chalice Extinguishing

"We Hold Hope Close" (Julián Jamaica Soto)

We close our time together with the words of Rev. Julián Jamaica Soto in "Spilling the Light":

In this community, we hold hope close. We don't
always know what comes next, but that cannot dissuade us.
We don't always know just what to do, but that will not mean
that we are lost in the wilderness. We rely on the certainty
beneath, the foundation of our values and ethics. We
are the people who return to love like a North Star and to
the truth that we are greater together than we are alone.
Our hope does not live in some glimmer of an indistinct future.
Rather, we know the way to the world of which we dream,
and by covenant and the movement forward of one right action
and the next, we know that one day we will arrive at home.

(Extinguish the chalice.)

For Lamenting and Setting Intentions to Heal White Supremacy Culture

Rev. Carol Cissel

This ritual is adapted from one written for the "Promise and the Practice of Our Faith" campaign, a set of worship and religious education materials published on the Unitarian Universalist Association's WorshipWeb to encourage Unitarian Universalists to listen deeply to and center the stories of people of color in our movement. It strives to create an opportunity for individuals, congregations, and communities to lament what we have lost, petition for a way forward, confess our hopes and fears, and then set intentions that honor the past but lean strongly into the future.

Materials

- ☐ Altar table
- ☐ Four smaller tables for stations
- ☐ Four tablecloths: black, white, light blue, and red
- ☐ Four large white candles
- ☐ Large clear glass bowl of water
- ☐ Small deep bowl for salt
- ☐ Stick to mix the salt and water
- ☐ Small cup
- ☐ Several pinwheels
- ☐ Small blank cards, such as index cards, at least two for each participant
- ☐ Pens or pencils
- ☐ Basket to collect cards
- ☐ Basket or bowl of small stones, at least one for each participant

☐ Two large clear glass bowls, one filled with white sand and the other with black sand

☐ Stick to stir the sands

☐ Tray and small bowls to make a traveling station

☐ Chime

Setup

The four stations of this ritual can be arranged in a number of ways: in a circle, along a wall, or in the corners of your space. Allow space for participants to move around them. The actions participants are asked to take are simple—dropping salt into a bowl of water, writing on a card, taking a stone from a beautiful basket, mixing black sand into white sand—but they are powerful.

The four stations are most effective in this order:

- Lament
- Petition
- Confession
- Intention

However, they can be approached in any order, according to your group's size, the space available, and the physical arrangement of your space. If your group is big, having everyone go to the stations in the same order will disrupt the ritual's flow and take a long time; encourage each person to move through them in the order that feels right. Do not fret: someone might need to begin by asking for help at the Petition station, and someone else might need to end by laying down their grief for what we have lost at the Lament station. Let them go where their heart needs to be.

Make trays with the ritual elements—small bowls of water and salt and something to stir with, a pinwheel, index cards and pens, and small bowls of black and white sand plus something to stir them with and some small stones—to bring to those with limited mobility.

Set up the altar table at the front or center of your space. Place the small cup on it, to be used at the close of the ritual.

Place the station tables in the locations you have chosen for them, and set them up as follows:

- Lament—Set the table with a black cloth, a large white candle in the center, a large clear glass bowl of water, a small deep bowl for salt, and a stick to mix salt gently into the water.
- Petition—Set the table with a light blue cloth, a large white candle in the center, and several pinwheels.
- Confession—Set the table with a white cloth, a large white candle in the center, an empty basket to collect cards, some pens or pencils, and two stacks of small blank cards. Label one stack HOPES and the other FEARS.
- Intention—Set the table with a red cloth, a large white candle in the center, a basket or bowl of small stones, two large, clear glass bowls of white sand and black sand, and a stick to gently stir the black sand into the white.

It's okay if you don't have the perfect bowl or the exact color of cloth. The important thing is to embrace the meaning and symbolism of the tables.

Also place an instruction sheet on each station. The sheet should name the ritual component (Lament, Petition, Confession, or Intention), explain its purpose, and describe what participants are asked to do and say aloud at that station.

Recruit five helpers (or more if you have a very large group). Post one at each station to offer assistance or gently repeat directions. The fifth will bring a tray holding the ritual elements of each station—small bowls of water and salt plus something to stir with, a pinwheel, index cards and pens, and small bowls of black and white sand plus something to stir with and some small stones—to anyone who requests it. These helpers need to be chosen mindfully and cared for (perhaps with a blessing ahead of time), because they're being entrusted with powerful work on behalf of the community. Have them practice what they're doing ahead of time.

This ritual is intended to be done without conversation or chatter. The author recommends that it be accompanied by music from the African American tradition, whether offered by a full choir, performed by a soloist, or recorded. The point is to fill the air with the music of African Americans and create a container to hold the ritual. Music will also dissuade general conversation. The murmuring voices of those speaking their laments or stating their intentions aloud are welcome. If needed, the helpers will speak gently to assist those using the stations.

Script

Opening Words

Dear ones, I invite you to enter a space of lament and intention. Over the years, our faith has not lived up to our deepest values. We have been harmed and caused harm through the white supremacy culture that is in the very air we breathe. Today we have an opportunity to lament what we have lost because of that, to petition for a way forward, to confess our hopes and fears, and then to set intentions that honor the past but lean strongly into the future.

The tools we will use are simple. The results we hope for are not.

We grieve what has been done. We honor, and we lament. This is what is past.

The ways in which we preach to each other, how we confess our dreams and desires, and how we begin to forgive ourselves are the present.

What we choose to do tomorrow, with intention, is our future.

There are four tables here in this room. Each has a purpose.

One table is for lament, allowing you to create tears of healing by mixing a dash of salt into a bowl of water while softly speaking aloud your sorrow for all that has been squandered and lost.

Another table provides a space to petition the universe, to ask for help as we move forward together, by blowing air gently into a pinwheel.

The third is a place to confess in writing your hopes and fears, for the power of the written word cannot be denied.

The final table is a place to give voice to your intention. Say aloud something you will do to move our [faith, community, world, etc.] forward, and then pour a little black sand into the bowl of white sand. Draw the stick through the sands, blending black into white, watching the black sand create a path in the white sand, and then mark your intention by taking a stone with you. Carry that stone as a reminder of your promise to take action.

Music will accompany you on this journey. As you are moved, and in any order, visit each table. Signal a helper if you'd like the stations to come to you. Let us begin.

(Sound a chime, and then have the music start. Participants make their way forward and move through the stations, until everyone has visited each one.)

Closing Words

(Sound a chime, and have the music fade. The helpers empty the basket of cards from the tray into the main basket and the bowl of tears from the tray into the main bowl of tears, and then bring forward the bowl of tears, one pinwheel, the basket of cards, the main bowl of mixed sand and the one from the tray, and a stone, and place them on the altar table.)

Together we have shed tears and lamented the past.

(Dip the small cup into the bowl of tears and then pour the liquid back into the bowl. Do this three or four times.)

We have petitioned the universe and asked for help.

(Blow the pinwheel, wait for it to stop turning, and blow it again.)

We have confessed our hopes and fears.

(Two or three times, lift several cards and let them fall from your hand back into the basket.)

And we have spoken aloud and promised our intentions by mixing black sand into white.

(Lift a bowl of sand up to chest height, hold it out toward the participants, and then lower it back to the table.)

Our work is not done. So much more is required of us.

The journey ahead is steep and littered with crevasses and boulders. Painful blunders await. Know this: We will make mistakes as we move forward and seek to serve each other. We will hurt each other unintentionally with our words and deeds. We will shy away from the fiery truth needed to truly change. And when we do embrace the flames of change, they will scorch our hearts and singe our hands. It will not be easy. But today we make a start. We have set our intentions [hold up a stone] and promised to move forward, together.

Blessed be, and amen.

For Blessing a Congregational Black Lives Matter Banner

Rev. Allison Palm

This ritual is written for a congregation to bless a Black Lives Matter banner and raise it on their church building. It could easily be adapted for rededication of a banner, or for other banners that a congregation might display on their building to declare their values.

Materials

- ☐ Black Lives Matter banner
- ☐ Optional: Materials to raise the banner during the ceremony

Setup

Participants should be gathered in such a way that those at the front can touch the banner. If you are able to set things up so that you can raise the banner smoothly during the ritual, that is ideal.

Make sure that all participants can access the space you are using for this ritual. This may mean you cannot bless the banner in the same place as you plan to display it. In this case, raise it after the benediction, instead of in the middle of the ritual as shown here.

Script

Opening Words

We believe that every person is worthy of love, imbued with inherent worth and dignity. Too often in this country, our institutions fall short of embodying this principle. Too often, Black people, Indigenous people, and other people of color are told in words and deeds that their lives do not matter.

We are called to proclaim that Black Lives Matter here in [name of town or city] and all across our country. When hatred and discrimination rise up, we are called to rise up in love and work for justice for all. For we know that none of us can be free until we all are free.

Today we join with hundreds of other congregations, communities, and organizations across the country in displaying a Black Lives Matter banner outside our church. Today we commit to working together, and partnering with those in our community, to dismantle white supremacy, both in our hearts and in our institutions. May the words on this banner remind us every time we see them of our values and our commitments.

Blessing

I want to invite you now to join me in blessing our banner. If you are close to the banner, reach out a hand to touch it. If you are further away, reach out and put your hand on the shoulder of someone near you, so we can all be connected for this blessing. If you would rather others did not touch you physically, feel free to move closer to the edges of the group and cross your arms over your chest to signal your wishes to others. We will include you in spirit only.

(Pause and wait for everyone to get connected, offering additional direction as needed.)

We bless this banner, and each other, with courage.
There are many who seek to silence those who would speak out on behalf of Black lives.
There are parts of our own hearts that fear speaking out.
May we be brave enough to speak and act in spite of our fears.

We bless this banner, and each other, with persistence.
The wounds of white supremacy run deep; they will not be healed in a day, or a month, or a year.

This is a long, hard road we embark on today.
May we find the endurance we need for the long-haul journey of racial justice.

We bless this banner, and each other, with solidarity.
This is not a time to go it alone. We need one another to do this work.
We need our partners in the community.
May we be guided by our belief in the interconnectedness of our liberation.

We bless this banner, and each other, with love.
For, in the words of Rev. Martin Luther King Jr.,
"Hate cannot drive out hate. Only love can do that."
May we harness the power of revolutionary love to drive out the injustice that surrounds us.

May it be so. Blessed be, and amen.

Banner Raising

(Plan ahead of time with your congregation's leaders to raise the banner as part of the ritual, if you can. You can include music here or just raise it in silence. If you can't raise it now, describe here the plans for doing so later.)

Benediction

Friends, today is only the beginning of our journey. May you go with courage, persistence, solidarity, and love, ready to move forward together on the road to freedom.

Go in peace. Go in love.

For Survivors of Sexual Assault and Harassment

Rev. Kate Lore

This ritual is based on the premise that sharing our stories of sexual assault and harassment is both healing and empowering. It was designed for groups of up to fifty people but can be adapted as needed.

It was created as a stand-alone healing ritual during the #MeToo movement for a congregation of 450 members. Members of the congregation's pastoral care team and representatives of a local organization working against domestic and sexual violence were present to offer additional support. A slightly modified version of this ritual was adapted for nonmembers of the congregation who were also seeking healing.

Materials

For the main ritual space:

- ☐ Large altar table
- ☐ Chalice
- ☐ Tea lights, at least one for each participant
- ☐ White craft sand
- ☐ Large tray for holding sand and candles
- ☐ Copies of the responsive reading

For the entrance:

- ☐ Large bulletin board covered in white butcher paper
- ☐ Large, fat-tipped markers

For outside:

- ☐ Fire pit
- ☐ Firewood

Setup

This ritual is designed to be led by four leaders, but can be modified to work with fewer, if necessary. Leader 1 should ideally have some formal training in pastoral care.

Recruit a handful of helpers—ideally, members of a lay pastoral care team or others in a formal role of community care. They will:

- Welcome participants and hand them a tea light.
- Introduce participants to the "bathroom wall" and encourage them to write something on it as they enter.
- Help usher people out to the fire pit and guide them through the ritual, offering emotional support as needed.

Darkness is essential for this ritual, as it affords more intimacy and safety when dealing with strong emotions.

In the main ritual space:

- Dim the lights and/or light candles all around the room.
- Set chairs in concentric circles, with the altar table in the center.
- Place the tea lights on the altar table.
- Set copies of the responsive reading on the chairs or distribute them in some other way.
- Recruit a few people to offer examples of assault or harassment, in case no one is spontaneously moved to speak.

At the entrance:

- Set out the paper-covered bulletin board and markers.
- At the top of the board, write "Bathroom Wall" in large letters, and under it write "(for expressing our innermost feelings about the people who harmed us.)"
- Write a few examples in advance, in an informal graffiti style, to give participants a feel for it (e.g., "I was raped at church camp and am furious over this betrayal," or "I never gave consent; it was rape!").

Outside:

- Set up the fire pit and light a fire so that it will be appropriately roaring for the burning portion of the ritual.
- Designate a helper to tend the fire during the ritual.
- Recruit musicians to play drums or musical instruments.

Have a helper on hand with a tray to receive and transport the tea lights of anyone who requests their assistance.

Script

(Comforting music—preferably live—should be playing as people enter.)

Opening Words

LEADER 1: Welcome, everyone, to this very special healing ritual. Here we will both speak and hear stories of our experiences with sexual violence and harassment. As many of you can attest, doing so is powerful. Not only does it demonstrate the gravity of the problem, it assures us that we're not alone; it gives us hope that the power of our joined voices can change norms and develop systems of accountability.

That said, I want to acknowledge that it may not be easy being here. We may be afraid of our scars. Deep emotions may rise to the surface. We may worry that we'll embarrass ourselves by crying or raging in public. We may even worry that our private pain might be shared with others outside of this room.

So let me begin by stressing the importance of creating a space in which people's privacy is respected. I ask that everyone here pledge to keep any specifics shared in this room confidential. Our stories are our own to tell. Nobody else has the right to share our stories without our permission. So if you are willing to maintain the confidentiality of the people in this room, please say, "I will."

PARTICIPANTS: I will.

LEADER 1: I also ask that you focus upon listening and being present to others when they speak. Please refrain from interrupting them or offering unsolicited advice.

So, welcome, brave ones. We're so glad you're here this evening, and we honor and salute you!

Chalice Lighting

LEADER 1: We light a chalice this evening as a way of marking our entrance into sacred time and space. Here in this sanctuary of ancient dreams, wisdom, and beauty, we gather now to grow, to speak our truths, to connect deeply with other, to heal and be renewed.

(Light the chalice.)

Responsive Reading

LEADER 1: Please join us in a responsive reading.

LEADER 1: To all of us who have been retraumatized by the public conversation on sexual assault and harassment.

LEADER 2: To our courage, to our silence, to our endurance, to our carrying of private shame we never should have had to carry; to our disappointment and betrayal when the perpetrator was someone loved, respected, or trusted, to our needing to remain quiet, to our sobbing in the night, to waking up numb, to our rage, to our loss, to our loneliness.

LEADER 3: To our witnessing victim blaming, to having to read asinine comments from broken, clueless people; to far too many people trying to put us back in the corner again, trying to silence our voices.

LEADER 4: To a stunning lack of compassion in the face of life-altering, body-altering events. And also to all those who have showered us with compassion, with hopes for our healing. To all of this.

PARTICIPANTS: To victims, to survivors: We believe you. We are with you. We are you.

LEADER 1: We honor and salute the sheer strength it takes to survive abuse of any kind. We salute everyone here for surviving. We honor everyone here for carrying grief, pain, and isolation in the face of unspeakable things.

PARTICIPANTS: We are not alone. And we are not to blame.

LEADER 2: We will not be put back in a corner. We will not shut up.

LEADER 3: We will not be blamed. We will not celebrate pedophiles and rapists and those who commit assault.

PARTICIPANTS: We will never be silenced again.

LEADER 4: Tonight we extend our love, respect, and healing energy to everyone here who has endured unspeakable things.

LEADER 1: We give you our total commitment to exposing and ending cycles of violence, predation, and harm.

PARTICIPANTS: One by one, we are breaking the silence. One by one, we are healing. One by one, we are changing our world and each other.

LEADER 1: Let us name the sacred nature of the work upon which we now embark. It is the work of generations. Tonight, we hold our ancestors and empower each other to stop the abuse.

ALL: This is our work in our time. Let us do it together!

Song

"Spirit of Life" (Carolyn McDade)

LEADER 1: And now we call upon the Spirit of Life to infuse our healing work tonight. Let us join voices in singing "Spirit of Life."

(Lead participants in singing.)

Roll Call

LEADER 1: For anyone here who feels that their story is somehow less important than others', who feels they have "gotten off easy" compared to others, that their experiences aren't shocking enough or awful enough to be shared—rest assured. We need your voice, too. Because all accounts of harassment and abuse are valid. None of them should be swept under the carpet. And while none of us should ever feel pressured to talk about the abuse we've experienced, it's important to note that there's a healing power in sharing our stories.

We won't have the time to hear all our stories tonight. What I'd like to do instead is conduct a roll call. I'm about to begin listing types of assault and harassment. If I name something that you've experienced, we invite you to raise your hand while saying "Me, too!" with gusto, as you are willing and able.

- Some of us have had to endure suggestive and unwanted comments—from bosses, coworkers, and people we don't even know.
- Some of us were sexually assaulted by strangers who robbed us of our innocence, our dignity, our sense of safety, our peace of mind.
- Some of us were sexually assaulted by people we knew and had trusted.
- Some of us were violated by family members or their friends.
- Some of us were sexualized by others before we ever reached puberty.
- Some of us feel like no matter how old we get, we'll never reach an age where we won't be sexualized.
- Some of us have had to endure unwanted sexual advances from people who had more power than us—in schools and other learning institutions, or in our workplaces, or in our congregations, or in our homes.

- Some of us have endured sexual assault or harassment without saying no, because we were too afraid for our safety or survival or because we simply froze up.
- Some of us said no, and it happened anyway.
- Some of us have suffered the humiliation of being groped.
- Some of us have been raped.
- Some of us have been humiliated by lewd comments made in the presence of others.
- Some of us have had to endure lewd comments in small, confined places where we felt trapped.

I got us started; now it's your turn. If you feel so moved, please share a type of incident that either happened to you or a loved one. Please be as brief in your descriptions as I have been. We're not looking for a lot of detail during this ritual; we just want to name aloud the types of experiences we've had to endure. And, like before, shout out "Me, too!" if you have had a similar experience.

(Don't be afraid of silence; give participants time to gather themselves and choose to speak. Still, if a silence lingers, discreetly signal your helpers to "seed" some examples. Let people name things until you feel the group has reached a natural conclusion point.)

LEADER 1: Thank you so much for sharing parts of our collective stories. Thank you for being silence-breakers, truth-tellers, and change-makers. Together we join our voices with people around the globe who are not only saying "Me, too!" but have decided that these abuses will no longer be tolerated. Let us all feel the power of saying this rallying cry. After I count to three, let us join voices in saying "No more!" One, two, three—

PARTICIPANTS: No more!

Burning Ritual

LEADER 2: As you were arriving, our greeters introduced you to our bathroom wall—a shared repository of our innermost feelings. I hope you had some time to write down yours. If you didn't, you are about to have another chance.

What we're going to do now is file out into the entrance and read the remarks on the bathroom wall. If you want to add anything, this will be your chance.

After a few minutes, we will then snatch off pieces of the butcher paper and burn them outside in the fire. The purpose of this ritual is to release the hold our injuries have on us; let go of any lingering sense of shame, guilt, regret, or self-doubt; and experience the power of people releasing their abuses together!

We will then file back into the sanctuary.

I ask that you remain completely silent for this part of our ritual. Our helpers will guide you through the process.

(When people go outside, the fire helper and musicians should be already stationed in a circle, drumming or playing music around a roaring fire. In their own time, participants will cast their pieces of paper into the fire. Make time to let them watch the embers float upward. When the time feels right, cue the musicians to fade into silence. Guide the participants back inside.)

Lighting of Tea Lights

(Once everyone has settled into their seats, continue.)

LEADER 3: We give thanks for the healing power of this community to release us from our silence and pain. Our work, though, is not yet complete. There are people outside of this space who have helped bring us to this point in time. And so we will now honor them. In a moment we'll invite you, if you wish, to come up to the altar and light a candle for someone who has inspired you or helped you in any way on your journey toward healing. You can say their name aloud if you want, or articulate your hopes and wishes.

We're going to take our time with this, so please don't feel rushed.

(Soft music begins. Participants come up one by one and light candles.)

LEADER 4: Thank you, everyone, for bearing witness to your own and each other's resilience and dreams for a better way. We're now going to sing a song that was written by Libby Roderick. She originally wrote it to comfort her sister, who had just been sexually assaulted. We sing it tonight to remind ourselves that we will not be defined or defiled by the ugly things that have been done to us. Let us rise in body or spirit and form one big circle as we sing "How Could Anyone."

Song

"How Could Anyone" (Libby Roderick)

(Lead participants in singing.)

Chalice Extinguishing

LEADER 1: Spirit of Life, we give thanks for the people in this room and for this time set aside for healing. Tonight we have come together to break the silence, to tell the truth, and to help each other heal. And what we've firmly established here tonight is that silence does break, truth does seek the light, and healing is possible.

Our secrets are beginning to breathe fresh air again and noticing they're not alone. In the comfort of this community, we have discovered that our power with one another is far greater than the power someone once had over us.

Spirit of Life, please help us remember this night, our power, our connections, and your steady presence in our lives. Amen.

(Extinguish the chalice.)

(Close with an invitation to a processing space if one is available, and share information about where people can get further support if they want it.)

For Trauma in the News

Rev. Heather Concannon and Rev. Allison Palm

This ritual is intended to be used on the Sunday following a major national trauma, devastating news event, or act of violence, with special care for events that affect or threaten the rights of marginalized identity groups. For instance, it could be used in response to mass shootings, verdicts in court cases centering on hate crimes or racialized shootings, Supreme Court decisions, or election results. It is intended to be used as a part of congregational worship and is crafted to be placed immediately before or after a congregational prayer or time for joys and sorrows.

Materials

- ☐ Altar table
- ☐ Floating candle
- ☐ Stones in a small basket or bowl
- ☐ Clear bowl of water

Setup

Review the script to decide how many stones you will need and what you will say for each one; adapt the script as necessary to fit your circumstances.

Put the basket of stones and the bowl of water on the altar table. Place the floating candle in the bowl of water. Try to use a candle that's large enough to be visible to all participants.

Script

Introduction

This morning we gather with heavy hearts
After the news this week of [insert specifics].
We are shaken once again
By the realities of oppression, violence, and suffering in our world.

We cannot offer easy answers to these hard truths.
    But we do know that when we hold these truths together, they are lighter
    And that, together, it is easier to move forward with resilience and hope.

Please join me in singing.

Song

"There Is a Love" (words by Rebecca Parker, music by Elizabeth Norton)

(Lead participants in singing the third verse once through.)

Water

This water symbolizes our interdependence, our community, and the Spirit of Love that surrounds us all.

Stones

Option 1: Concepts

These stones [lift up the basket of stones] represent the heaviness that we feel in holding this news.
We place the stones in this water
Because we know that they are lighter when we hold them together.

(One by one, name specific concepts related to the event. These might be feelings, such as rage, sorrow, frustration; or biases, such as misogyny or racism; or the names of groups or communities affected. You can simply list them, or phrase them in statements like "Today we bring [feelings] for the ways this attack reminds us of [concept]." Place a stone in the water for each thing that you name or sentence that you say.)

Option 2: Names

These stones [lift up the basket of stones] represent those who were killed in [name the event].
As we place these stones in this water
And read the name of each person who was killed
We surround their families and loved ones with the love and care of this community.

(Read the names ones by one, placing a stone in the water for each.)

Song

"There Is a Love"

(Lead participants in singing the third verse once through.)

Candle

We hold on to our faith that in the end, love has the final say.
We light this candle
In hope that [name specific hopes and visions],
With a commitment to [name specific actions or commitments],
And with faith in the love that holds us and will not let us go.
Let us sing again.

Song

"There Is a Love"

(Lead participants in singing the third verse once through.)

Crafting Your Own Rituals

This book contains over seventy rituals, but there is no limit to the moments in our lives, and in the lives of our communities, that we might want to mark with a ritual. We have offered rituals for many common and uncommon moments, but we also hope that this book will inspire and guide you to creatively develop rituals of your own for all the events, transitions, sorrows, and joys that you may want to honor. The steps below outline the process we use to craft a new ritual.

Step 1: Grounding the Ritual

Before you begin to think about what a ritual will look like, identify its overall purpose and its spiritual, emotional, and theological goals. Some questions to ask yourself at this stage are:

- What is the ritual for? What transformation are you facilitating, or what transition are you marking?
- Who is it for? Who will be participating? What words, actions, music, and symbols will have meaning for them?
- What do you want participants to experience? How do you want them to feel when they leave?
- What part of your and your participants' values or theology does this ritual reflect?

Step 2: Embodying the Ritual

Once you are clear about the goal of the ritual, think about what words, actions, music, and symbols might embody that goal best. These elements are what take us out of our heads and into our bodies, making us participants rather than merely audience. You can read more in the introduction to this book about the importance of the embodied, participatory nature of rituals.

Consider what the participants will do to embody the values or theology you have identified as the core of the ritual. What tangible object or action will help to embody this transition or transformation? Look through the rituals in this book for examples and ideas. Will you have participants handle bubbles, glitter, clay, stones, water, or something else? Will they write, eat, plant, light candles, hold hands, sing together, keep silence together? Choose an action to serve as the centerpiece of your ritual. Be sure that it suits your context, and that it is appropriate for your participants, keeping in mind their likely range of abilities, cultural and religious backgrounds, attention spans, etc.

Step 3: Framing the Ritual

The next step is to build out the rest of the ritual. Choose readings, songs, prayers, blessings, and so on to support the ritual action that is your centerpiece.

Start by thinking about how the ritual will begin. How will people feel as they enter the space? Will they know what you and they are about to do, and why? It's important to briefly explain the ritual and its importance before launching into it. This is a moment to help ground participants in what is about to happen and to help them begin to do their own meaning-making. Be sure to speak in a way that meets participants where they are; consider what language and level of complexity is appropriate in this setting. Use the first few elements—opening words, chalice or candle lighting, a reading or song or unison recital—to help participants enter into the spirit of the ritual and find meaning in it.

Once you have oriented participants and grounded them in the ritual space, you can move on to the central ritual action. Make sure to tell participants clearly what they are supposed to do and why. Leaders sometimes forget that others don't know the ritual as well as they do, and when participants are confused or unsure they cannot fully enter into the rich meaning-making experience of the ritual.

After the central action has taken place, be sure to give people adequate time to transition out of the ritual space. An abrupt end can feel awkward or jarring. Take time to summarize what you just did, the transition you are marking or the transformation you are facilitating; reiterate the meaning-making you have offered and underline the values you have affirmed. Give people some space to integrate what just happened. This can be a good place for music or a time of silence, followed by closing prayers, blessings, benedictions, or chalice extinguishing words to help close out the ritual space.

Step 4: Leading the Ritual

Even the most beautifully written ritual can fall flat for participants if it is poorly executed. The "Practical Tips for Rituals" section of this book offers in-depth practical advice for rituals. We recommend reviewing it before leading your ritual.

Acknowledgments

We have so many people to thank for helping to bring this book into being. We are grateful to the people and communities who inspired our love for rituals:

The UU youth and young adult communities who introduced us to one another and taught us that good worship can center ritual instead of a sermon, who encouraged us to experiment with ritual and liturgy, and who gave space to grow as liturgical leaders.

Katie Tyson, whose life and love for Unitarian Universalism continues to ignite our own passion for this faith, whose legacy lives on in our lives and in our ministries, and whose death left us with a longing for a container to hold our grief and remember her well.

Rev. Leanne McCall Tigert, who taught our Pastoral Care and Counseling with Couples and Families class at Andover Newton Theological School in 2012, where the idea for this book first took shape.

All the congregations and communities we've served who have generously welcomed our experimentation with rituals in worship and beyond.

We are grateful for all of the people who helped turn our dream of a ritual resource book into a reality:

The sixty-one contributors who shaped this book through their writing, their experiences, and their love and care for our faith. We thank them for all the wisdom and creativity that they have shared, and for the many emails from us that they responded to over the last four years.

Our editors at Skinner House, particularly Mary Benard, who helped imagine the shape of this book and was instrumental in its development, and Larisa Hohenboken, who helped refine everything into its final form.

The Skinner House Equity and Accountability Panel, who helped us wrestle with Unitarian Universalism's legacy of cultural appropriation in rituals. Their insight and thoughtfulness about how to approach this project responsibly made this book so much richer.

Rev. Liz Weber, who helped us think about how to more deeply incorporate accessibility into the book and the rituals.

Rev. Aisha Ansano, who helped to ground the practice of these rituals in covenant, offering insight into how to use these sacred words and acts with care.

We are grateful for our colleagues and friends who supported us along the way:

Our favorite Facebook group, the 20s & 30s Women+ Ministers, who have been an invaluable source of emotional and practical support. Thank you for cheering us on, for brainstorming terminology for everything from ritual participants to liturgical elements, and for doing important scientific candle floating tests when we were away from our candle stash.

Our many colleagues and friends who have encouraged us, listened when challenges arose, believed in us even before we ourselves did, and reminded us of the need for this book in our world.

And finally, we are grateful for our families and households who accompanied us steadfastly on this journey, offering listening, encouragement, hours and hours of childcare, cozy snuggles, and inspiration, and who, most of all, loved us through this process:

Tristan, Olympia, and Hosea.

Justin, Keyes, Em, Rebecca, Alec, Matt, Evan, Micah, Amy, and Sharon.